# Ema's Odyssey

## Shamanism for Healing and Spiritual Knowledge

# SANDRA HARNER

Foreword by Michael Harner

North Atlantic Books
Berkeley, California

Published by
North Atlantic Books                    Cover image: Eliks/shutterstock.com
P.O. Box 12327                          Cover and book design by Suzanne Albertson
Berkeley, California 94712

Printed in the United States of America

*Ema's Odyssey: Shamanism for Healing and Spiritual Knowledge* is sponsored by the Society for the Study of Native Arts and Sciences, a nonprofit educational corporation whose goals are to develop an educational and cross-cultural perspective linking various scientific, social, and artistic fields; to nurture a holistic view of arts, sciences, humanities, and healing; and to publish and distribute literature on the relationship of mind, body, and nature.

North Atlantic Books' publications are available through most bookstores. For further information, visit our website at www.northatlanticbooks.com or call 800-733-3000.

MEDICAL DISCLAIMER: The following information is intended for general information purposes only. Individuals should always see their health care provider before administering any suggestions made in this book. Any application of the material set forth in the following pages is at the reader's discretion and is his or her sole responsibility.

Library of Congress Cataloging-in-Publication Data

Harner, Sandra, 1939–
    *Ema's odyssey : shamanism for healing and spiritual knowledge* / Sandra Harner.
        pages cm
    Summary: "This enchanting, poetic recording of one woman's experiences while in a shamanic state of consciousness is a must-read for students and practitioners of shamanism, and will have broad appeal for spiritual and New Age readers interested in personal growth, self-discovery, and alternative healing modes"—Provided by publisher.
    ISBN 978-1-58394-663-3 (pbk.)
    1. Shamanism. 2. Spirits. 3. Mind and body. 4. Mind and body therapies. I. Title.
    BF1999.H37519 2014
    201'.44—dc23
        2013008346

1 2 3 4 5 6 7 8 9 UNITED 18 17 16 15 14

Printed on recycled paper

## Praise for *Ema's Odyssey*

"No where else will you find a more compelling and illuminating account of the inherent wisdom, spiritual democracy, and transformative power found within the experience of shamanic journeying—the most ancient of spiritual practices! Not only a must read for students and practitioners of shamanism, but for anyone, personally or professionally, who is interested in spiritual liberation, personal growth, self-discovery, and self-healing."

—ANGELES ARRIEN, cultural anthropologist and president of the Foundation for Cross-Cultural Education & Research

"*Ema's Odyssey* captivates and delivers us into the sparkling mystery of our very existence."

—BARBARA BERGER, LAc, acupuncturist and specialist in the healing benefits of microcurrent therapy

"A powerful and inspiring collaboration filled with wisdom and sure to touch the heart."

—RANDY CHERNER, founder of the Cherner Institute, a center for the practice of somatic education

"This book is an important map of the far reaches of inner territories, as well as an expression of the intricate and rich poetry of the soul."

—CHRISTINA GROF, PhD, author of *The Thirst for Wholeness*, *The Eggshell Landing*, and coauthor of *Spiritual Emergency* and *Holotropic Breathwork*

"*Ema's Odyssey* beautifully demonstrates the visionary, healing, and transformative power of the images and experiences that can emerge during shamanic journeys and shows, for the first time, how these experiences can evolve and can resolve multiple issues over multiple journeys."

—ROGER WALSH, MD, PhD, University of California, Irvine, author of *The World of Shamanism*

*To Michael*

# ACKNOWLEDGMENTS

First and foremost, deserving of our appreciation and admiration are the indigenous shamans themselves, who keep shamanism a living tradition against great odds and despite an encroaching modern, technological, industrial world. They preserve the knowledge of their forebears, who introduced them and guided them on this spiritual path for the benefit of their communities—a path we also inherit, however tenuously.

We are obliged to travelers, scholars, anthropologists, missionaries, and other curious individuals who have recognized and recorded these practices. To those individuals of the present time who seriously undertake the study and experiential practice of the ancient shamanic methods, we owe sincere gratitude—they show great courage, as Western culture is largely separated from these spiritual roots. Contemporary shamanic practitioners show that the remnants of this heritage can be and are being authentically revived for service in our times.

Those who have been strong advocates and supporters of this endeavor, I deeply thank. They include, most particularly, Frances Vaughan, who early saw the unique contribution of Ema's verbatim, direct spiritual experiences and who has remained a source of inspiration. I am grateful to Barry Schlosser, who helped me probe the various possibilities for sharing Ema's journeys, as well as technological opportunities best suited for their presentation. His support and guidance have been instrumental in the evolution of the project. Myrtle Heery, friend and colleague, lent a critical ear in helping me preserve the authentic voice of Ema's immediate experiences. Many students, clients, and others have helped bring this work to fruition by their interest and love of the journey process and of Harner Shamanic Counseling (HSC). For them I have great respect and pleasure in remembering our work together.

I am grateful for the help given by Dr. Baron A. M. F. to the Shamanic Knowledge Conservatory for aid in archiving Ema's journeys. In addition, I appreciate Norman and Michael Benzie and the Samuel Lunenfeld Foundation for supporting the Foundation for Shamanic Studies, in particular the research of Shamanism and Health projects that I conducted. I am thankful for grants by the Betsy Gordon Foundation, which reduced my administrative responsibilities at the Foundation for Shamanic Studies and made it possible for me to apply myself to *Ema's Odyssey*. Coleen Burrows Judson, Lou Judson, and Aimée Lunier brought the recorded and handwritten transcripts to digital form for editing. Gizelle Rhyon-Berry organized the ethnographic materials of the Shamanic Knowledge Conservatory, which aided my search for appropriate examples of indigenous journey experiences. The help of these four was essential to this project. Susan Mokelke's interest and enthusiasm for the project encouraged me throughout. Of course, none of this would have been possible had Michael Harner not brought shamanic journeying to Westerners and without the singular method he developed for teaching journeying and using the simultaneous narration technique in HSC.

I am indebted to my editors, Wendy Dherin and Vanessa Ta, who have shepherded this book through the publication process with care. I am grateful to the staff at North Atlantic Books and, in particular, to Richard Grossinger, who understood and remained committed to Ema's personal cosmography, seeing it as comparable to the rare ethnographic records of indigenous peoples, such as those tales related to Franz Boas by Mr. George Hunt of the Kwakiutl People.[1]

To all of them, and especially to Ema, for her permission to publish her journeys here, in the hope that they will inspire others to make their own spiritual search, I offer my sincere thanks.

---

1 Franz Boas, *Kwakiutl Tales* (New York: Columbia University Press, 1910).

# CONTENTS

# EMA'S OVERTURE

As a Westerner, I had my doubts about shamanism. But severe pain, caused by arthritis, led me to try. I happened to come by Michael Harner's book *The Way of the Shaman* and tried the journeys on my own. It worked quite well. Even though, I must admit, when I went through my first dismemberment I almost gave up. Journeys of cruelties like the one I experienced, I did not appreciate at that time and only many years later did I understand the purpose.

When my husband passed away, I was shattered. Subsequently, I found that I had difficulties to journey. Then, by chance, I attended a seminar on shamanism led by Michael and Sandra Harner. I asked Sandra to be my teacher and have studied with her for almost eleven years.

From then on, in our work together, the Harner Shamanic Counseling (HSC) journeys started out for healings physically and understanding of the Soul. But over the years, I was taught so much more than that. Often, my Spirit Guides let me know things I did not understand. Sometimes weeks, months, or even years later gave me the right understandings.

Through the teachings, I came to appreciate Buddhism. Bodhisattvas took the pain to teach and guide me without my understanding who they were. (Before HSC, I had little prior knowledge about Buddhism.) In 2009 I had a spiritual breakdown. A few months later I had a certain awakening. I walked through the gate and my mind opened.

I have journeyed into limitless space, have been embraced by emptiness, and have been allowed to see certain mysteries.

I am in awe and so very grateful that my Spirit Guides and Bodhisattvas find me worthy—that at my old age I can take a glimpse of something words cannot always express.

My heartfelt thank you goes to all my Spirit Guides, the Bodhisattvas, and my teacher Sandra Harner who patiently, without interference, let me evolve.

—EMA

# FOREWORD

This is a unique and inspiring story—a woman's shamanic adventures in other worlds over ten years, narrated and recorded as they happened. By narrating her experiences while in those realms, the anonymous Ema offers the reader the opportunity to be with her step by step as her magical odyssey unfolds under the listening ear of Sandra Harner, her experienced shamanic counselor.

What is Ema's odyssey? It could be called the heroine's journey, remembering Joseph Campbell's "the hero's journey." But recording such an experience as it happened is probably not something he ever envisioned. With this book, we enter someone's evolving spiritual life as never before, a life of surprises, poetry, eloquence, and love. This is myth in the making.

*Ema's Odyssey* offers many exciting lessons. First are the individual lessons learned by Ema in response to her specific mission in each shamanic journey. Then there are broader lessons, such as Ema's discovery of her intimate spiritual connection with other species, species who compassionately teach her in the journeys. Further, she learns that there is a progression in her knowledge as she sequentially advances in her journeys, eventually achieving cosmic union. Then there is the lesson of what is to be her personal path, which appears to be Buddhism, but then takes a surprising turn. Following the lessons she received, we see her blossoming into spiritual independence and personal self confidence, made possible by the careful noninterference and patience of her shamanic counselor in keeping with the principles of Harner Shamanic Counseling (HSC).

That noninterference is illustrated by Ema's use of the word "guide," a mediumistic ("channeling") term, with regard to the beings who advise and heal her. That they heal is an indication that they are more than guides, and in the parlance of core shamanism would be called by other terms, such as "power animal" and "teacher." But Ema did not significantly train in shamanism prior to undertaking shamanic counseling, and Sandra Harner wisely did not attempt to "correct" her. By letting Ema exercise her independence in such ways during their individual sessions, Sandra was giving her the gift of ever-greater spiritual autonomy and evolving self confidence.

Besides Ema's story, there is another important lesson of this book: the simplicity and power of HSC, designed to help individuals attain happier, more fulfilled lives through the wise counsel and help of compassionate spirits, the *real* counselors in the system. Many clients are satisfied with only a few weeks or months of sessions with a shamanic counselor before working entirely alone. Even then, they can find it useful to visit the counselor regularly to adhere to the HSC system and maximize its benefits. This is the path that Ema chose, and her ten years of working with Sandra may be a record.

We owe a debt of gratitude to Ema and Sandra Harner for giving us, the readers, the opportunity to share this beautiful and instructive adventure in nonordinary reality. I also personally thank Sandra for the many years she spent leading the teaching of this spiritual system and for providing us with the first book devoted to it.

—MICHAEL HARNER

Summer 2013

# PREFACE

Saints and mystics, revelations, origin myths, and heroes' journeys, as well as ethical and spiritual guidelines, speak to us from ancient times and far-flung lands and peoples. Sometimes zealously exported beyond their source, the lessons have become formalized and structured into entrenched "truths." With time and distance, these individual "revelations" become generalized "teachings" for the many—solid, monolithic, and divorced from unmediated, personal spiritual sources of knowledge and healing.

Now, shamanism—that most ancient of spiritual practices, long obscured by powerful state religions and politics—is reemerging and opening the doors to *individual,* direct spiritual experiences. While lost in much of the world, it tenaciously survives in a few remote frontiers. If we lose it, we lose a fundamental gift of what it is to be human and to live with nature. Fortunately, thanks to the shamanic journey and its individualized treatment in Harner Shamanic Counseling (HSC), we have access to tools to reestablish a genuine and personal connection with spirits of another reality. *Ema's Odyssey*—a transcribed collection of one woman's shamanic journeying experiences using this technique—is a testament to the transformative power and personal spiritual liberation made possible by HSC.

How do Ema's journeys happen to be available to us? Ema has given permission and generously cooperated in sharing her shamanic journeys publicly, with the condition that she only be identified as Ema, the name given to her in her journeys.

Ema is a modest, even shy woman who was 60 years old and widowed for about a year and a half when she requested training in shamanic journeying. For most of her adult life, she lived a conventional lifestyle.

She had completed high school and was a housewife. Her knowledge of shamanism was quite limited and her background made acquiring such information in the course of her daily life unlikely.

At the time of her first appointment with me, in 1999, she had already read *The Way of the Shaman* and had journeyed with success using the exercises in the book. After the death of her husband, she found, to her dismay, that she was unable to journey to her satisfaction. By chance, for she is not given to taking workshops, she attended a one-day introduction to shamanism and experiential shamanic journeying, after which she approached me, saying she now wanted more individually tailored training in shamanic journeying. She said she was on a spiritual search. We agreed that I would introduce her to journeying according to the HSC protocol. Her shamanic journeys reveal her acquiring skills and knowledge similar to that observed in many.

In her journeys, Ema enters a trance state, as evidenced by her changes in voice speed, tonal quality, and loudness, for instance. She demonstrates a capacity for ecstatic experience. She descends to the Lower World and ascends to the Upper World, where she has a number of classic shamanic experiences—initiations—such as special relations with helping spirits, in both human and animal form. She communicates and even dialogues with them. She sees them, hears them, feels heat, is healed by light, is given gifts and instructions for rituals, and experiences transformation. She also receives powerful personal spiritual teachings.

Her journeys are recorded in the moment, thanks to the wonders of electronic innovations in technology—not as diaries or retrospective accounts. The journeys are entered deliberately—using tested methods that work, that keep the journeyer safe. Remarkably, her experiences—while emotional, profoundly personal, and specific—also carry messages of practical, ethical, and compassionate social value.

Familiar life challenges, health, and healing are prominent in Ema's journeys; eating problems, self-defined emotional issues, curiosity-driven explorations, and spiritual matters are some of the purposes for Ema's journeys. The revelations in the course of her journeys are often deeply wise. Sometimes they are obscure until later, either upon reflection or in further journeys. Their vitality, diversity, and specificity demonstrate both universality and nce.

Ema's shamanic counplace from late 1999 to 2010. The rihile specific to her, alsn to shamans and nolustrate the speciand practice the metund. They are also ences over an extenss of readers' religiouive, they can engage is.

These hose who study indis to those noted for nord of experiences is resuch as those on which comparative religimythology studies are based. Poets, storytellers, and artists may find inspiration in her imagery and expression. Ema's lyrical language, as she shares her immediate, ongoing journeys, is reminiscent of the well-known connection between the Greek muses and the arts, including poetry. Think, too, of Homer's *Odyssey* and other tales of a hero's journey, here all the more remarkable for its contemporary, everyday context.

Researchers into states of consciousness stand to benefit from the journeys too, while linguists can observe the verbatim language of a multilevel trance state. Some may consider these narrations to be similar to channeling by mediums. There is even a hypnotic quality, when Ema is in a deep shamanic state of consciousness and speaks of sacred unity with beauty. For those engaged in psychedelic research, these journeys can also provide an orienting framework for content and normalizing their own firsthand experiences.

Information is here to be plumbed by psychologists, both traditional and cutting-edge. Exposure to these descriptions of direct personal spiritual experiences enriches the theoretical perspectives of Freudian, Jungian, transpersonal, humanistic, existential, and cognitive therapies.

Ema's journeys model a process available to almost all who choose to explore it. The ultimate goal is cultivation and confirmation of each individual's spiritual autonomy, for in shamanism the interpretation of the meaning of a journey lies exclusively with the one whose journey it is. Hence, the content of the journeys serves to show the *potential* to access another reality, and to experience it in each individual's own genuine way.

The person inspired to travel the path of the shamanic journey has available his or her own unique personal experiences, which reflect a larger basic human capacity that exists from past to present to future, across cultures. This fundamental element often draws us closer to understanding our deep unity and interdependence. With this can come greater compassion for our fellow beings and the planet itself, which sustains all.

—Sandra Harner
Mill Valley, California
Summer 2013

# Introduction

## HARNER SHAMANIC COUNSELING

Shamanism is an ancient and widespread system of personal knowledge obtained through a deliberate change in state of consciousness, commonly called "ecstasy" in religious studies.[1] Making journeys to other worlds is a distinctive characteristic of shamanism and facilitates two-way communication between an individual and many kinds of spirits.[2] In this trance state, the person's soul leaves his body and ascends to a world above or descends to one below. Classic shamanic experiences commonly include other exceptional events, such as having a partnership with helping spirits, undergoing transformation, and dialoging with gods and spirits.[3] Traditionally, these are expressed within the manifest mode of each culture.

Core shamanism moves beyond the culture-specific to a more underlying, panhuman transcultural shamanism. The term, originated by Michael Harner, is defined as consisting of "the universal, near-universal, and common features of shamanism, together with journeys to other worlds, a distinguishing feature of shamanism."[4] As he notes,[5] this altered state of consciousness reflects nonordinary reality, in contrast to the regular, ordinary reality of daily life in the ordinary state of consciousness.

When the altered state is undertaken within a shamanic perspective, Michael Harner calls it the shamanic state of consciousness (SSC).[6] Cross-culturally, this state is usually aided by sonic driving,

---

1 Franz Boas, *Kwakiutl Tales* (New York: Columbia University Press, 1910).
2 Michael Harner, *Cave and Cosmos: Shamanic Encounters with Another Reality* (Berkeley, CA: North Atlantic Books, 2013).
3 Mircea Eliade, *Shamanism: Archaic Techniques of Ecstasy* (New York: Bollingen Series 76, 1964).
4 Harner, *Cave and Cosmos.*
5 Michael Harner, *The Way of the Shaman: A Guide to Power and Healing* (San Francisco: Harper and Row, 1980).
6 Ibid.

achieved through a repetitious percussive sound like drumming, or, in a minority of cases, by the use of various mind-altering substances, sometimes termed entheogens. Harner also found that recorded drumming, when properly used, was as effective as live drumming in altering consciousness.

In the early 1980s, Harner created Harner Shamanic Counseling (HSC),[1] a system to help people work on problems in their lives.[2] The design consists of five basic journeys that stress methodology and are presented in a one-to-one setting of HSC counselor and client. Journeys are accompanied by repetitive drumming and sessions unfold in a tutorial fashion, with a progressive series of designated journey tasks. The methods are experiential and based on the journey technique of classic shamanism.

The clients make their own shamanic journeys into realms of nonordinary reality, where they directly access information, spiritual wisdom, and guidance in answer to questions in their own lives. These five firsthand, direct experiences in the SSC are structured in a sequence that teaches a method for changing one's state of consciousness from the ordinary, everyday waking state to the altered state of consciousness of the shamanic journey. In effect, the sessions are set up as a series of initiations, in which the client learns to interpret the experiences and to move deliberately and confidently at will between the altered state of the shamanic journey and that of everyday waking consciousness. The instructions systematically acquaint the client with fundamental tools of access to information through journeying, accompanied by the sonic driving of recorded monotonous drumming, which is heard through earphones.

Essential to this process is the *simultaneous narration* technique. In it the client relates, out loud, the ongoing experiences in real time, which is recorded. While the client is narrating the journey, the counselor, also, is

1 He applied the name "Harner" to distinguish it from other activities being called "shamanic counseling."
2 Michael Harner, "Shamanic Counseling," in *Shaman's Path: Healing, Personal Growth and Empowerment,* ed. Gary Doore (Boston: Shambhala, 1988).

making a written record of the narration and observing and noting client behaviors while journeying. The most frequent activities are changes in expressive voice, but others may include such things as crying, laughter, carrying a special object, moving around, and making gestures. Western clients report that they tend to have more vivid and intense experiences when they use simultaneous narration than when they do not. The experiences can even be more vivid than with a live drum.

The simultaneous narration of HSC has indigenous precedents. A singing narration of the shaman's visions while he or she experiences them is reported in the ethnographic literature, and I have had occasion to witness it during a curing session by an Achuar shaman in 1969 in eastern Ecuador. Likewise, in the eastern Peruvian rain forest, shamans sing their journeys. For example, these lines sung under the influence of ayahuasca announce the arrival of spirits of hummingbirds.[1] When the shaman sings, he is singing along with the spirits.[2]

> Hummingbirds, hummingbirds, they come running
> Hummingbirds, hummingbirds, dark appearance
> Hummingbirds, hummingbirds, all our brothers
> Hummingbirds, hummingbirds, they all hover
> Hummingbirds, hummingbirds, group without blemish

In classical shamanism, clients go to the shaman, who does the spiritual work. In HSC, the clients learn the method in order to journey for themselves, learning to become their own shamans for this type of journey. This restores spiritual power and authority to the clients through their direct experience and deepest knowing.

HSC is a unique system with specific innovations consistent with Western society, employing electronic technology in the service of reclaiming individual and cultural loss of direct spiritual experience. The client becomes a practitioner of divination shamanism by combining

---

1 Gerald Weiss, "Shamanism and Priesthood in the Light of the Campa Ayahuasca Ceremony," in *Hallucinogens and Shamanism,* ed. Michael Harner (New York: Oxford University Press, 1973), 45.

2 Ibid., 44.

the classic shamanic journey, recorded drumming, and simultaneous narration of the journey as it unfolds.

There are a number of other innovations used in HSC as well. Electronic technology provides recording of drumming to induce auditory or sonic driving,[1] which facilitates the journey to nonordinary reality. Using headphones to hear the drumming has the practical consequence that it doesn't disturb the neighbors, and more to the point, permits recorded simultaneous narration. Recording the journey allows for review, future reference, refinement, and analysis. It is difficult to remember all, or even part, of the information obtained in the SSC of a journey.

Typically, the shaman journeys in darkness. Covering the eyes with a Mindfold[2] effectively provides complete darkness, thus screening out visual distractions and making it easier to see the imagery that arises. Otherwise, a bandanna or scarf can be laid across the eyes for the same purpose.

An underlying principle is that the counselor is a counselor of *method* primarily. As little content as possible is presented, so the trainee or client can fully experience his or her own journeys and their contents without preconceived expectation or undue influence from others. The *real counselors* are the teachers and power animals.

Some preparatory and exploratory work begins to familiarize clients with nonordinary reality, its resources and terrain, and the methodology for journeying. Then the counseling sessions are devoted to seeking an answer to a question the client brings. Learning how to frame the question is central to the process. The client makes the journey once the question has been clarified and refined. Finally, the client alone interprets the journey and the answer to the question. Only after a person has achieved a classic shamanic experience does the counselor discuss it, and then only in terms of the trainee's direct experience.

---

1 Harner, *Cave and Cosmos*: 42–45.
2 This is a commercially available eye mask. It is called a "Mindfold Relaxation Mask" and may be obtained from www.Mindfold.com.

The shamanic counselor takes a less and less active role as the client's skill increases, for the main objective is that the client becomes autonomous in the whole process. HSC is a method of personal empowerment in which the client acquires the ability to directly obtain spiritual wisdom and practical information. It is a *spiritual method of counseling,* a time-tested way of working with the human mind and spirit and involving the whole person, as well as the mind's visionary and analytic abilities. This is consistent with the basic concept of classical shamanism—that one can gain direct access to spiritual insight.

## An Overview of the HSC Process

HSC is a programmed series of journeys that introduce the client to the shamanic journey for divination. The shamanic counselor teaches a method. The nonordinary reality spirit helpers, teachers, and power animals are the true counselors.

A preliminary session introduces the trainee to the system and its technological features; orients the individual to the process; and secures informed consent. The explicit agreement is that the services offered are for the purposes of teaching a productive method of journeying and providing feedback on adherence to the method, not as a class in shamanism. These clarifications at the outset guide the work that follows.

The procedure includes recorded drumming.[1] The client journeys in darkness for the previously determined purpose and narrates the experiences, which are electronically recorded. At the same time the shamanic counselor is writing down the narration and noting the client's behaviors. The counselor does not interrupt the client's journey. Immediately after the journey concludes, the client offers a brief summary or interpretation.

Together the client and counselor listen to the playback of the recording. Then a discussion ensues. First, without interruption, the client

1 Usually Track 1 or 2 of the CD (Side A of the FSS Journey Tape) *Michael Harner's Shamanic Journey Solo and Double Drumming,* No. 1, provides the sonic driving for the client's journey. Ema chose to use No. 7, *Shamanic Journey Multiple Drumming.* They are available in digitally remastered CD or MP3 formats at www.shamanism.org.

reviews, evaluates, and interprets the contents of each journey, especially with regard to the original, stated intention for that journey. The shamanic counselor's discussion focuses on the client's methodology and in-the-moment behaviors, so the trainee fully integrates his or her own journey with confidence.

The counselor may ask open-ended questions, to provoke thought and guide a client in what to look for in interpreting the journey. The counselor may also note and indicate material that may have been "edited out" in the client's discussion. For example, "What do you think *X* meant in partial answer to your question?" An advantage of following these detailed steps is that the client observes his or her own behaviors and experiences in the SSC, including qualities of consciousness, and recalls and retains many experiences that otherwise might be lost.

The counselor discusses a possible shamanic context for the client's experiences only after the fact of the client's journey experiences and the client's interpretations of them. The intention is to engage in the shamanic, not psychological, psychotherapeutic, or other perspective. Psychology and shamanism are distinctly different, each with its own basic assumptions and each worthy in its own right.[1] Likewise, this system does not mix other spiritual systems or terminology from them. For example, the term "guide" is typically used by mediums in channeling, but not in shamanism. In shamanism, the term "guide" normally refers to a helping spirit that leads the journeyer from one place to another in the journey.

The exercises are presented in the following sequence. The first journey is to the Lower World to meet an animal waiting there. In the second journey, the client returns to the Lower World, asking a question of the animal. The purpose of the third journey is to go to the Upper World to meet a tutelary spirit or "teacher." The fourth journey challenges the client to return to the teacher and ask a question that is personally important. The fifth and final journey of the series is to seek advice on

---

1 Sandra Harner, "Presence in the Shamanic Journey and in Existential-Humanistic Psychotherapy," *Shamanism* 20, no. 2 (2007): 25–30.

how to implement in everyday life some information from the previous journey. A task may be repeated in ensuing sessions until the client has mastered its methodology, before moving on to the next stage. The first and third journeys are fifteen minutes long, while the rest are for thirty minutes. During the period of the five journeys, clients are not to journey between sessions. The purpose for this admonition is to maximize continuity and the learning opportunity for the client by keeping the content of the journeys constant between the client and the counselor.

Having acquired the objectives and skills posed by these five tasks, the beginning client has key tools with which to continue to journey independently, without further need for the shamanic counselor. In each exercise the client has an opportunity to refine the methodological elements of journeying and to practice them. From accumulating journey experiences, as in Ema's case, the client makes interpretations and learns vocabulary, resources, and cosmology of realms personally encountered in the SSC. The changed state of consciousness sometimes leads to ungrammatical and slurred language. The client may experience quite unfamiliar events, some of which may be considered cross-culturally widespread, classic shamanic experiences.

## HSC JOURNEY 1

On instructions from a kingfisher, he lets himself fall into the hole of the earth and comes down dead on the bottom of it. Rain coupled with sunshine make him wet, and through this he is revived.
—A TORADJA SHAMAN'S JOURNEY TO THE LOWER WORLD[1]

This first HSC journey is one of exploration. Its purpose is to help the client begin training in journeying and to instill confidence in the process, as well as to begin to learn the terrain of nonordinary reality. Instructions for this journey are simply for the client to go to the Lower World to meet an animal, explore, build a relationship, and return when

1 N. Adriani and Albert C. Kruyt, *De Bare'e Sprekende Toradjas van Midden-Celebes (de Oost Toradjas)* [The Bare'e-speaking Toradja of central Celebes (the east Toradja)] (Amsterdam: Noord-Hollandsche Uitgevers Maatschappij, 1950).

the drumming call changes to indicate that it is time to return to the starting place in ordinary reality. The counselor briefly orients the client about three core fundamental elements in the shaman's world. These are two states of consciousness (ordinary state of consciousness (OSC) and the altered state of consciousness or SSC), two realities (ordinary reality and nonordinary reality), and three worlds (Upper World, Middle World, and Lower World). In the Upper World and Lower World there is only nonordinary reality. They are solely spiritual in nature, while the Middle World has both aspects, ordinary reality and nonordinary reality.

To get to the Lower World, the client is instructed in advance to find a natural opening in the earth that is a place she has seen in ordinary reality, hence in the Middle World. She is to use this place to go down to the Lower World. Typical places are a cave; a body of water such as a lake, pond, or well; a hole in the ground or in a tree trunk.

Upon starting the journeying process, the client is instructed to relax and state the journey's purpose three times, out loud. The client is to see or feel herself going into the opening and moving downward. As the journey begins, the client is to start describing her experience in detail. She may find herself in a tunnel or tube with light ahead. She should put out a very strong telepathic message that she is asking an animal to be waiting for her on the other side. When she comes out into the light and meets the animal, she should visit with it and explore the Lower World. She should keep an open mind and avoid preconceived ideas, staying in the journey and narrating what's happening until she hears the change in the drumbeat. Then she should say "thank you" and "good-bye" and retrace her steps, back to where she began. Once the drumming recording has ended and before the Mindfold is removed, she should summarize in two to three sentences what has happened in the journey.

## HSC JOURNEY 2

In an Iban initiation, the witch-doctors lead the aspirant into an apartment curtained off from public gaze by large sheets of native woven cloth. There they assert they cut his head open, and take out

his brains and wash and restore them. This is to give him a clear
mind to penetrate into the mysteries of disease and to circumvent
the wiles of unseen spirits.
—AN IBAN SHAMAN'S INITIATION[1]

The second journey builds on the first. The instructions are for the
client to journey to the Lower World to ask the animal a question of
importance to him.

There are ways to frame the question that increase the likelihood
that he can maximize his understanding of the journey as an answer to
his question. The content and final form of the question itself comes
from the client.

The question needs to be of clear *personal* importance. These are
often about relationships, career, or health. Ethically, the question should
be only about the client; he should not invade the privacy of others by
asking questions about them, unless they specifically ask him to do so.
Divination journeys are best when they are about things the client has
been working on in ordinary reality for a while—that he has put in his
own time and effort to resolve.

He should create one simple question, but should avoid yes/no questions. If it is a question that implies an answer of "yes" or "no," he will
miss the opportunity for a fuller answer.

In the same sense, clients should use "should" questions with caution. They also call for a "yes/no" answer. Instead, clients should take
personal responsibility for their decisions. A more useful approach is
to ask, "How could I . . . ?" Or, "What could . . . ?" Another good way to
frame questions is to use one of the following: "How . . . ?" "Who . . . ?"
"What . . . ?" "Where . . . ?" "Why . . . ?"

"When" questions are problematic; by their very nature they involve
matters of time. As Michael Harner noted, Waldemar Bogoras coined
the term "outside of time" to describe the journeys made by the Siberian
shamans he studied.[2] This useful phrase reiterates a difference in

1 Edwin Gomes, *Seventeen Years Among the Sea Dyaks of Borneo: A Record of Intimate
  Association with the Natives of the Bornean Jungles* (Philadelphia: J.B. Lippinncott, 1911).
2 Harner, *Cave and Cosmos.*

concepts of time between ordinary and nonordinary reality. Further, when referring to the future, prophecy or prediction is involved, a notoriously complex issue even when a person is very experienced in divination.

The question should be unambiguous and yet in the client's own words. He should first ask himself: Is this what I mean to be asking? Is it clear?

The client should also not use conjunctions like *and* or *or*. Otherwise, once he gets an answer, he won't necessarily know what part of the question the answer is addressing.

Once the question has been determined, the client is instructed that he will be making another Lower World journey, using the same ordinary reality entrance and looking for the same animal in the same place as in the first journey. He is instructed that once the animal is found, he should ask his question immediately.

Once the journey begins, the client should remain with the journey until the drum calls him back. He should explore the Lower World, getting to know the terrain and its resources. When he hears the callback, he should return immediately, retracing his steps as precisely as he can remember, but quickly.

Unlike the prior journey, before removing his Mindfold, he should summarize the answer to his question, *not* the journey itself. This should be brief—one sentence is best and no more than two or three sentences.

## HSC JOURNEY 3

At last I climbed a tall tree, where I wept myself out, and being quite exhausted by pain and weariness, I remained hanging in the branches of the tree.

All at once I heard a voice near me, and perceived a black form hovering over me. "Who art thou?—Why dost thou weep?" the form asked me.

"I am a poor Indian lad," I replied, "and I weep for my mother."

"Come, follow me," the black figure said, and took me by the hand. It walked with me through the air with one step to the next

tree . . . then she put out the other foot, and we reached with the second step the top of a tall young birch. . . . And thus we stepped out again, and with the third step came to the foot of a tall mountain. But what appeared to me three steps were, in reality, three days' journeys. . . .
—CHIPPEWA JOURNEY TO THE UPPER WORLD[1]

The client may not be ready or may not be "finished" with the last journey. It's a very personal matter. She may want to repeat the second journey, especially if she did not journey or did not meet an animal in the Lower World. She can also repeat the first or second journey later.

The third journey is to go to the Upper World and find a teacher in human form. In many ways it is similar to journeying to the Lower World. It, too, is a journey of exploration. One obvious difference is that she moves up, not down.

More specific to the Upper World journey are these instructions: To start, find another place that you know in ordinary reality in the Middle World, in nature, that sets you to move upward. A person may choose to jump off a treetop or mountain; go up smoke from a chimney or campfire; go up a tornado, a ladder, stairs, whirlwind, or rainbow; or get an animal to take you up.

How she proceeds to go up will come to her when the journey begins. All she needs at first is to plan, before the drumming begins, the place in nature that is to be her starting point.

She starts moving up, putting out a very strong telepathic message that "I want a teacher in human form to be waiting for me in the Upper World." The way she knows she is entering the Upper World is that there will be a transition layer, between the Middle World and the Upper World. It may be like a cloud layer, tissue paper, a membrane, or a pool, for instance. She may feel herself pass through it.

She is to go to the first level, look around, and see if someone is waiting for her. If not, she goes to the second level, and then the third and

1 J. G. Kohl, *Kitchi-Gami* (London: Chapman and Hall, 1860).

on, until she finds someone, a teacher in human form, who she can visit. She is then to ask, "Are you my teacher?"

If the teacher indicates "no," then the journeyer continues to move upward, passing through subsequent levels until she meets a spirit who acknowledges being the client's teacher.

If the response is affirmative, she stays in the Upper World with the teacher, narrating her experiences, and returns when the drumbeat calls her back, retracing the path she took to get there. When she is back in ordinary reality, before she removes her Mindfold, she is to make a short summary of the journey, and if she meets a teacher, she notes on what level of the Upper World they met.

## HSC JOURNEY 4

"Now say; whither wilt thou now—down below, whence thou camest, or up above? The choice is left thee."

"Yes, yes," I replied, "I will go up; for that I have fasted."

The four men seemed pleased at my answer, and the fourth said to me, "Ascend!" He pointed to the back of my stone seat, and I saw that it had grown, and went up an extraordinary height. There were holes cut in it, and I could climb up as if on a ladder. I climbed and clambered higher and higher, and at length came to a place where four white-haired old men were sitting. . . .

"Receive this box with medicine. Use it in case of need; and whenever thou art in difficulty, think of us, and all thou seest in us. When thou prayest to us, we will help thee, and intercede for thee with the Master of Life. . . ."

—AN UPPER WORLD JOURNEY FROM KOHL'S REPORT ON THE CHIPPEWA[1]

This fourth journey is a divination, for the client to get an answer to a question that is personally important. His mission is to return to the Upper World and ask his question of a teacher, preferably the one he

1 J. G. Kohl, *Kitchi-Gami*.

met in the third journey. This can be the same question he asked the animal previously and can be a "second opinion" or a clarification. He may have a natural evolution of a question from a previous journey or an entirely new question.

Following his path as in the third journey, he goes from the same Middle World starting place to the same teacher and immediately asks, "Are you my teacher?" If the answer is "yes," then he asks his question.

It is important that he is quite observant of the very *first* thing the teacher says or does after he asks his question. It is the essential answer to the question. The rest of the journey adds to that answer—it is valuable to stay with the journey until the drumming calls him back. The elaborations and enrichment of the answer are very useful.

The client should always go first to where his teacher is. If the teacher is not there, he has tacit permission to look elsewhere for another teacher for the answer to this question. Remember to repeat the question three times at the outset—before the journey begins and after the drumming starts. Repeat it exactly to the teacher.

## HSC JOURNEY 5

> The medicine-men of the Kumgaingeri (Coomgangree, a Bellinger River tribe [of Australia]) went to the mountains at set seasons of the year. Whilst they fasted and endured privations there for months, "wild stones" (quartz crystals) were placed in their insides by Ulitarra (the first man, who became their god). The large rock-crystal is the symbol of their Great Spirit.
> —FROM ELKIN ON THE IMPORTANCE OF QUARTZ CRYSTALS
> AMONG SOME AUSTRALIAN ABORIGINAL PEOPLE[1]

In this final HSC journey, the instruction is to make a journey to seek advice from the helping spirits about how to bring into action in ordinary reality an answer received in a previous journey. Ideally, the client asks the teacher in the Upper World how to implement in ordinary

---

1 Elkin, *Aboriginal Men of High Degree* (New York: St. Martin's Press, 1977).

reality the answer given in the journey just prior to this one. In these journeys we get a lot of information. The purpose here is to learn how to put it to use.

Although the task is stated for the client to journey to her teacher in the Upper World, there is flexibility here, for teachers may be found in either the Upper World or the Lower World and may be in human, animal, or other form. Whichever the client chooses, she should always use a starting place in ordinary reality of the Middle World. The critical point is that she work with a helping spirit that has proven reliable in answering her questions.

Helpful to the client is to keep her question narrow, so that she is able to do the prescribed actions. Some examples of ways to ask her question include but are not limited to the following: What can I do in ordinary reality to . . . ? How do I implement the information in my journey to the Upper World (or Lower World) about . . . ? How can I do this in my ordinary reality life?

The task is to integrate information with action—to bring the information obtained in nonordinary reality into practical everyday life. To be the ordinary reality shamanic counselor in this process is a singular and awesome honor.

## Spirits

As this is a spiritual practice, the question of spirits arises. In general, each helping spirit is perfect for the individual with whom there is a connection. This relationship may be defined as a partnership, in which the individual and the helping spirits collaborate for purposes of healing, power, maintaining health, and divination or obtaining knowledge. Neither dominates the other.

As said before, commonly, the spiritual beings may take the form of an animal or human. However, they may also take other forms, such as plants, crystals, and other elements of the known and unknown universe. The tutelary spirits called "teachers,"[1] usually appearing in human

1 Harner, *Cave and Cosmos.*

form, may also appear in animal form. They are especially resourceful in matters of healing and access to information, whereas other helping spirits in animal form largely specialize in matters of personal spiritual power. To maintain health, keeping in touch with one's power animal serves to continue the power connection and to indicate if one's power is weak.

Typically any individual spirit animal brings the power of its entire species. For example, "Bear" is usually not a specific kind of bear, but rather all bears, and their collective power are "Bear Power." Beyond that, any specific designation of the nature of that power is an individual matter. It is imperative that clients get empirical data from the facts of their own direct experiences.

As a person continues to work with these helping spirits in service for beneficial ends, a mutual familiarity develops between them and with it comes increasing power in both spiritual work and in their ordinary reality lives, as you will see in the evolution of Ema's journey work.

## After Harner Shamanic Counseling

With the completion of the tasks of the five introductory journeys of HSC, the client has enough rudiments of shamanic journeying to proceed independently.

The counselor—as witness, consultant of method, and source of information about shamanic experiences that arise—monitors the client's journeying skills. In addition, the counselor notes if the client is able to critique his or her own methodology. Finally, is the client able to make interpretations that are meaningful to him- or herself?

It is not always easy to move from one phase to the next on schedule, so an introductory journey may be repeated, as needed. Ideally, throughout the five initial sessions, the client takes more and more responsibility for the whole process, including the equipment. While not technically part of the original protocol, adding a final, autonomous HSC journey can be helpful. When the client feels ready to work entirely alone, the client and counselor may review together a recorded independent journey narration, taped analysis, and written notes for discussion and feedback.

Some options at the conclusion of the five basic tasks of formal HSC that may encourage spiritual independence and support the client's growth are ongoing meetings or occasional "booster" sessions. The benefits of the latter extend to even the most experienced journeyers, as there is a tendency to get relaxed in technique, or use journeying not for themselves, but only in service for others.

In Ema's case, after the first five journeys she chose to begin journeying outside of sessions and to return for an occasional formal HSC session. She made all the Part II journeys in follow-up HSC sessions. Since Ema chose not to master the recording process, there are no recordings or transcripts of journeys she did outside of our meetings together. They took place after her initial formal HSC journeys and were interspersed throughout the recorded journeys of Part II. Journeying remains an active and integral part of her way of life.

# Guide to Reading the Journeys

The language of trance, as in Ema's journeys, is quite different from ordinary, everyday usage. In the ordinary state of consciousness, Ema's grammar is quite correct and coherent, but in the shamanic state of consciousness, it may be neither. Besides the limits and problems with conveying sound, emotion, and emphasis on the written page, particularly when working with direct transcription, there are features that may even be diagnostic of the trance state itself. One of these is pace; for instance, when Ema is deeply engaged in the journey, her spoken words are often very, very slow. This I indicate by placing each word on a separate line. Tonal quality or loudness tends to get very soft and quiet. At times, Ema indicates that she cannot continue narrating, for much language gets lost when Ema is in a deep trance state. When repeated words or phrases do not add significantly to the meaning of the text, I omit them.

To indicate the approximate pace of the narrations, I've explained the conventions in the following table.

| Convention | Significance |
| --- | --- |
| Ellipsis at end of phrase or sentence | Word or thought fades out or is incomplete |
| Ellipsis within a sentence | Unfinished word, phrase, or sentence |
| Ellipsis on a line by itself | A long pause |
| Comma | A short period or pause |
| Comma at the end of a line | A longer pause than a line break |
| Semicolon | Pause longer than a comma but still part of the ongoing current narration |
| Period | End of complete thought or sentence and a full stop |

| Convention | Significance |
| --- | --- |
| Line space | A very, very long pause |
| Multiple line spaces | Silence, no narration |
| Lowercase at start of new line, in middle of sentence | A mid-sentence pause |
| Uppercase at start of new line | New sentence |

In addition to different font styles for Ema as narrator or observer, Ema in dialogue with spirits, and dialogue from spirits, another feature I employ to help the reader is indentation. The level of indentation indicates who is speaking in the narrations and dialogues.

> Far left margin = Ema's narration or description or thought to herself
>
> Single indent = Ema's words to spirits
>
> Double indent = spirits' words to Ema

When Ema is narrating as observer, the narration may continue onto the next line; initial lowercase then starts the first word of the slightly indented new line, unless it is a proper name (like "Turtle") or "I."

After each journey there is a "Reflections" section with several parts: Ema's Quest or purpose of the journey; her response, immediately after the journey; and her interpretation of the journey after listening to a replay of her narration. Frequently, she offers an evaluation statement in addition to, or instead of, an interpretation. Her quotes are excerpted from extensive post-journey discussions and presented here in parts as an aid to the reader, not as a formal template in HSC.

# PART I

## EMA'S JOURNEYS WITH HARNER SHAMANIC COUNSELING

# A New Way to Learn

Purpose: Journey to the Lower World to meet an animal.

I am
walking to the tree and jump down into the tunnel.
Really dark.
Very dry.

I'm just walking.
Oh, the *Native* is there.

> Yes, I think I should go to the Turtle Cave.

> . . .

> All right.

So I am just going to the tunnel to the right,
to the tunnel cave.

There's water.
Kelp is there. I may as well lie down.

> Turtle, I wish you could help me with my leg.

> . . .

> No, no pills anymore.

> . . .

> I know, yes, I . . .

> . . .

> Yes, I did.

> . . .

> I know, I decided since you don't eat any meat, I may as well
>   stop it, too.

> . . .

> It's really nice. Do you want me to stay longer?

I'm walking now through another cave.
I used to go there when I needed thinking.
I am in a larger cave.
Bluish-silver light. And I am supposed to sit on a round rock so
   the light hits me full force.
I'm supposed to sit upright.
The light seems to penetrate my whole body.
Some healing power to my joints.

   Yes, Vulture, I'm supposed to talk . . . I'm with a teacher.

   . . .

   A new learning experience.

   . . .

   I know.

   . . .

   Yes, I know. But I didn't get anywhere.
   You know that.
   Does it mean you abandon me now?

   . . .

   Yes, I see.

   . . .

   I know. All right.

The blue light is all over. Actually it is within my body. Makes
   my joints feel all warm.
Vulture thinks I talk too much.
He said he is going to leave, but he'll be back. And I really need
   him. Turtle is gone. I seem to be all alone in this cave. I don't
   like it.

I seem to be sucked up in this hole where the blue light came in.
Seems to be the same spot.
The old oak tree.
Vulture is flying overhead,
he and several others.
Maybe I should walk, try to climb up the old oak tree.

Very nice, Vulture. Yes, I can see.

I am looking into Vulture's eyes. He has very steely, strong eyes.

He wants me to be strong.

That's what I'm here for.

I think,

to be strong.

Don't you think?

. . .

Yes, I know.

. . .

Oh, thank you for the feather.

I will take it with me.

. . .

Yes, I will have a fire tonight.

. . .

Yes, I will use the feather.

. . .

Yes, I have some sage.

. . .

Yes, I will burn it.

Thank you.

. . .

Yes, yes.

That is a strange

I feel as if I am an acorn. I am an acorn.

Oh, my, now I am stuck here on the tree, I guess.

Pretty windy, suddenly.

The sky starts to get dark.

Now starts to rain also.

The whole branch I was on came down.

The

river.

I am traveling and traveling, traveling. Now I am stuck.

I am here, still after all these
probably months. I don't know. It seems I am *becoming* a tree.
It must be years. I guess that is possible. I seem to be a tree, a
    *small* oak tree.
I seem to *grow...*
More
the size
of
twenty years.
Well, I am a grown oak tree now.
I feel so *strong,* so different.
Oh. I have to leave now.

The drum is calling me back. I better run fast.
Through the cave, the big one, the small one, Turtle Cave.
    Thank you.

---

## 🐢 Reflections

Purpose. Journey to the Lower World to meet an animal.

Ema's Response. "This is my first journey."

Ema's Evaluation "Yes." [In response to a query as to whether she
was able to journey, Ema said with surprise that she was able to
journey].

Ema's Interpretation. "I am always grateful and forget, take it for
granted . . . you [the ordinary reality counselor] make me understand this is really something special."

Counselor's Comments. In the first five tasks of HSC, the primary goal is to establish a systematic methodology that provides
an armature for Ema to journey effectively by herself. Although
this is Ema's first formal HSC journey session, she had previously
made some journeys based on reading *The Way of the Shaman*.

Consequently, she brings some initial familiarity with the non-ordinary reality associated with shamanic journeying. She seeks training through HSC to increase her journeying skills, including interpretation. The HSC focus on methodology provides a framework for her mission.

Here she journeys to the Lower World and returns with the drumming signals, roughly retracing her steps. Notably, she engages in dialogue with two residents of the Lower World; however, she narrates only her side of the conversations, losing the words of the spirits. She demonstrates in this journey the classic shamanic experience of journeying to other worlds, as she journeys to the Lower World. Furthermore, she converses with spirits and transforms from acorn to tree.

As Ema already has some basic journey skills, her initial challenge is to integrate simultaneous narration of the journey, including its purpose and both sides of a dialogue, moving beyond "reporting" to active engagement. Also, she has ahead of herself the task of briefly summarizing (in the present journey) or interpreting her journey (in later journeys) after she completes it, in terms of its intention. In the first HSC journey, there is a lot of methodology to remember. Here she did not state her purpose at the beginning or report anything just after the completion of the journey, and after the replay she was at a loss as to what to say. These points then become a matter of methodology about which the counselor reminds the client. This is also an appropriate time to educate the client about using context-specific terminology, such as "helping spirit" rather than "guide." It may bear repeating, however the client may or may not be concerned with such semantics. The primary matter here is that she is able to journey to the Lower World, meet an animal, and begin to narrate. For each client, each session proceeds according to what his or her individual methodology needs are.

# Seeking Wisdom

Purpose: Journey to the Lower World to ask the animal a question of importance to you.

*How can I obtain wisdom?*

*I like to meet Snake to ask how I can obtain wisdom.*

*I like to meet Snake to ask how I can obtain wisdom.*

I am walking down to the oak tree. And
I see that the tunnel is slightly wet, but
I jump in
and walk
slowly
through the lava tube.
It is fairly dark, but I see in the far distance,
like a pinhead,
a light.
Sort of yellowish, actually.

So I just
think I walk toward that light. And I'm walking. Smells mossy.
  There's lots of water in the cave,
in the tunnel today.
In effect, I'm walking in water, actually. Just a little bit.
I am splashing.
And the moss,
oh, it smells very good. Mossy and earthy. I guess I'm in for a
  long walk because it's still a pinhead.

This is the first time that I ask

before I do the journey.
And I wonder whether Snake will appear and help me.
I'm just walking and walking
and walking.

Oh! Now I'm there.
It's not a cave, actually, but it seems to be surrounded.
It's an area surrounded by
rocks.
And in the middle, a circle,
is a fire.
It is a cold fire.
I mean, it just has flames,
but, it doesn't seem to be hot at all.

Strange. I'm all alone. I'm all alone.

Snake, I would like to talk to you.
I know I haven't seen you for a long time.
I wonder whether you can help me.

I'm still alone.

Vulture! So you have come. Thank you.

. . .

What? You mean I have Snake on me.

. . .

Yes, that is true. It is around my head.
I didn't see it, of course.
Since you both are here. Maybe you heard my question.
What do I have to do to become a wise person?
You know how uncomfortable I am when I have to talk to
workers.

. . .

Yes, I know.
But how can I study that? I mean, I cannot read books to find

out. Yes, I could study and go to the library and find out
how certain things are done.

   . . .

Yes, I know.
That is just so labor-intensive,
I mean, and then when I talk to them about it,
they tell me that it's wrong and . . .

   . . .

Of course, I'm serious. Yes.
Vulture seems to
have turned away. He disappeared. And
Snake obviously was
around my head.
And it's now that I sort of feel the tightening.
He's tightening. She, or he, I never know.
I think Snake is both.
She is tightening and tightening my brain.

Then, *Ugh!* It just
burst open!
Strange
yellow, gooey, syrupy stuff is coming out of it. It's just flowing
  down,
right into the earth.

   Snake, what does that mean?

    . . .

Yes, I know. I do
think too much about things.
I know it is not necessary. I know, but I can't help it. I think
  about it at night and it just won't go away.
I know
it is for me
to do
it on
my own.

What is coming out of my head? It is still coming.

What is it?

. . .

You mean, this will clear my mind?

All this mass that has accumulated over the years.

It's coming . . .

. . .

Yes, well, that makes sense.

I had no idea that it was so much.

Alas,

I thought I had cleared my mind before, but,

yes, you are quite right. I should start with a clear head.

Thank you for squeezing this out of me.

My head feels so much lighter.

. . .

You want me to go

where?

. . .

Right.

I am supposed to go through the meadow.

It seems to be a small pond there

with a tiny cascading waterfall. It is really tiny.

Do you fit?

. . .

I'm much too big for that waterfall.

. . .

All right, I will sit underneath.

Ahhhhh! How nice.

It just comes down

on my head and my face, my shoulders, my whole body.

I'm submerged in water.

Turn my neck.

Now.

Ah, the water is just
trickling
on my head.

    Oh, take all my thoughts of heaviness away.
    Let me think clear and precise.
    Don't let my brain be cluttered again
    with useless thoughts and anxieties.

      . . .

    Snake, I had no idea that you can swim.

      . . .

    You want me to follow you
    swimming?

Snake asked me to follow her. We are swimming in the pond.
  She wants me to dive down. Deep, deep down. Oh, it is so
  muddy in here.
I don't seem to need air.
I mean, I can breathe right here
in the water and the mud. I go deeper and deeper and deeper
  and deeper.
Ah! I am back
in the lava?
In the tunnel?
In the lava tunnel.

    Does it mean you want to get rid of me?

      . . .

    You want me to go back?

      . . .

    Ohhh,
    I am supposed to follow you.
    This is a very, very deep pit.
    I can't go down there.

Oh! There are hundreds of snakes making the rope for me to
  climb down into this dark, dark, dark pit.
And so I am just climbing down

and climbing down
and climbing down.
Still, still.
It seems to be no end. And it is *so* dark. I can't see anything.
Now, I seem
to have arrived at the bottom
of this pit.

I wonder what I am supposed to do here in this dark pit. I can't
  see anything. It is pitch, pitch dark.
I feel snakes all around me. They are *all* over me. I don't know
  what they are doing.
They just seem to
massage me.
They seem to squeeze my *whole* body. It is as if they
*squeeze* the water out of my body,
or some kind of liquid.
They're still on me,
squeezing some kind of liquid out of my body.
My arms, and my chest, and my stomach, and my legs.
Or, maybe they are massaging me.
I really cannot quite make out
because I can't see anything. It is so dark. But, it feels, actually,
  very nice.
Snake tells me to look to my
to my navel.

              . . .

    Yes, I see the light. Oh, yes! There is my blue light. Now I can
      see where I am.
It is a pit
with ferns and water; little water rivulets are running. *Beautiful*
  maidenhair fern.
How wonderful it is here!
    Why am I here, Snake?

Why am I here, Snake?

No answer.

No answer.

I am sitting here

in the dark.

The snakes are still around me, but they have gone off my body.

They just seem to be on the ground, lying.

It seems to me as if we all sit here to meditate, because there is
   nothing else to do. So I sit and meditate. I am to concentrate
   on the light that comes from my navel, so I try to concentrate
   on that beautiful blue light that sometimes surrounds me

when I need help. It is warm. Oh, and it gets lighter and lighter
   and lighter.

And now I am in the meadow again.

Strange. I seem to be so much lighter.

I mean,

my body seems to be

so much lighter. My brain,

I,

seems to be so different.

Not *clouded* anymore.

   Snake, what does this mean?

I am all alone, Snake has left.

I wish Turtle were here. Turtle could explain to me what it
   meant.

But Turtle is gone.

Actually, Turtle was never there, was she?

I just sit here

At the meadow. The sun is shining. This would be the right
   grass for buffalo, but there is no buffalo in sight.

The drum is calling. I have to go back.

   I want to thank you all.

I have to go to that yellow-lit place, in order to get back. I can't
   really find it. I wonder where it was.
I have gone through so many . . .
OK, I better go. I don't want to go into the pit. OK, there's the
   yellow light. Now, I'm in the tunnel.
I better hurry.

And
I'm back.

---

 ## Reflections

Purpose. Journey to the Lower World to ask the animal a question
of importance to you.

Ema's Quest. "I like to meet Snake to ask how I can obtain wisdom."

Ema's Evaluation. [Ema makes no initial response just after concluding her journey. After her counselor asks if she obtained an
answer to her question, she says, "Yes." Later she summarizes as
follows.] "I should empty my brain of the thoughts I have . . . they
probably interfere with my seeing clear. I just should throw out all
the . . . worries I have . . ."

Ema's Interpretation. "I think I cloud my vision by worries which
are not really there, is what it meant."

Counselor's Comments. Continuing to narrate only her side of
conversations, Ema questions both Snake and Vulture. Notice that
the question as she states it in the journey differs from what she
originally framed at the outset. In addition, she asks further questions that build on the theme of obtaining wisdom, while working
with the answers she is given. She is careful to follow the methodology for stating the question or purpose at the outset, beginning
and ending the journey, returning according to the drumbeat signals. Notably, Ema offers thanks, expressing gratitude to the spirits.

Her efforts are rewarded with Snake's answer to her question.

Methodologically, for each journey, the aim is for the client to volunteer her immediate response (either a brief summary of the journey or the answer to the question, depending on its purpose) to the journey just after she completes it; then, after hearing the playback, she gives a more considered response or evaluation of her journey and whether or how the journey applies to the original intention. Finally, in further discussion, the client consolidates her interpretation or understanding of the meaning of her journey, if she can do so at this time. Prompts from the counselor are appropriate early in the process to help the client learn the methodology; it becomes the responsibility of the client to use these reminders in her own way as the sessions continue. This is a model that varies considerably from client to client, as each develops her own way of working with her journeys.

# Lavender Tea

Purpose: Go to the Upper World to find a teacher in human form.

*I want to go to the Upper World to find a teacher.*

*I want to go to the Upper World to find a teacher.*

*I want to go to the Upper World to find a teacher.*

I try to go down to the oak tree.
It's somewhat slippery.
And so I'm here now.
I'm looking down into the tunnel; it's all wet.
Actually, it's quite foggy.
The fog just goes, sort of envelops me. It seems to try to lift me.
  Maybe I should climb up the oak tree myself and just see
if I am on top of the
branches, maybe.
It's kind of cool up here.
It seems to be some kind of a
ladder or something coming down.
I think I just climb this ladder
and go up.
And up. Just climb.
Mmmm, it's so light. I seem to be so light.
I hardly have to hold on to the ladder.
It goes faster and faster and faster. I am going up very quickly
  now.

Isn't cold anymore, either. It's just
very pleasant.
Now I seem to float. I just seem to float. I just seem to float in
  the air.

Ahhh, and just see all these interesting formations of clouds
and fog.
I really can't see much at all. It just seems to be foggy.

Clouds.
The clouds seem to have sort of
*crystals* on them. It shimmers.
It's so beautiful!
But when I touch it, it
seems to disappear. I mean, the crystals seem to be
*air,* also.
I better don't touch them because they look so nice
just to see them.

How nice it is to just *flow*
*weightless,* through
the sky, I would say. It must be the sky.
I'm still floating.
Floating, floating.
Ahhh.
The crystals
seem to get *bigger* now. At first, they were very small.
Now they seem to get
*bigger.*
They have this sheen to it.
I wonder where the source of the light is that shines on the
crystals. I just kind of
*push.*
This is a big crystal. I really
should look at this crystal closer.
I put my finger through it.
It must be a mirage, because when I put my finger into it, it
doesn't seem to be *there.* I mean, I can *see* it, but it seems to be
clouds, because
it has no substance. And yet, they *are*

*crystals.*
I cannot quite figure this out,
there is a light, but I do not know where it comes from.
Maybe the light is
within the crystal.
I am in the clouds, but the crystals and everything is just foggy.
But, the crystals seem to be
a sort of light,
the source of light.

I am supposed to look for human.
Otherwise, I think I would just ask the crystal
whether the crystal
would be a teacher.
Well, I may as well ask.
Or maybe *not.*
Hmm. I don't know what to do. I just don't know what to do.
Should I? I *think* I see the Native. He seems to walk out right,
right out of the crystal.

> Is it really you? I have been asked to come to the Upper World.
> Are you a mirage, also?

I think I better try to touch him. Yes, it was a mirage, because he
  sort of
disappeared. He became clouds.

Now, somehow my brain plays tricks on me. I think I so badly
  want to find someone, because I'm told I should. *Oh, dear.*
I think I better relax and just
*float.* Ohh.
It's not so terrible if I don't find a teacher. It really isn't. Since it
  is so foggy, I can't really . . .
Can't see anything.
Even if I would look, it would be so difficult. But, on the other
  hand, I'm *supposed* to look.
All right. I may as well just get myself

a look.

If I could just find out where the source of light. I have the
feeling, if I could just go where the light is.

Ah! My goodness! I just *bumped* into Great Grandmother's
kettle. I guess she isn't here because
it is cold. Normally, she has always herb tea in it. I just wonder
whether I should make some tea for myself. All right,
I just put lavender
into it,
lavender
and water.
And now, I just take this crystal and put it underneath,
Please give me one fire, so I can have some tea.
Hmmm. It smells really good.
And it bubbles. I think I can drink some in a minute.
Yes.
Now I'm going to drink it. Mmmmm!

I think I was dehydrated.
Ah, my body seems to
become full and,
ah, that feels so much better having something warm in me.
I just wonder,
Great Grandmother doesn't seem to be home.
Well, I suppose I just leave. I wish I could take some tea along. I
just take a cup.
Take it along.
The fog is
lighter now. It's not as dense anymore.
Not as heavy
But, I still can't see anything. I still can't see anything. I mean,
no human form.

I wonder if I call Vulture.

I could maybe be faster up here
to find him. He has this good eyesight.

> Vulture, I'm in the Upper World. I'm looking for a teacher.
> Please help me to find a teacher.

Vulture, I think . . .
I think he doesn't hear me. He's probably busy.
There *are* some formations in the
distance.

They are *trees.*
*Pine* trees,
slender and tall.
I think I'm sort of tired.
I may as well go to them, just sit at there.

Sit down here.
I'm supposed to
look for a teacher,
but nobody is here. I've looked anywhere and I'm so tired now. I
    still don't have the strength I would like to have.
Oh, I still have some
tea. Why don't I just finish it?
Mmm. That *does* give me strength.

The drum is calling. I have to go back.
I just float back. I see Great Grandmother's kettle. And I just
fly and float
down and down and down and down and down.
Plop!
I'm back.
I'm back.
Ah.

> Thank you. That was a wonderful trip.

##  Reflections

Purpose. Go to the Upper World to find a teacher in human form.

Ema's Quest. "My purpose is to go to the Upper World to find a teacher."

Ema's Response (or summary just after her journey). None.

Ema's Evaluation (in reply to counselor's prompt about whether she met her purpose for this journey). "No. Too comfortable, nice."

Ema's Interpretation. "It was a wonderful journey actually . . . I felt so nice . . . I was just floating . . . I think I didn't have the urgency to find a teacher . . . discipline to the task at hand, purpose for this journey. . . . It felt so nice to float."

Counselor's Comments. In this journey to the Upper World to find a teacher, Ema starts from a place she knows, hoping to find a teacher in human form. She does enter the Upper World. Within the journey she observes that she would ask the crystal she encounters "whether the crystal would be a teacher" and decides against it in order to adhere to the stated objective of this journey. Although she did not find Great Grandmother in the Upper World, Ema did find Great Grandmother's usual place and kettle and made for herself some lavender tea, which was warm and refreshing. She herself notices that she loses her focus on her primary purpose—to find a teacher in the Upper World. Upon reflection, she also makes the astute observation (above) that she "didn't have the urgency to find a teacher." Attention to the methodology gave way to the pleasure of her experience in the journey.

# Crystal Wisdom

Purpose: Go to the Upper World to ask the teacher an important question in your life.

*I like to ask why I am not able to eat the right foods.*

*I like to ask why I am not be able to eat the right foods.*

*I like to ask why I am not able to eat the right foods.*

Please receive me.

I think I go again,
down to the oak tree.
Ah!
Ohhh.
It's foggy again.
I'm climbing up the oak tree and I'm
just waiting for the ladder to come. There it is.
So I'm
climbing up the ladder.
Higher, and higher, and higher.
And higher.
Now, I'm suddenly light as a feather again.
And I seem to float
in this foggy environment, but it
is not at all cool or wet.
It's dry!
Dry.
A dry fog or mist
and

it is
a *smell* of *spring,*
like spring flowers.
Mmmm.
I have to fill my lungs
with this wonderful fragrance.
It makes me light
and airy.
Ahhh! What a wonderful feeling to float.
Not be earthbound.
Oh, it is so light.
So airy.
Ahh Ohhh.

I'm just *floating.* Ah! I seem to be caught up on the
small crystals.
Ah!!
They all seem to chatter. I mean they all seem to talk.
Some voices come out of there,
like children.

> Now, listen, I need a teacher. Do you think you can
> point me to a teacher?

They want me to come in
and play with them.
That is really not what I had in mind.

Ohh.

I don't know. Somehow
I'm pushed away.
And now I'm floating again and floating.
Now the bigger crystals are
in sight. *There* is that big crystal.

> Oh, Crystal, you want me to come inside.

I'm stepping inside the *huge, beautiful,*

white,

no, *clear,*

clear crystal. I'm supposed to sit down.

 Crystal, will you be my teacher?

I didn't get an answer, but I seem to be wedged

in this beautiful crystal.

So I will just say my

question.

 Crystal, why am I not be able to eat the right foods?

 I know it is so important to keep my body healthy.

 What can I do? *Please,* let me know.

Nothing is being said, but

I am

to *concentrate.*

Deep, deep within my inner self,

to the *very* deepest, inner self.

To the

very

deepest

inner

self.

I see *emptiness* in there. Emptiness. Why would I be empty?

It should be filled.

There seem to be a big hole there.

 How can we fill the hole, Crystal?

 How can we fill that hole?

 How

 can we fill

 that hole?

It seems to me as if

crystals are forming in that deep hole.

Light, light blue. More and more *tiny* crystals.
More and more
tiny crystals
forming
within my deepest self. Clear
and clean
and *powerful.*
Ahhhh!
What a *strange feeling!* They seem to form a ball.
The outside is
flat. The inside
seems like a round ball.
It's rolling around.
And rolling around,
rolling around. I don't know whether this is the *life force,*
making it going up and down, up and down.
This is something happening,

I don't quite grasp.
It's more than I can understand, but it *feels* so *terribly important.*
Oh, why can't I grasp what is going on?
I don't understand, but it feels important. Please, let me under-
    stand.

    Crystal. Please let me understand.
    What is happening with me?
    What is the meaning?
The crystals
are a wise entity.

    Is that what you m . . . ? That's what you say.
Saying.
Really
seems to
vibrate. Seems to vibrate. Crystals
bring knowledge.

Knowledge.
Knowledge.

> How can I use this knowledge

> for my eating habits? Is there any way I can use this
> knowledge?

I should take time?
> Time for what?
>> *Take time,*
It seems to vibrate.
>> *Take time*
>> *Take time.*
> For what? For what? For what?
>> *Take time,*
It says.
Crystals are wise. They give me knowledge. To take time.
> To take time to prepare the right foods, is that what it means?
>> *To take time to think things through,*
> Ah.
I have the feeling as if the crystals sort of dissolve.

There's a cool wind.
I seem to be in a flat field
all by myself.
The crystals are all gone. It's
light and airy, but I can't see
very far.
Now,
the drum is calling me back. I
try to go back
through the field of small crystals.

I see a crystal in the
background.

It looks like the crystal I have. I guess I'm supposed, I'm to
concentrate on that one.

I have to go.

I have to go.

I really have to go.

I go down the ladder.

Down the tree.

Ahh! And I'm back. Just in time, I may add! I arrived with the
last beat.

Oh, God! What a journey!

##  Reflections

Purpose. Go to the Upper World to ask the teacher an important
question in your life.

Ema's Quest. "I like to ask why I am not able to eat the right foods."

Ema's Response. "Oh, God! What a journey!"

Ema's Evaluation. After reviewing the replay and discussion, she
says, "I felt the crystal was the teacher for the day . . . I really didn't
get an answer . . . they said . . . I am to concentrate, I am to . . .
deep, deep within my inner self, to the very deepest inner self, to
the very deepest inner self."

Ema's Interpretation: "Incredible journey at the point this crystal
forms and within me . . . unbelievable moment . . . life force . . . I
was that . . . the words fail me to describe it. . . . Blue seems to be
a healing color for me."

Counselor's Comments. Ema decides to try again to find a teacher
in the Upper World, this time in the context of the fourth exercise,
to ask a question that is very important to her. As in the previous
journey, a ladder provides her access to the Upper World. Crystals
are again a prominent feature and Ema acts on her prior thought,

asking the big crystal to be her teacher and posing her question just as she had originally planned.

In the prior journey, Ema tasted lavender tea and felt its warmth; in this journey her sense of smell becomes apparent. For the first time, Ema narrates both sides of this dialogue, as she searches to understand the answer. With the drumbeat, she returns as she went, concluding that she "really didn't get an answer." Recall that with the recorded narration, Ema can replay the journey and continue to consider what answer to her question might be embedded in the journey. Notice that there is no prompt for Ema to give a response, evaluation, or interpretation. This is to determine whether Ema is able to initiate this part of the process on her own, which she does.

# Floating in Infinity

Purpose: Make a journey to the Upper World to ask your teacher how to implement in ordinary reality the answer given in a previous journey.

*How can I work with the Energies in ordinary life?*

*How can I work with the Energies in ordinary life?*

*How can I work—the Energies in ordinary life?*

> I go
> down the
> *wet* slope toward the oak tree
> and, the oak tree is
> really wet today.
> I have to be careful that I don't slip. So I just go *up* the oak tree
> to the *very* top
> and the *ladder* is already waiting for me today. So I'm going up
>    the ladder.
> Higher and higher.
> And higher
> and higher. Gee, that is a very long,
> Higher still.
> The fog seems to be so heavy. It
> seems to *weigh* me down.
> Seems to me as if I can't really
> get up there.
> I'm looking. Suddenly, something seems to
> take me under the arms and seems to sort of *pull* me up.
>
> And now I'm

floating.

Now it's dry.

Dry and light.

Ahhh.

Ahhh.

It's

airy.

I'm floating.

*There* are the small crystals and I just seem to float *by* the
crystals. Higher.

Much.

I seem to be

looking down on them this time. I'm looking *down* on the
crystals.

I cannot at all reach the crystals.

I seem to be so light

that I seem to be just floating. Even *by* the *huge* crystal. It seems
to be

*down* then. So, I am in a different area.

I really would like to meet the Native

and my [great-]grandmother, too. Because they

told me that I should use the Energies

in ordinary life. And even though I think I *do* it partly, but

I seem to have to remind myself all the time.

I wish I could just be more mindful about my surroundings and
understand that they are

*all*

*Energies.*

Precious, mysterious Energies. But I am in a completely different
surrounding now. I seem to be *so* high up.

I seem to be in *space,* because

it is like the night sky. It is very dark blue.

And I seem to leave the

area
with the crystals
*far, far* behind.
It is like a tiny, tiny, silvery dot. And I seem to be in space. I
    mean, it feels like a
*huge, huge*
globe.
So huge I don't even have a word for it. Infinite.
I seem to be in a blue
infinite
space
and I just seem to
float in it.
Back
and forth.
And back
and forth.
It is
*dark* blue but
still seems to be a
light source.
I wonder where the light source is coming from?
I *think* the light source is coming from me.
Yes.
I
seem to be
a *glowing*
*entity.*
This is *just*
strange. But, like a light
is coming from me. Like a star maybe
but very much smaller, of course. And yet it seems to light the
    infinite space,
because I can see far.

Far.
And little dots of lights. They are coming
sort of
closer.
God, I should feel lonely really, because I seem to be so alone,
   but I don't feel lonely at all this time.
I feel just being
*happy.*
It is just such a wonderful feeling. I can breathe
this *marvelous*
air
or *energy.*
I wonder whether if I am floating in energy,
in *dark, blue infinite energy.* That's exactly what I am in
right now.
It is an *absolutely* marvelous feeling.
I just wonder what that means.
I should probably have asked before
I left, that I wanted to meet the
Native.

Something says to me,
         *Be flexible. Enjoy, enjoy, enjoy.*
The whole space is filled with this,
         *Enjoy. Enjoy.*
Yes, I am going to enjoy.
I'm just floating
in this
*marvelous*

*infinite*

*ocean*

of energy.
It is *so great.* And I am all alone.

And it feels so freeing.

Whatever movement I want to do, I can do freely.
I mean, I can whirl fast and I can go up and down
and around.
It's just amazing
how wonderful it feels.
How *wonderful* it feels!

> Vulture, I don't believe it!
>
> What are you doing here? I mean, here?
>
> . . .
>
> Yes, I know. I should have visited you, but I,
> I'm sorry I didn't.
> Is this energy I'm in? I mean this . . .
>
> . . .
>
> Yes, I thought so.
> Vulture, I have to leave. The drum is calling me back. I promise
>  I will
> visit you. I promise. I have to go. I have to just go very fast.

Vulture is taking me on his wings.
And so, we fly.
And we flying and flying and flying and flying and flying, flying.
Now we are
back in the
world of
mist.
We are still flying together. And now he just drops me.
And I am back.
I go down the tree
and I am back.

## ⬤ Reflections

Purpose: Make a journey to the Upper World to ask your teacher how to implement in ordinary reality the answer given in a previous journey.

Ema's Quest. "How can I work with the Energies in ordinary life?"

Ema's Response. "I cried the whole way through."

Ema's Interpretation. "Be flexible . . . enjoy. . . . That was energy. I should use the energy here and enjoy . . . go with the flow of the energy. This whole journey . . . was to tell me to relax . . . not take it too rigid . . . take it easy."

Counselor's Comments. Ema develops her question from a prior journey in which her teacher tells her "to work with the Energies." In this journey, she asks how to do that in her daily life of ordinary reality.

Experiencing joyous crying in the journey and in ordinary reality awakens her to the personal benefits of free-flowing energy. She needed no prompt to make an immediate response to her journey or to develop her interpretation of it. While her emphasis is on her felt experience of this emotionally powerful journey, she comes to a meaning specific to herself. This underscores the importance both of leaving the interpretation of a journey to the journeyer and of the counselor not interrupting with the client as she journeys.

# PART II

EMA'S JOURNEYS AFTER
FORMAL HARNER SHAMANIC
COUNSELING SESSIONS

JOURNEY 6

# To Heal the Spirit

*What can I do in the ordinary world to heal my spirit?*

*What can I do in the ordinary world to heal my spirit?*

*What can I do in the ordinary world to heal my spirit?*

I'm going down to the oak tree and
try to go through the opening. It
seems to be like a little river in there, so I
just go in and my feet are *all wet.* So I'm
walking down the tunnel.
Moss has formed on the sides of the tunnel. It's really nice. It's a
  nice earthy smell.
I would like to speak to Turtle today. And,
I would like to *meet* her. I thought I would meet her in the
meadow near the brook, but I
really forgot how I got there.

> Oh, Turtle, you are already there.

> Oh, Turtle, this is . . .

Turtle is *huge* and *black*; she wants me to sit
on her. And now
we seem to swim. We seem to swim
through the *tunnel!* I did not know that there was so much water
  in here, but
here we go,
swimming.

> Turtle, I have the feeling that my spirit is broken. I just wonder
> whether you can help me
> to heal it. I mean, myself, in the ordinary world?

Turtle says I should wait till we are

where she wants to go with me. So, we are swimming. And now
we go

to the Turtle Cave.

Oh, yes.

The Turtle Cave is a medium-sized cave and it has lots and lots
of turtles in it.

They all need healing.

Oh, I see so many

that have a cracked shell.

Maybe I should heal them first before I do anything else. What I
do is

I just pick up some

seaweed that is all over

on the ground in this cave and put it on their

shells and it heals

right away.

And here are some small turtles. Oh. This one seems to be as if
somebody has bitten off

one of the little feet.

So I also put some

seaweed on it.

I think I just put seaweed

on all the turtles that are in here. There seem to be a

dozen.

Fifteen, altogether, I think. And then there is one in the corner,
in the dark corner.

Okay, let's see what happen to you. Oh.

She wants me to sit next to her.

You want me to repeat
my question.
I would like you to help me
to heal myself in the ordinary world.
I mean to heal my spirit, you know.
I think my spirit is broken.

Turtle is putting seaweed all over me. It is the *big* turtle. She is so
  *big* that she can regurgitate
seaweed over me. It comes out of her mouth like
coming from a spout of a fountain, which is actually a very nice
  *feeling*. It is *not sticky* at all. It is just
a very nice *clean* feeling and it is a wonderful ocean smell
  about it.
     No, I don't really know
It was asked whether I know what
spirit is, whether I know where my spirit is located.
     No, I don't know. I mean,
     I don't really know
     what spirit is.

     I really don't know
     even whether my spirit is broken. I think
     I just said it. Because I personally feel so
     unhappy
     with my health.

I'm supposed to lie down now. I'm supposed to
*concentrate*
on my body,
to lie in this
bed of seaweed.
The seaweed is just swishing over my body. Water,
there is water. Also, it seems to be
sort of a
hollow. And so, I'm lying actually
in an
indent in a sort of a pool.
     You say to me that I should take more time, but I thought I did.
     . . . the seat of the spirit.
I'm just lying there and Turtle, both of the turtles, are sitting and
  watching me. I just don't know.

I don't *feel* I should ask again 'cause they know what I would like.

But they don't answer.

Turtle, what is spirit? Tell me, what is spirit?

*Spirit is also a life force*
*within*
*all of us. It is within the trees and the rocks,*
*the food we eat,*
*the animals.*
*Everything is spirit, everything is spirit, you see. Everything*
*is spirit.*

How can one heal spirit? Turtle, how can one heal spirit?

*Take your thoughts off.*
*The invading*
*thoughts you have. Push them aside. See your future in a*
*bright way. Don't struggle with the past. It is gone. Look*
*for the future. Look for the future.*

Do you think I have a future? Turtle?

*That is up to you. That is up to you. Spirit holds it all*
*together. Spirit holds it all together.*

I think I still don't quite understand. It means that the oak tree outside my home
has a spirit
because it's alive.
But the rock has a spirit too,
so it must be also alive in some way. Does it mean I should be more mindful of nature?

. . .

I have tried it. I thought I did. But you think . . .

. . .

It's not thorough enough? I think I'm mindful in the Lower World about the spirits of nature. But in the ordinary world I get distracted. Is that what you try to tell me?

*Yes.*

I thought
I remember you said I should travel to the Lower World every
   day,
every night,
but I haven't done it.
In other words, you really have the time
to receive me on a daily basis?
In other words, what you are saying is
if I want my spirit to be healed,
I have to go to the Lower World more often to be reminded
   how to live in the ordinary world,
so that I won't be distracted.
Yes, I know, I'm in the position to do that.
Yes, I know, I'm very fortunate that way.
Thank you, Turtle. I think I finally understand
what I have to do. As you know, I was quite desperate.

It is a *wonderful* feeling just lying here
and have the seaweed
swishing over my body. I could stay here forever. It's just so
   wonderful. Ahhh!
Turtle motions me to go with her.
So we
walk through the cave. And through a sort of whirlpool. We just
   get transported toward the ocean. With a *plop,*
I'm in the water.
It is sort of a, what can I say, lagoon. The water is very shallow
and we are swimming toward the beach. Ah! The sun is *warm.* It
   feels nice on my skin.
This is an area I have been before
because I know the cave and I also know the beach here. There
   is a round stone, a rather big round stone like a wheel. And I'm
   supposed to sit on it. I'm supposed to meditate.
The sun is shining on me. It's sort of a bluish light that comes
   from the sun. And my whole body is in this blue light.

I am to *meditate*
about what I have just learned.
That spirit
is everywhere. In the trees, and in the rocks, and in the animals.
Even in the furniture, even in the cup I am drinking tea out.
Everything is spirit. *Everything* is spirit. Once one understands
that everything is spirit, the healing *has* to occur.

Yes, it is still so new to me. I think I still don't quite grasp it,
but maybe I do.
I mean yes, maybe I do.

I try to really go very deep, deep down into myself. My whole
body is a light blue. I can see into my body. It is as if I am
crystal. It's like crystal. I can see my heart beat. I can see my
veins.
I can see my stomach, my spleen.
I see all my organs but I cannot see my bones. I only see my
organs.
My heart seems to be,
I don't know, my heart is so dark.
My heart needs a lot.
*My heart needs lots of blue light*
to make it lighter.
To take the heaviness away from it.

Where does the spirit sit?
In what part of the body?

*There is no one spot where your spirit sits; you are all spirit.*
*Spirit is in all of you.*
Spirit is in my heart. In all the organs.
Now I seem to be myself again. I mean, my bones and my flesh.
And everything is intact again. And the blue light has
disappeared.
*Time* has gone by and it
is

getting dark. It's getting dark. Seems to be a *glow* coming from
  my body.
I am sitting here and it is dark.
And I'm glowing. I seem to be the light
source
for my immediate surroundings.
Turtle is there. She is digging a hole
to put her eggs in!
She's laying eggs!
    Oh, Turtle, I had no idea!
She wants me to help put sand over the eggs. So I *really* put my
  hands into the *sand*. The sand is cool and a little bit *wet*. I put
  it over the eggs.
White
tiny little balls.
They look like
golf balls. A little bit slimy.
Now Turtle wants me to lie down. And I lie down. Now she is
  putting
the last egg she has. She is putting [it]
into my belly button.
    Ahhh, Turtle.
    Ahhh.
The egg is within me now.
    Oh, Turtle, the drum is calling me. I have to go back.
    Thank you I will take care of your egg.
I need to go *down* the water spout into the cave. And now I'm at
  the tunnel. I'm going fast
And I'm going fast. There's the opening.
And now I'm back
in the ordinary world.

##  Reflections

Ema's Quest. "What can I do in the ordinary world to heal my spirit?"

Ema's Evaluation. "My goodness! . . . I think I don't quite understand it. It seems to be such a difficult way."

Ema's Interpretation (after reviewing recording). "What I understand is that spirit seems to be probably in everything. I mean spirit is . . . we are surrounded by spirit. Everything has . . . has . . . spirit. . . . Everything is spirit."

Counselor's Comments. This is the first journey after the formal HSC sequence. The first five journeys establish a baseline of mutual understanding of a methodology and orientation to shamanic journeying. Beginning with this, the sixth journey, Ema determines the stated purpose and where and from which spirit she seeks an answer. From this point onward, all journeys are set by Ema. She decides their purpose and the specific question. The counselor continues to make a handwritten record of her narration and behaviors as she journeys, as well as to handle the mechanics of recording. Ema uses the recordings, but chooses not to get involved in managing the equipment. The tutorial aspect of HSC is now limited to methodology and shamanic context observations *after the fact*; that is, after Ema completes her journey and discusses it. Clearly, the use of the summary statement immediately after her journey is taking its own course, in Ema's own specific way.

Comments on the journey become the vehicle by which further ordinary reality teaching proceeds, keeping in mind that Ema is developing her own style for effective journeying in her own way, and to inform without judging her journey work. Likewise, interpretation of content is her responsibility alone.

When she has difficulties in technique, ethical issues arise, or she has a classic shamanic experience, these points become the subject of discussion. Creating an environment that promotes her spiritual autonomy is at the forefront. Guidelines or reminders of what others find helpful and why, and fundamental principles like not using the journey for harmful purposes, respecting the privacy of others, and experiencing the reality of spirits help Ema refine her journey practice, while emphasizing that her journeys and her interpretations are perfect for her individually and not necessarily a message for others, even if they seem suitable as general rules. The first five journeys establish a baseline of mutual understanding of a methodology and orientation to shamanic journeying.

Ema's compassion for others (e.g., Turtle and Vulture) and her gratitude are repeated refrains as she proceeds in her journeys. Here she comes asking for healing for her spirit and in the process of the journey expresses compassionate healing first to the turtles she finds need healing. Throughout the journey she develops her concerns about her initial question and receives deep wisdom from her helping sprits, extracting a significant interpretation of their message to her, as well as details beyond her original question.

# Journey on Balance

*What was the meaning of the sun and moon shining on us at the equinox?*

*What was the meaning of the sun and moon shining on us at the equinox?*

*What was the meaning of the sun and moon shining on us at the equinox?*

This is my question I would like to have answered on my
   journey today.

I am going toward
the oak tree and
I look in the opening. There's the tree.
There's a little bit of moisture in there, but I can jump right in.
I am in the tunnel. It is dark.
Very dark.
I can't see anything this time.
Normally, I think I sort of
had some light
coming from within me, but it doesn't seem to be at all there
   today, so I just have to go toward the wall and sort of feel
     my way
in the dark. The wall is all moist and mossy. Soft at times where
   the moss is.
And then jagged
where the
raw lava is coming through.
I don't really like this darkness at all.

I'm just walking.

I think I just sit down and concentrate. Maybe I can get some
  light from in myself.

I just

touch my area

where I feel that my energy is.

And now

I can see where I am. I have almost made it to

the tunnel that leads to the Turtle Cave.

But for whatever reason I don't think I'm supposed to go there
  today.

I just go straight.

There is no light inside this time. I wonder if whether I'm
  supposed to be in the tunnel today.

I think I better sit down again

and just wait.

I wonder what I should do.

There is a little lizard opposite the wall. I think he wants me
  to follow him. Sort of greenish, teeny little lizard. He's just
  running along

across the wall. I really have to go fast in order to keep up with
  him.

And now he disappears

within a crack. He wants me to follow him. I really have to
  *squeeze* myself through that crack.

Ah, I cannot quite make it.

Now I'm through! Ha!

Sort of a

grayish

teeny little

cave-like

place.

Light

seems to shine through.

Windows!? That's amazing. There seem to be windows.

It seems to be like a church hall, actually. I'm supposed to sit in the middle.

Is this the lizard? It seems to be the lizard standing right in front of me.

> Should I ask you then?
> At the equinox
> I was with the Native.
> I wonder why the sun and the moon
> were shining on us
> at the equinox. I really would like to know the meaning of it.

It seems to me as if the same is just happening again to me.

On the left side

I feel warmth.

All around my left side of the body. Nothing on the right side

But it's all lit.

The left side of my body

seems to be almost in flames.

I just *have* to go to the other side.

Ah, gosh!

I thought I was burning to death.

But now on the right side

it's ice-cold. My bones seem to become brittle. I can hardly think. I just have to get to the other side. *I have to find the balance point.* I just

balance.

> Is that what it means? Balance. To balance myself.
>> *Yes.*
> Please show me the spot
> to sit so I can balance myself. So that I will not be burned.

At the moment I feel

I'm dying.

I'm dying. Oh!

Vulture is there. He had opened up my brain with his beak
and he's taking my brain out.
Ah!
He's just picking it. It looks like a long sausage in his mouth.
  And more,
and more. He's emptying my skull completely. Oh, my God. Ah,
  my God.
    Vulture, what are you doing?
Oh! He's *taking* my brain and
put it into
some kind of a cauldron or . . .
It's a big pot.
And he's putting it in there. And, now he's *cooking* it. That's not
  possible. That is just not possible.
And, now he's putting ice pieces into it.
Now it's not Vulture anymore. Now it's the Native. He seems to
  *wash* my brain. This is just not real! But that's exactly what he's
  doing. He's washing it
in hot ice water.
In hot ice water. That's exactly what he's doing. The water is
  steaming
but ice is in there, too.
Now he's taking it out. He comes back to me
and he puts it back into my open skull.
Oh. He puts it in so carefully.
Ahh. Everything right in its place.
Clean. Clean.
Ahhh, my brain.
    Native, does it mean
    a new start? A new beginning?
    Thank you. That is a wonderful thing.
I think I could use a new start.
A new beginning.
Balance.

But it is *very* difficult
to keep the right balance, is it not?
I seem to be in the middle of it.
     Is that what you say?
     I was in the middle of it. Then give me the tools to stay
     balanced. Please give me the tools to stay balanced. What
     should I do? What should I do in the world of reality?
I am still standing in this church. Have asked the question, but
I am all alone now. The question has not been answered.
   However, it has to do with balance. To find the fine point of
   balance.
This is something I have to work on.
Ahhh!
There is a
big black rock in the church hall.
It's not a *real* church hall. It is just a big hall, I would say.
   Because it has no altar or nothing in it. But it has these big
   Gothic windows. But I think on the north side is this *big, big*
black rock.
It looks like obsidian. It's shiny. I would like to go and touch it.
   So I'm going up to this
big rock.
It's huge! It is as big as a house. And it has
wonderful,
wonderful look. However, I have to be careful. It has sharp
   edges. It's glassy. It can hurt.
It's not something you touch. It's just something you just see
   from far. I'm stepping back and looking at the beauty of it.
Now toward the east.
I wonder.
I see *another* stone,
sort of orange.
*That* stone

seems to be more friendly. I can *touch* it. But it is *very* brittle. I
  better I don't touch it because I just
have the feeling I'm destroying it.
It seems to be I am supposed to look at the four corners,
  because now I am looking south. South seems to be far away.
  I'm supposed to follow *south*.
I am going out of this
big hall.
South. I am going south.
Toward the sun. The sun is setting. It's a *beautiful red* glow. It's
  friendly. It's just the right warmth.
It's a beautiful red ball. It sounds unreal, but I am touching it.
  It's like a *soft* . . .
No, it's not soft.
It's polished. It's so polished that it feels, actually, soft. That's
  exactly right.
It can't be the sun. It must be something else. It is
a sphere, I guess. Because I can *touch* it. It is not really
*that big*.
It's the size of a . . .
How big can I say is it?
Now it's suddenly getting bigger.
Maybe it was the sun after all.
Maybe here where I am, the sun is *different*. I don't know. I
  think I'm thinking too much. I really should enjoy. I just put
  my *arms around the sun*.
It is
a wonderful feeling. It is
soft.
It *shines*.
I look red. I'm as red as the sun.
It seems to me
as if I am sort of incorporated
into the

*setting* sun.

Now the sun is *turning,* and I am turning with the sun. And I
see the area I came from. It looks like a little pearl. I have the
feeling I am above. In the sky. And I'm looking down. It's
something that looks like a pearl

A shiny, silvery pearl.

Or is that?

I don't know.

It's so far away. I have the feeling that's where I'm supposed
to be.

I'm just walking away

from the sun. Walking toward the pearl. I'm walking

on air. Very effortless, very effortless.

It is too big for a pearl. Ah.

That is the *moon!*

What a *strange* happening. When I came closer to the pearl, it
turned out to be the moon.

Silvery. It's surrounded by mist. I wonder whether I am
supposed to go closer. I always like the moon. *I always liked the
moon.*

But it is obscured. I wonder whether I am not supposed to get
closer? But I feel I

want to get *closer.* Silvery.

Light

surrounded by fog and mist.

I just stepped through the mist

and through the fog.

There's nothing there! Does it mean that

that is the moon? It seems that the fog is just going through my
body. Every vein makes me light and airy. And, in effect, I seem
to be fog, myself.

I just seem to swirl around.

And swirl around.

And swirl around.

Maybe it is not the moon. Maybe it is something else.

Nothing to hold onto. Nothing to hold onto.

I feel that I am not in control any more. I'm just
*swirling back and forth,*
around and around.

Around and around.

Around and around.

Balance. The moment I thought "balance," it was as if I fell into
something. Something hard. The fog has disappeared.

I am in the

Light

Place, but I do not know where I am.

It is a

clean place. It looks as if I am sitting on a

white . . .

It could be a crystal, a huge crystal, absolutely huge.

I have to leave.

The drum is calling me back. I have to go back. I wonder what
it meant?

Oh, how did I get here?

Vulture, I do not know how I got here. Please help me back.

There's Vulture. He's just taking me by the neck and he's flying
with me.

I am closing my eyes. And, he's just throwing me down.

And back I am.

What a complicated journey!

---

 **Reflections**

Ema's Quest. "What was the meaning of the sun and the moon
shining on us at the equinox?"

Ema's Response. "What a complicated journey."

Ema's Interpretation (after reviewing recording, and quiet prompt to interpret). "Now that I listen to it, it wasn't complicated at all, because what I think it tells me is, 'Balance.' I have to look for balance. That's the meaning of the sun and the moon, the hot and the cold, because my whole journey was around balance."

Counselor's Comments. Without prejudicing Ema's response, the counselor quietly asks (after the replay) if she now has an interpretation of the journey in answer to her question.

Many of the titles come directly from what Ema inscribes on the tape recording, upon replay outside of the session—her reminder to herself about the contents of a given journey and the meaning to her in retrospect. Hence, the title here, "Journey on Balance," is an allusion to the meaning she found in the journey as an answer to her question. From a spirit helper, she seeks aid in interpreting its meaning. More questions build in response to the initial question, and so it goes, alive and continuing, leaving the impression that the question is unanswered, because another and another replace it. By reviewing the recording outside of the session, Ema further learns that the answer is clearly enfolded in her journey, which she enters fully, without reservation, alive and engaged in nonordinary reality.

# Healing Tears

*I like to meet Turtle today to see whether she can heal my eyes.*

*I would like to meet Turtle today to see whether she can heal my eyes.*

*I would like to meet Turtle today to see whether she can heal my eyes.*

I'm going down the slope
toward the oak tree
that has the opening. And,
I look into the opening.
Everything is dry today, so I just jump right into it. It's dry.
  It has almost the smell of summer, like dried grass. I am going
  down the
lava tunnel. And when I walk it seems to be
I have this hollow sound. The whole lava tube seems to be
  dried out.
The sounds
of my steps are almost hurting my ear
It's so *loud* and *hollow.*
I just walk
along
the dry
lava tube. I'm walking and walking. Walking.
I just wonder whether Turtle will meet me today. This is the first
  time that I have really
asked for
Turtle to see me. I am just walking, but suddenly it seems to be
there is a wall and I cannot go any further. It seems to me as if I
  am at the dead end.

I think I probably should go back then. For whatever reason,
  where I came from
has also closed. I seem to be in a
small
cubicle
surrounded by this lava.
I think I better sit down. Maybe I should just wait.
Seems to be sort of *warm* underneath where I'm
sitting. It's a nice warmth. A nice warmth comes from the lava
  walls. I have the feeling as if I am in a
sort of a cocoon. It is nice and warm. I better be careful not to
  fall asleep because it is just so comfortable.
Looking up, I see a huge spider.
It's not really huge. I mean, the body is small, but the legs are
  very long and spindly. And it just seems to go in and out, in
  and out
through a small opening. I just wonder whether if I can get out
  of this
opening there. I'm just climbing up
to a little spot where the little spider went through
and
looking out. Everything is dark. I don't know whether I want to
  go. It is dark. I don't even know how deep it is.
But now looking down, it seems to me as if water is seeping
in from down below.
Water with
white foam on it. It's really a beautiful sight. The
black lava on the white foamy water. Coming higher and higher
and higher.
I think I
have no choice but
going out of this little hole
if I don't want to drown. But I think I just wait still a little bit.
No.

But the water is coming higher and higher,
and higher yet. And now my feet are getting wet. I think what
  I will do is I will just let the water get out and then just ride on
  the wave. Maybe that's the best thing to do. And see where the
  water brings me.
But the water just suddenly stopped.
And now it's emptying again. What strange! I wonder whether
  I will ever be stuck here. I just don't have the guts to jump
  into this
black nothing.

Now the water is
filling this chamber again.
Foam. It's mainly foam. I wonder what it feels like? I just jump
  into it. Ah, what a nice feeling, that foam all around my body. I
  really like it. It smells really of ocean. And it is so
beautifully white.
What a *marvelous* feeling. I think I see
little baby turtles
squeezing through the cracks
where the foam came in. *Many* of them
One, two, three. Oh, my goodness!
There are so many. I'm afraid it will fill the whole cubicle. Now, I
  sit right on top of them.
I just sort of get lifted by the masses of small turtles.
Higher and higher and higher.
It just fills the cubicle more and more.
More and more.
There seem to be more and more coming in. I cannot see it
  because I sit on top
of the turtles. I really don't know what is going on. Pretty soon I
  will just be squashed.
I just wonder, I should try to
open that hole a little more so that the turtles [get] out, too.
  Otherwise they will be all be squashed.

I just have to

see whether I can.

I don't have any tool.

Maybe I can

*break* this little . . .

I just broke off a little piece of lava.

And still a little more. And, now I'm just pushed through that
  hole

with all the multitude of turtles.

It seems to be

this hole we went through seems to be the entrance

to *another*

tunnel. It is very small tunnel. It is just

for

the size of the turtles. So, I must have really *shrunk*
  tremendously.

And they are just pushing me

with them

through this tunnel. Their little feet are just flapping all over the
  place. It's really funny. They *smell* so *nice*. They smell of sea
  weed.

I really have this longing for eating some seaweed. I just wish I
  could find some seaweed. On the other hand, I think I better
  watch where we go.

Now there seems to be some kind of a spring. And the turtles
  jump right into it

and

are spiraling

*up.*

So, I better do the same.

I just went into this little *world* of water. And,

oh, my goodness! I really have to hold my breath.

It seems to be a very long way up through the water, but I can
  see that it gets lighter and lighter and lighter.

Ah!

There we are

in some kind of a

*lagoon.* The water is salty. *Lots* of seaweed. I just rip some of the
seaweed off and eat it. It tastes awfully good.

These are huge fronds of seaweed. By gosh, I've never seen them
that big. The water is really shallow

and one can just lie in it.

And so, my body sort of

swished around with the waves coming and going, and coming
and going. Coming and going.

I must have closed my eyes

because now I open it and I

see

Turtle's face right over me.

> Hi, Turtle. As you see, I brought all the babies with me.
> I'm sure you know about my eyes. But I just wonder
> what I can do to take the pressure off
> of my eyes. I do not want to end up blind.

Turtle is looking at me

with her sweet eyes.

She looks sort of lovingly. I've never seen her looking
at me like that. It's with a certain tenderness in her eyes.
*Very, very* sweet.

And now, drops come out of her eyes

and they fall exactly into mine.

And more drops.

Clear, watery drops come out of her eyes. They are falling right
into mine. And more, and more.

Ah, it is a resting feeling for the eyes. Even though I can't see
anything because it is all blurred because of her tears or the
liquid comes out of her eyes that sort of

makes everything

watery. But it is

very healing.

It is *very* healing.

A certain *peace* over me. It is a *marvelous* feeling.

Now, I

try to open my eyes again. Turtle is gone. She went to the beach.

I think I follow her.

Somehow, I'm not walking on two legs: I'm just crawling like
    Turtle. I have the feeling that I should be like Turtle. And so,
    I'm just crawling

on my hands

and my knees. And it is a very nice feeling to be so small and just
    crawling in the sand.

It is *really nice.* The *sand is warm.*

Turtle is

digging a small hole and she wants me to . . .

into this hole. I must be *small* again, because the hole she dug is
    really not very big. So I guess I am,

I don't really know what I am at the moment.

I almost have the feeling that I am a turtle myself, but, on the
    other hand, I do have

my legs and my arms. But my stomach seems to be sort of

like a turtle's.

Strange. Now she is putting *sand* over me.

All over my body.

Only my head is sticking out. Exactly.

I really don't like it because I have the feeling I can't breathe.

I think I try to get out.

Turtle wants me to stay.

    I just have to take the sand off my chest, Turtle, because I
        can't breathe. The sand is too much for me.

But she wants me to stay. And suddenly

something is growing on my chest. Like a turtle shell. And
    so that

keeps the pressure off my heart

area. This way I can sit in the sand.

This is sand healing? This why you want me to sit here?

Well, I'm not so sure because I see that actually
the water is coming
closer and closer. Because

I think the tide is coming in, Turtle. I can't be in this hole here!

But Turtle wants me to stay. So, the water is just washing
over me
and washing over me.

Swish, swish, swish. And now suddenly I just seem to *plop* out of
that sand. I seem to swim
on my back on the water. I just don't *believe* it. I just feel so help
less. I am swimming on my back and
I can't turn around.

Oh, gosh. I have to hold onto the seaweed.

Ah! My God.

Here, now I'm on my back. Now, I am on my tummy. And I
can swim. Oh, the turtles are swimming around. They seem to
have a wonderful time. I really ought to join them.

They swim
and paddle so lovely in the water.

So, I just go among them. And, I just swim in circles and up and
down. Eating seaweed. It's marvelous.

Just marvelous.

I wonder where Turtle is. She went up
the beach. Higher up
where there is no water, where the tide can't reach her.

I just wonder whether she wants me to follow her.

So I just go out and follow Turtle up the beach.

Now, Turtle is sitting upright, almost like a human being.

And the Native shines through Turtle. And now, Turtle just
becomes the Native.

Hi. It is nice to see you again.

I have not been journeying for a long time. I get distracted and

I'm so tired in the evenings, I just can't do it. I know it would
be good for me to do it more often.
Just to meet you. And for you to teach me.
The Native just looks at me. He speaks very rarely, very rarely.
Very rarely. He's pointing
to an area. I think he wants me to go
with him.
We are just walking through a desert-like landscape. Very hot.
Beautiful sand. Beautiful sand dunes. There are markings in
the ground and we seem to follow it. I do not know. They
could be the markings of a snake. I'm not sure. But I think I
once saw it
in a movie. They surround us. Strange. I'm sure that's what it is.
I think a snake was here before us, and we just seem to follow
the snake. I mean the
printings in the sand.
I do not know.
The dunes are so high
I cannot see. The dunes are almost like Hell and where we
really are.
The sand, it doesn't give at all.
It is so hot I really
want to stop.
The Native just points ahead.
I am really sweating now. It is really hot.
We are just walking,
just following the trail.

Now the drum is calling.
I have to go back.
I am just racing back.
Diving down into the darkness
to the cubicle.
The cubicle opens up and I'm quickly back into the lava tube,
and getting out the oak tree.

## 🐢 Reflections

Ema's Quest. "I would like to meet Turtle today to see whether she can heal my eyes."

Ema's Response. "If one thinks about it, it may be healing was giving tears or whatever the liquid may be. It was from her eye into my eyes. I still think she meant to heal me."

Ema's Interpretation (after reviewing recording). "I think the meaning is, yes, she would like to help me. She did obviously something for me. Maybe she is reminding me that I should fight it (those terrible drops I don't like at all) and take it."

Counselor's Comments. At last, in this journey, Ema addresses the journey as an answer to her question. As Ema vividly describes, she faces fearful challenges, feels cold and warmth, experiences the sense of sight, taste, movement, darkness, beauty, has the sensation of foam, and notices size changes. She helps the turtles and learns how different spirits communicate with gestures. Further, she sees Turtle and the Native merging. Maintaining disciplined journeying, Ema returns with the drumbeat's call to return to ordinary reality. She arrives at a tentative meaning for herself and concludes that this is an important journey.

# The Power of Seaweed

*I would like to thank Seaweed for its healing power.*

*I would like to thank Seaweed for its healing power.*

*I would like to thank Seaweed for its healing power.*

I am
going down the slope. Through the dry grass. To the oak tree.
  And I
slip through the
hole
into the darkness.
I am
walking.
It is the lava tunnel. Very dry today. Very dry.
I seem to be barefoot, because I don't hear
the noise of my steps.
Yes, I'm without shoes. Huh! Strange. The
lava seems to be so worn down. I am looking at it. Must have
been worn down by thousands of
people
or
spirits. Because it is really
so worn I
don't have to worry to hurt my feet. No jagged edges.
I don't know, I just seem to concentrate on the *ground* this time.
There are
at some spots some water seems to come out
and run little rivulets
over the lava.

I just walk.

I wonder

whether I should go to Turtle Cave today. I may as well just walk
  to the Turtle Cave.

I am walking

and walking.

It's a long way today.

I couldn't have missed it. *There* it is.

It seems to be empty

today.

Water

is in there. And seaweed

is swaying

with the

wave motion. I am just sitting down. Something just presses me
  down, so I am lying in the water

and have the seaweed gently

going over my body.

    Seaweed, for all these years you have taken care of me and I
      have never thanked you for it. I would like to thank you

    for taking care of my pain. I like to thank you

    for your power of healing.

    And I would [like] very much if you could

    give me

    your power of healing, for the future, because

    I still need it

    for balancing. For cleaning. I still have toxins in my body, I
      know. They are getting out slowly. I would like you to
      help me

    with that. And mainly my eyes. I wonder whether

    I am using the right

    seaweed for it. My question is, "Is it important to have a
      certain seaweed, to use, or can it be

    any seaweed?"

The water is
coming a little higher
and higher
and higher. I am *standing now* in the cave. And the seaweed, for
   whatever reason, seem to *grow* on me.
It is a wonderful feeling having this
*cool seaweed*
*around me.* Around my legs. Around my body. Around my arms.
   Around my neck.
It seems to be as if my *hair* has become
strings of seaweed. Only my face is free.
It seems to me, that
the *current* has become so strong
in the cave that I am
carried away by the current.
It seems to
push me toward
where the whirlpool is.
And, sure enough, I am right
*there.* And now I *am sucked* up
into that lagoon. It is not daytime today. Normally, when I am
   here, the sun is shining. But today
the *moon* is out.
I see.
I see lots of
sea turtles
at the beach. Many. Oh, so many! I have never seen *that many*
   sea turtles. And they are all
*grown-ups.* I mean, they are not babies. It's a multitude of sea
   turtles. *What a sight.* What a *beautiful* sight.
I myself
seem to *float*

and float

and float

and float
on the water. There are some turtles in the
lagoon. And they seem to *nibble* on me. My gosh!
It is a funny, ticklish feeling.
Well, I may as well stay.
It seems to me as if I
am somewhat . . .
No, I still have my legs, and I still have my arms. But also it
    seems to me as if this is all, as if my arms and my legs are
*seaweed.* I almost feel
as if the seaweed has taken over my body, in a way. I guess this is
    why floating so wonderfully
in the water because
I don't really have to do any motions. I mean, I just seem to
    float.

> Turtle
> It's me. I'm not
> the seaweed. You shouldn't eat on me.

The turtle is just determined to eat.
It's my left leg. He's just nibbling on my left leg.
Well, maybe it's for a *purpose.* And now, *another* turtle comes
    and she is nibbling on me, too. On my right leg.
Whatever they eat, it seems to grow *right back.* Because there is
    really nothing missing. It's just is a *ticklish* feeling. It seems
    as if the
seaweed has *grown*
onto me
and I can feel when it is eaten,
but it grows right back. Because it's just in beautiful, long
fronds.
It's like fern. It's just
a very nice feeling. I wonder whether I should try to

put some seaweed on my face, on my eyes. I am just lying on
  my back.
I cannot be on my belly at all because I'm
immediately thrown the other way, and I'm really floating. And
  it is *so wonderful.* I'm putting some of the fronds that
seem to be my hair
over my eyes. And here I am lying in the
water and the moon is shining on me.
Ah,
that is a *very wonderful* feeling.
    Seaweed, I thank you for your power. I thank you for your
      power for healing.
Ohh.
    I just wonder. Do you want me to honor you? Tell me what I
      can do
    to honor you. Tell me what I can do
    to honor you.
Everything is still. I just seem to hear little
noises from the
sea turtles.
It looks as if they all
want to come into the lagoon.
Yes, they are all coming into the lagoon.
And I feel,
while they are coming in,
I feel sort of
*drawn out.* Out toward the beach.
So here
I'm sitting
in
a little hollow.
Looking at myself, I am full of seaweed. It is
sort of draped *around me.* And even though it is cool, I am not
  cool because the seaweed seems to

keep me just at the right temperature.

I just

seem to just

want to soak in

the seaweed. Right within my body

to the very core. It is *so beautiful.* It has this

silvery look

in the moonlight. And it's shiny

like silver.

I have the feeling as if I'm seeing myself from above. I mean,

I can see myself sitting on the beach.

A silvery kind of figure. Completely enveloped in

seaweed.

And now, Sea Turtle is coming out

of the water.

She wants me to

take some seaweed

off me

and give it to her to eat. So, I sort of

peel off

the seaweed

and feed it

to Sea Turtle.

She eats *very fast.* I give her these.

The fronds seem to be really huge.

Endless. They are

wrapped

almost without

an end in sight around my body. And she is gobbling and

gobbling and gobbling and gobbling. I really can't go as fast

as she gobbles the seaweed up.

I think I better stand up.

And so I am now twirling and twirling and twirling around.

Really very fast, very fast, very fast

so that she can get

the seaweed. And around, and around, and around. It seems to
  be as if I sort of

have become

like energy. Like a *swirl* of energy.

I just go so fast, so fast, so fast. So very fast.

I have the feeling as

she is eating so fast

that,

and *I* personally,

I think I have become

like an *energy.* And she is eating me right with it. And I seem
  to be

right in Turtle now.

Because it is *very* dark.

I think I am *within* Turtle.

Strange.

It's like a . . .

What can I say? Like a cave maybe. It's *warm* in here

and it *smells* of seaweed

and ocean.

But now I see a light

and

I seem to get

sort of pushed out

of her mouth again. It was as if she sort of

spit me out. And

here I am

on the *beach.* Myself again. No seaweed around me.

*Completely naked.*

That was a *strange feeling.*

> Turtle, I really wonder
> what I can do for Seaweed
> to honor Seaweed.

I ask it, but it really didn't answer. Would you know what is
appropriate?
Sea Turtle is just looking at me.
Sea Turtle has never spoken to me, actually. She just came as of
late into my life.
Nothing is being said but she is looking at me
very intently. I seem to be *small* because
I am
sitting right at eye level
with
Sea Turtle, because I'm sitting and I look right into her eyes.
So, I'm just
stroking her head. It is such a beautiful
sea turtle
and the eyes are *so mild*.
Seem to be all kinds of
*splinters* in her neck, like
as if she
got
stung by a
sea eagle or something. I think I better take those out.
One. Two . . .

Did you have a fight with the sea eagle? Look at all these
stickers in you. And here are some more. Gosh, look at this!
I must have taken about a half dozen of these. There are some
more here.

Oh, my goodness, you must have really been in pain! Oh,
come here.
There's still one over here.
I better take a look at you. Let me look at your feet. No, that
seems to be okay.
I think I better look at [your] tail, also.
It's a cute little tail. That is all right.
No, they were just at your neck, weren't they? Maybe I put
some seaweed on that,

on that place there where you had the stickers,
so you won't get an infection.
I have to dive in the water in order to get some seaweed to put
around
Turtle's neck.
Ah. Turtle.
It seems to me that
the moon is gone
and the sky is getting light. Then it will be a little warmer. 'Cause
I am sort of
coolish at the moment.
I am sitting in the water now, because the water is warmer than
the air. And Turtle has sort of followed me.
Turtle isn't saying anything.
Maybe, I don't have to
do anything for Seaweed. Maybe, if I just
*thank it* as I did,
maybe that is enough.
So be it.

Turtle and I, we are just sitting together in the water. We seem to
be alone.
At least I can't see the other turtles, if they are there
they are just
far
enough away that they won't disturb us.
The sun is coming up and I am going out
lying on the beach
and
get warm
by the sun. Ah! What a wonderful feeling.
What a wonderful feeling.
The sun is just . . .
I think I better sit up.

It's
warming my brain. And
my face,
my upper body, my arms, my fingers.
My chest, my stomach area.
The *drum* is calling me back. I *have* to leave.
My legs
and my *feet*. Ahh. I am all warmed up but I have to leave.
    Thank you. Bye!
So, I am just
swimming toward the whirlpool and down to the Turtle Cave.
  And
I better race
through the tunnel, as fast as I can.
And I am still running and running and running.
And, now I'm out.
Now I'm at the oak tree.

---

 **Reflections**

Ema's Quest. "I would like to thank Seaweed for its healing power."

Ema's Evaluation. "This time I think I really achieved what I wanted to do, more so than what I ever thought would happen."

Ema's Interpretation. "I am sort of seaweed myself and still I was I. . . . if not seaweed itself, then host of seaweed. I seemed to become energy."

Counselor's Comments. Ema carefully observes and narrates this journey, thanking Seaweed and requesting Seaweed's power for healing. This latter part she adds to her original intention and asks further questions of Seaweed. She makes the acquaintance of such classic shamanic phenomena as *becoming* seaweed, having an out-of-body experience, feeling warmth and coolness, changing size—fully immersing herself in nonordinary reality in the Lower World. When called, she returns with the drumbeat, offering thanks.

Ema is beginning to integrate evaluations and interpretations into the immediate response just after concluding her journey. Ema states that this journey is a signal achievement and she identifies with Seaweed while retaining her own sense of self—a self become energy.

# From Seed to Tree

*What might be the most enriching way for me to go now?*

*What might be the most enriching way—for me to go now?*

*What might be—the most enriching way—for me—to go—now?*

I am
walking down
the hillside
to the big oak tree. And, I find it locked.
It is completely closed.
I cannot go in here.
I wonder whether that means I should go to the Upper World.
I am trying to get up, but I . . .
I just can't
get up this tree.
I just can't.
I wonder whether this is the wrong tree.
Maybe I have to look for another
opening this time.
I
have another tree in
mind. So I have to go up the hillside.
Have to climb over a fence in order to get to this
oak tree. It has a huge
opening. And I just
go into
this
oak tree
opening.

This is not at
all a familiar
area. And instead of being lava,
this seems to be a
an earthy tunnel.
It is earth. It is earthy.
It is a *very* small tunnel. I have the feeling that I
have become small because
I have to crouch.

I am not getting anywhere. I am not getting anywhere.
I think I better *sit down* and just *wait.*
I really
would like
to have an answer
for the future of my
life here on the ordinary world.

It seems to me I can see that an opening is being dug by worms.
Lots of worms are there. At least
they seem to sort of soften the soil for me so I can sort of,
in effect, go there. As a matter of fact
I have to dig myself a little bit.
But
they seem to soften the soil for me. And, I think I just
do that. I'm just there. The soil feels *cool* on my skin and it has a
   wonderful
earthy fragrance. I really like this kind of
work.
Just
with my hands I push the soil aside.
It doesn't seem to go anywhere either.

I seem to be caught in this tiny little earthen space, because
   from where I came

it seems to have
closed off itself. So, here,
I feel just like a
little cocoon
in the earth. Just a tiny little thing. Or, and in effect I have the
  feeling I am a seed. Because it seems as if
I split open and
something out of me
is
going upwards
through the soil. And now I can see some light. I am reaching
daylight. I am reaching the warm sun.
Ah, my goodness! That's most certainly a blessing. I was really
  not very comfortable down there.
I seem to be a . . .
I wonder . . .
I am a plant
And I'm still growing. And I'm still growing.
And now I seem to grow leaves.
It looks like oak.
I think I am an oak tree. A small oak tree.
I'm
looking at my surroundings.
It seems to be in a mountainous area. There's a little stream
  going right
by where I am.
And,
it seems to be winter because
everything is white. Snow.
I still have my leaves on. So I seem to be a
deciduous.
I'm not a deciduous.
Yes, I still have my leaves.
I cannot quite express what happens. It's just

the tree seems to grow in winter. I mean, I
seem to be
suddenly
a rather big tree. And now it seems to be,
I don't know, I
guess it's summertime.
Because the little river seems to be completely dry.
Now I seem to be really an *older* . . .
oak tree. I seem to be huge.
There is a nest on top of me and birds seem to be there.
An old oak tree, because I seem to be huge. There is a nest on
  top of me and
birds
seem to be there.
Small little birds.

This is very hard to explain. This is really very hard to explain.
It is as if I sort of
have become an acorn. And,
there is
very, very heavy wind.
Very, very heavy wind. And the
river, the little brook or whatever, it has started to run again.
It is not only windy, it *rains* very hard. And, ah, I am being an
  acorn and
I am in the river now. I must have fallen. And I am in this river.
  And, I am just *washed* away
by the current of
the river.
This is not a river. It is just a small
rivulet.
It's actually become almost a
small little river.
I'm just *pushed* off

against rocks and all kinds of . . .

I don't know what's going to happen to me now because I am so
    small. I'm just this little

acorn. And I seem to be sort of *wedged*

against some kind of . . .

It looks like a big

rock.

I don't know what it is. It seems to be a big rock. And I am sort
    of wedged between.

At *least* I can rest for a while.

This was not really a very good trip

in the river, because

I felt almost sick.

I'm just being here between the rocks. I really have

to do this. Very strange.

Why don't I just *relax*?

I'm just

still between the crack

and it seems to be

winter again because there is snow all over.

And

I feel snow on me, too.

I just look up to the sky and I see.

I look in the eyes of . . .

*Beautiful, beautiful* dark eyes.

I think it is a squirrel.

And it just

*picks* me up

but it doesn't seem to eat me. It just takes me

to another spot.

This is a mossy area. I mean, where I am now there seems to be
    no snow anymore, but it's lots of moss. And it just

puts me in one of these *nice mossy* beds.

And after this wild ride and this waiting, I am finally at a soft spot where I really like to be and just dream and look up in the sky. I am surrounded by trees and I just can see the sky through the tree tips, which just filter through. And it is a wonderful, wonderful feeling.

I don't feel at all vulnerable anymore, because I feel *secure* here in the moss.

And in effect

I can go deeper,

sort of wiggle myself even deeper into the moss, that I won't be visible to anyone. This is really a, a very good, *very* good space.

> Snake, you have helped me before.
>
> I am here in this mossy area
>
> and I wonder whether you could help me. I don't know what the future will bring.

Nothing happens really.

This

journey seems to have taken a lot out of me. I feel I need really to recuperate.

I have to sort of think it through because,

thinking back,

it seems to be that a lifetime has

sort of gone by.

The drum is calling. And I have to go back. I really don't quite know [how] to.

I think I have to go back to the river.

I have to find the area where the oak tree is. And go down to the earth.

Now I have to dig myself out. And going through the oak tree.

And I'm back.

## 🐢 Reflections

Ema's Quest. "What might be the most enriching way for me to go now?"

Ema's Evaluation and Interpretation (after reviewing recording). "I think I got an answer . . . Why don't I just *relax*!"

Counselor's Comments. Ema keeps the focus of her journey on her own self; she does not meddle with the lives of others. Humble, grateful, polite, modest, and ethical, she uses good form in journeying. She is engaged in the journey and in problem-solving the challenges the journey poses. She experiences herself as an acorn or seed becoming a tree, the passing seasons, and the new acorn arising. With the drum call she returns in reverse order to her starting point in ordinary reality.

Ema has discerned a meaningful answer to her question about how to proceed in conducting her life now; that is, she interprets the answer to be "relax." This journey provides an educational opportunity. First, is the presence of the helping spirit necessary when asking a question? It is for her to discover what is so in her case. Second, notice that this theme of growing from acorn to oak appeared in her first HSC journey. When a theme repeats itself in ensuing journeys, it may be an especially important message for the journeyer to give it further attention.

# A Former Life

*Did I really have—a former life in a—lava environment?*

*Did I really have a former life—in a lava environment?*

*Did I really have—a former life—in a lava environment?*

I am, somehow,
drawn to the oak tree. I brought a branch
from today.
There is a tiny
hole
in that oak tree and it is sort of a wound, which I have treated
   the other day with sulfa. And I am sort of
drawn to that
area, which is halfway up the oak tree.
And I'm just looking at it and I seem to be sort of
sucked into *this*
small hole.
And
now.
There seems to be a ladder
within the tree
and I am just climbing down the ladder.
And down and down it goes. It is an endless ladder.
Endless. But I see *very* far. In the *very far* distance I see a
light
the size of a pin.
So I have the feeling I really have to go a long, long time.
I seem to be surrounded by
roots. Some of them sort of want to hold me. I have to get
   myself free

in order to

go to this . . .

I don't know. I am just there. They are just holding onto me so
   strongly that

I really don't have the strength to

go any further.

But, there's Turtle!

    Turtle. How are you? I haven't seen you for so long. You are
   not the same turtle I met at the mud bath. You are just not.

It's a different turtle.

The sea turtle probably. No, it really isn't.

It is a smaller turtle from all the other turtles I have visiting me
   before. But she sort of

is biting all the

roots away from me and motions me to follow her.

So I just crawl behind her

in the earth. It

seems to be some kind of a . . .

What can I say?

It is a tunnel,

an earth tunnel,

and I seem to be the size of Turtle. It is a small turtle.

Not that small, but

maybe, oh, fifty pounds.

Maybe [a] little less. It's not as huge as the other ones.

Now we are settling in a

kind of cave

and she is looking at me.

    Turtle, I came here today to ask
     whether
     it's really true that my former life was in a lava environment.

She is looking at me with her big eyes.

In her eyes

I suddenly see

*endless* lava fields.

Her dark eyes. *Endless* lava fields. Endless. Beautiful. Silvery
   shining. It is dark. It is moon. They are shining some of the
   lava. Silvery moonlight, shining on them. It is really *very, very
   beautiful.*

I can't make anything out

but the endless lava fields. Way in the back

seem to be activity.

Getting closer. Lava is spewing out. It is [a] small hill

where the lava comes out.

I see some people nearby. They made some

sort of an altar

with fruits on it.

Bananas and

papayas and

rubies. It's a *very red fruit.* I am sort of drawn to this red fruit.
   It's the size of an apple but it is

very soft like a berry. Something just makes me to break it open.

I'm to *taste* it. Tastes lemony. Very sour. And the juice

sort of runs over me

and

leaves a

red, almost bloody

liquid behind

on my skin, on my arms. My arms look

as if blood is . . .

And on my feet . . .

It is dropping on my feet.

I now take the fruit and just

put it all over my body. I am just smearing it all over me. And
   someone is helping me to smear it

on my back and my legs.

I am completely red, like the fire.

I hear drums.

I just feel the urge to dance. And I am dancing. And I hear
strange singing. And the singing comes out of me. And the
singing comes out of me. And the singing comes out of me.
And the singing comes out of me. And the singing comes out
of me.
I feel slightly exhausted but
I have the feeling I *have* to dance.
I have to dance. I can't sing anymore. I am completely
exhausted. Even do I think my brain
feels I'm still dancing but I see myself
on the ground.
I think I have fainted.
I see myself on the ground
and
an older man is pouring water over me. The water seems to
go through my skin. The water goes
through my skin.
My body was completely depleted
of liquid, I think. Because when I saw myself lying, I seem to
be just
skin and bones. But now I see myself
getting
my normal shape back.
I'm filling out.
And more water is poured over me and more water is poured
over me. And still more water is poured over me.
And over the horizon I see the sun
coming up. A *small* sliver. The sun is *blood* red. Like the fruit
I had in my hands, before.
I have the feeling I should sing again.
But it is a different song that is coming out of me. I sing
but I don't really know the words. I am forming words, but I
don't know the meaning.
But the sun is going higher and higher. What a *marvelous sight,*

the sun! What a marvelous sight,
the sun!

I seem to be alone. The people seem to have left.
There is one person left. He seems to be the *same*
*old man* that poured the water over me.

> Tell me, what was the meaning of all this? What was the
> meaning of all this?

He smiles,
not saying anything.

> Please tell me, what was the meaning? Because I came here
> to find out
> whether
> my former life . . .

Things happen to me and I cannot quite
make out.
He's talking to me but in a tongue I can't understand. He's
talking very fast and I just don't understand him.

> Yes, yes. I have come from another . . .
> I have come from another world.

He says to me that I have always lived here. He doesn't under
stand why I'm asking a question like this. But then he tells me I
will have visions. Because that is my purpose here.

> But where is here? Am I on an island?

It doesn't seem to be very important for him to answer. He says I
am in a place. No, he says I am in *the* place.

> *In the place,*

he says.
He feels that
many visions will come to me, he says. Because I am *chosen.*
Many visions will come to me
but
they cannot be all interpreted.

> But I still need to learn. You said yourself, I'm just . . .

You just initiated me.

He still talks to me in a tongue I don't understand.

He motions me to go around the fire.

So, I am just walking around the
hill.

The lava I am walking on is cold. So I'm walking around.

I have to clear my head. I really don't know what to make of it.

I should have asked him whether he's my teacher. He probably is
my teacher. But it is very unfortunate that I don't understand
him.

So I'm just walking around.

He motions me I am walking wrong, the wrong way
around. I have to go clockwise. I should start in the east. So I am
starting in the east. I have to clear my head. I just have to clear
up my head. Oh, there is so much happening. That's not right.
It just isn't right. I *have*
to start in the east. Walking to the south. Walking to the south.
I have
to start in the east. Walking to the south. Walking.

Finally I seem to have adjusted some
and I am walking to the southern part of the hill.

Now I am walking to the western part of the hill.

I wonder whether I should *think* something or *say* something.

I cannot mindlessly walk around.

But somehow I am sort of *pressed*
to walk to the north. I am walking toward the north.

A *huge, huge* vulture is there, in the north. He seem to be waiting
for me.

It is a different-looking vulture from all the other vultures I have
ever seen. Maybe because he's so huge
and he doesn't have dark feathers. His feathers are light.

He motions me to sit down
toward the fire.

Red lava is pouring out. *Beautiful* to watch. The north is the
  farthest away from
the pit. It's not really a pit.
It's just a hill
really. And it comes out of the
top of this little hill. *Very slowly,* it oozes out. *Marvelous,*
  *beautiful lava.*
It is wonderful to watch. How it comes
out of the deepest,
out of the very deepest.
I motion to go further away. And still sit further away.
I am quite a ways away now. Maybe a mile. Maybe two.
I am not walking.
As if
Vulture is *carrying* me
further and further away
to the north, to the north, to the north.

I seem to be on a high plateau. Because looking down, I see a
  landscape, a green landscape, with a river
going through. From above, the river looks really very tiny,
like a creek. Like a very small creek. The water looks like a
silver band.
Beautiful to watch. The valley is green. Very green and lush.
I don't necessarily have the desire to go down there. But Vulture
  sort of is . . .
He's not insisting, but
I see in his eyes that he wants me to go down.
He picks me up in his beak
and just
flies with me. Ah!
I'm a very small,
small entity.
He puts me down.

The silver banded river turns out to be a very *wide*.

The drum is calling. I have to go back.
> Oh, you have to help me to go back.

Vulture is taking me again and flying up towards the lava fields.
So I have to race over the lava fields as fast as I can.
And Turtle seems to be waiting for me. She's kind of pulling me
into the earth.
And she's just motioning me to go on her back. Actually, she's
just crawling very fast. Very fast. Very fast
to the oak tree. And I'm back.

---

##  Reflections

Ema's Quest. "Did I really have a former life in a lava environment?"

Ema's Response. "I'm not sure I got an answer. It seems to me that
I was shown a part of the life I might have lived, way back then.
Maybe that was it—the answer. It's mysterious."

Ema's Interpretation (after reviewing recording). "I don't know
quite what to think. He talked in a language I didn't understand.
Very mysterious. Partly, I didn't understand him or I did understand him partly. . . . Turtle most certainly helped me. . . . Initiation
there . . . danced until I collapsed . . . saw myself lying there . . . he
thought I was having visions. . . . He didn't understand I come
from another place . . . the future."

Counselor's Comments. This new question about time does not
involve the future and does not refer to a specific time; it appears
that Ema is learning for herself about the mystery of time within
the journey. She is left at the end of this one unsure that she got
an answer.

Even experienced journeyers appreciate the usefulness of each
part of the HSC process, if they have had the chance to learn it.
They frequently need to remember that the discipline of the formal

structure of the journey process, stating the purpose, starting and moving up or down, stating the question before and during the journey, the drumbeat signals, and returning by the same pathway, serve to facilitate and contain the journey experience so that the journeyer can feel safe and allow for uncertainty, with curiosity and steadiness. The post-journey replay is also very supportive of the client's work, for hearing the journey while the client is in ordinary reality often provides more information and clarity than the client can muster while in the SSC.

# Merging of Energies

*Where do I go from here?*

*Where do I go from here?*

*Where do I go from here?*

And I would like to meet Turtle in the Lower World to help me with the question.

I'm . . .
Try to go down the hill, and I seem to be ankle-deep in all the
   leaves that have fallen from the last storm. It is wet
and I seem to be barefoot because the oak leaves
prick
my feet, so I think I probably should go a little faster,
so that my weight will not
step too
heavily in these leaves.

I think I just ran too fast because I cannot find the oak tree
I normally go into.
A little lake has formed
at the
bottom of the hill
and it seems to me as
if I
should dive into it. And seeing myself, I seem to
be without clothes at all. Not only barefoot, I also don't have
   any clothes on. So I think it's meant to, for me to
just dive into this little pool, or pond of water.
So I'm

diving right into it. And there seems to be an opening. And I go
   right through that opening.
I'm still in the water but for whatever reason I
can *breathe* in the water.
It seems to me that I am
sort of being *shot* through this tunnel. I don't do any swimming
   motions. I am just being shot through it. And still,
I'm seeing myself being
shot through this
endless tunnel.
I don't understand, I don't experience it myself.
But I seem to *see* myself.
I have my eyes closed. And now, I seem to have come to a
dead end.
The water is seeping
through that wall and I seem to become water myself. I'm just
   seeping through this
porous rock. It's dark rock. It seems to be lava rock but very
   porous. And it is very easy for me to slide through.
Being on the other side,
I still seem to be water. When I pry my way through all the
   other rocks
that are
in the landscape.
These are also lava rocks, I think, and they are so porous that
no river is forming.
The lava rocks seem to be like a sponge. I am sort of sucked
   into it.

I see myself in a little
drop of water. And, more and more water forms
around that drop, and
I feel like being in a very
*big* water drop. I mean, it just seems to expand

and I am right in the middle of it.

I seem to be a very small
entity, like a seed. But, I have human form, but very small, but, I
  mean it is me.
It is I.
It is I? It looks like me. My age, everything, but very minute
and
the *drop*
of water,
which has expanded, is swirling around and around and around.
It is
sort of playful almost. It's very
playful.
It looks very playful.
I see myself
from another spot.
I seem to
look from above. Seeing myself in that drop.
Very happy. I wish I could be
down there
where I am.
While I do see myself
and I would like to be in my body,
I cannot because the water does not let me through.
It is like a very strong wall. I cannot penetrate it. I cannot get
  to myself.
I can only watch. I can watch my body but I cannot get to it.
The
water
drop is . . . very beautiful. It has *beautiful, beautiful* colors. The
  colors of a rainbow.
And I sit on this beautiful rainbow-colored drop, trying to get
  to myself, that is

hidden in there. Not hidden,
I can see it, but I just can't get to it.
I just can't get to it.
I should make an effort to get to it. Maybe Turtle could help
    me. But,
Turtle is nowhere to be seen. Nowhere to be seen.
However, a lizard is coming.
A small lizard
and, I think
even though
I lie on that drop, I seem to be invisible
to the lizard.
Maybe it is my
spirit only that is looking at the
body inside
that raindrop.
I don't really know.
At least the lizard does not see. He's not at all afraid, and what
    he's doing now is he just
leaps.
He just drank the drop.
The lizard took the water, and
exposed the
body.
He's not interested in the body at all. He just leaves
my body there.
The body is
even smaller
than
it was when I saw it
through the
raindrop. It is minute. And I am afraid it may just
disappear, because it is so
*tiny.*

And I don't seem to be able to do anything.
I am not
mass.
I mean, I don't quite know how to explain it, but
I'm just energy, I guess. I'm not a body. I only can see what
   happens, but I cannot help. But since I have energy I wonder,
   maybe I can put some energy around
the tiny being
which is I.
And so, I just blow some energy toward this
tiny little thing. It is like
the size of a
corn really.
But everything is there. The hair, the ears, the nose
the hands, the arms, the legs, the
toes. Everything is just absolutely *perfect, just absolutely perfect.*
   But it is just very small.
The energy I'm sending
envelops this little
corn
and it swirls it around
sort of slowly.
And with each turn, it seems to grow.
And with each turn it seems to grow.
Now *I* seem to be
this.

Now I see it from the point of the
small entity.
It is actually a very nice feeling. I'm just
swirled around and around and around and I seem to grow.
And I am
really growing
quite a bit

and very fast.

Now suddenly, I can stand, and

where

the river and the rocks seemed to be huge, I now can bend down

and pick up the rocks.

So I

from

a small corn,

I have become a *real*

person. Or, I would say I was real then, have become a

grown-up person, that can handle

rocks and

*be* in this beautiful

area

with

water.

The water is

trickling

over the stones, over the rocks. These are not lava rocks

  anymore. It seems to be a

a rocky mass that does not let the water through, because the

  water just runs over them. And I just

have the feeling I should just walk

with the *stream.*

And the stream has become quite

large now and I can actually swim in it.

It is *nice*

to swim. I am actually

more carried by the

force of the water, which is not *too* strong, but just forceful

  enough to

bring me to different areas.

I have to

be careful I don't bump into the

rocks that stick out in the

river. I now have to keep my eye out that I won't be hurt. But it
   is very *easy* for me to maneuver, *very easy*.
Even though I am now
my normal size. But I have very sharp eyes and
the water has made me very
slick, so that I can
move around these boulders
very easily.
I have not seen Turtle yet.
I really wonder
where Turtle might be.
I'm just pushed forward
by the force of the water. It is a wonderful feeling really. And I
   am on the lookout for Turtle. I do not know whether Turtle
   would be in the water
or on land.
I seem to come to a beach
because suddenly there is sand underneath. And
way down from [it]
is the ocean.

So, the force of the water seems to go right into the sand. And
   just a little trickle
seems to make it to the ocean. So I am sort of pushed out in
   the sand, and
which at first I thought there were lots of boulders, there seem
   to be turtles. The whole beach seems to be full of turtles. They
   make strange noises.
And
they all of them seem to . . .
The *drum* is calling. I have to go back.
I have to go back.
I just go back
where I came from.
I have to go against the stream of the water, rather quickly.

I cannot quite find my way
but now I seem to be
coming through that little
pond. And I'm back again.

---

###  Reflections

Ema's Quest. "Where do I go from here?"

Ema's Response. "What an interesting journey that was! . . ."

Ema's Evaluation. "I do not know if it gave me the answer to my question."

Ema's Interpretation: "Again, a journey where I am reborn." (later, in discussion) "I have to embrace the part of myself that's missing."

Counselor's Comments. Ema's sensory engagement expands even more in this journey as she feels the wetness of water and she enters at a new starting place. She also experiences a variety of kinds of movement, such as walking and running, diving, being shot from a tunnel, seeping, sliding, and prying through a barrier. Being able to breathe underwater and becoming water are surprising miracles, which she tries to understand as she ruminates about solving her problem. Just as there is more in a given journey than the client can narrate, so there is more in the narration than client and counselor can discuss. This is for the best; it is the client's work to do. For the shamanic counselor there is so much that is tempting to share that it is wise to remember restraint. It is not necessary to exhaust every possibility for discussion. It does happen that Ema begins the next session with a discussion of her thoughts, observations, and questions about this journey. Ema's answer is here; her understanding of it may grow over time and with experience.

---

# Problems with Eating

*I like to go—to the Lower World to meet Vulture and ask—him—the question, "Why can't I get—a grip on my eating?"*

*Why can't I get a grip on my eating?*

*Why—can't I get a grip—on my eating?*

It seems to be
dark. It is very dark and I go down the hill to find the tree.
There.
It's a glowing light that seems to guide me toward the entrance
and, I just slip right through.
And it is sort of a green,
a teeny greenish light that seems to lead me
through the tunnel.
And, the tunnel
goes downward.
And now
it was just a small downward
walk.
And now
it is on even
ground again.
Now I see light
and I am
at the desolate area.
I haven't been here for a long time. It's still the same.
I am on
a plateau and I can see the
river down below. It is windy. And Vulture is

waiting for me
on the plateau. He's sitting on the
square house, made of stones.

> Hi, Vulture. You know I have my problems with eating. I put
> the question to you, "Why can't I get a grip on my eating?"
> Please help me with that.

Vulture is hopping down from the building. He's coming
  toward me.
His eyes are
very staring,
sort of
have an icy-cold stare in a way.
I have the feeling as if he wants me to focus on his staring eyes.
I look at his eyes,
cold, but sharp,
Cold
but sharp
like steel.
The eye is a gift,
have an immensely strength in them, a steely strength.
A steely strength that makes me really
straighten up.
I'm opposite Vulture
and I'm standing up completely straight. Steely straight. It is
as if a cool wind is going through my body that comes from
  his eyes.
Strange but the wind is very . . .
It is a cleaning wind.
I'm standing in front of Vulture. And the wind goes through my
  whole body. It seems as if the flesh has fallen off my body and
  just the bone structure is there.
The skeleton.
And the wind just goes through my bones.
And I am still staring. His eyes.

I am not mesmerized.

That I can't say,

but it gives me pleasure to see

in these steely eyes because it seems to give me strength. It
   strengthens

my skeleton.

> What is the meaning of this, Vulture?

I think what Vulture is conveying that I should strip everything
   away

from my being. Everything I have ever known.

I should let go of everything I have ever known.

I should

strip away

everything I have ever learned. The pattern.

The pattern. The pattern.

That is too much, I don't think I understand it.

> You have to be slow. You have to . . .

> You have to make me understand slowly.

> What are you really saying?

Vulture

is not really talking. But when

I still look at his eyes and

I get a message from there, but

I cannot quite comprehend what

I know it is so important, but I don't think I'm getting it. It is
   way above my head. It is just way above my head. I don't get it.

I think what it means is that

what I have learned, from when I was born, I have to go *all the
   way back* to there and strip

whatever I have learned, I have to strip it all away.

And, I have to start from completely new again. Because all the
   patterns I learned

are of no use.

I have to start anew. I have to strip away what I have learned

from my parents.
But I can't possibly invent myself.
What I am hearing is that I have within
my skeleton
generations and generations of
other beings, other cultures. I have a lot of different cultures in
   me from
the
dawn of
life. I mean from the beginning of
creation. This is all within me,
in my bone structure.
And I have to let go from the life I have been living. I have to try
   to open the lives from
former being.
      Is that what you are saying?
I still try to comprehend what I am told, and, I think I am
   getting it, but
I still cannot
express it rightly, I think. I cannot express it rightly.
I think Vulture is saying not try to express it.
I should just get it within my system to understand that I should
*forget* the patterns I came
in this my latest life. I should try to explore
some former lives.
No.
I should NOT try to explore former lives, but I should under
   stand that I had former lives and that they are as important as
   the one I have now. That I should not think
completely and utterly think that *this* life I have now is my most
   important. All the lives I had before
are as important. And I should try to
combine,
no, not combine.

What do I do with the message you are giving me then? What
has it to do with my eating?
I think that Vulture is saying that my eating is of no importance,
as long as I understand
*what* I am.
Not even where I came from.
What I *am*.
What I am made out of.
What Vulture says, once I understand
what I am, what I am made of,
the matter.
Vulture,
he feels
sorry for me that I'm so
obsessed with my eating. That is of no importance.
I should concentrate on . . .
On the *being*. Why am I?
No, not why I am here. What exactly? It is too complicated.
Vulture says it is not complicated at all.
He is *hitting* me so hard on my skull.
It seems to be, it's not splitting, but he seems to really hack holes
into my skull.
He wants to open my understanding.
I have no pain, but he has split open my skull.
There is no matter, I mean, there is no brain in there. It, it is just
a skull. And still he felt he had to open it
to let energy in there.
Energy from past times.
Energy to make me understand that
I should try to understand.
I have to go over this again. I don't get it.
Vulture, I just don't get it.
I should widen my horizon. I should not be concerned with
this life. With the pattern I have gotten. I should understand
that the bones, that everything

has in it

Energies from

way back.

Try to understand

that that is of more importance to know.

But it is important to have a healthy body for me. I mean, I can
die over this. Because I am not healthy.

I have not looked into Vulture's eyes for a while so he just makes
me to look back into his eyes. There is so much strength in his
eyes. It is such a

steely blue, and whenever I look into his eyes, it just makes me *so
strong.*

He's standing on my feet, to be sure I'm concentrating.

I feel his talons

On my bones. It is as if we are one. And he

makes me look into his eyes.

It seems to be as if the *marrow* goes out of my bones, too, now.
The marrow

is just oozing out.

Not only

one life is important. It is *all the lives* from the past. They are all
within me and I should be aware of it. There is no reason to

go back in the past, but the awareness

that there is

a long past within my bones, that is the main thing.

But how can that help me?

I think that

I should open up to

the big picture.

I think he split open my skull to have

my mind-set escape,

my mind-set

from this life I'm living now. He has let it escape. So that I'm
starting with a completely new mind-set.

Is that possible? I mean, in ordinary life, is that possible? I can
  imagine that I can do it here, but in ordinary life?
     Vulture, is that possible?
He wants me to concentrate
on the wider picture. He wants me to understand that I am
  made out of
millions of years of
particles.
That this is a minute part,
absolutely minute part.
     Yes. Yes. And I will die
     and then
     a small part will come up again, forever, will it?
That probably would help me to see things differently. I never
  saw it that way, actually. I never really did see it that way. Now
  Vulture is stepping off my feet. And his eyes have lost his steely
  stare. Actually, he has very beautiful brown eyes.

Some other vultures are coming now. And they are sort of
  standing around me and flapping their wings.
A certain
calmness. And it seems to me that
I am growing my flesh back on my body. Starting at my feet and
going upwards. I feel that my
skull is filling with brain. And it is closing. And, my hair is
  growing back and I am
as I was before. But with more knowledge.
With the knowledge that
I'm made out of
millions of years. Millions of years of knowledge, which I still
  have to learn, but
this is *not*
the beginning and this is not the end. Where I am right now.
And I should concentrate

and explore
the picture, the whole picture
of the past and the present and the future.
I feel . . .

The drum is calling. I have to go back.
    Thank you, Vulture. I think you have helped me a lot. Thank
      you so much.
The green light is waiting for me at the entrance of the cave and
  I am following the green light
down the tunnel.
Down the tunnel.
I'm still running and I'm still running.
And I'm back.
The drum is still calling, but I'm back already. I must have run
  very quickly.

---

##  Reflections

Ema's Quest. "I like to go to the Lower World to meet Vulture and ask him the question, 'Why can't I get a grip on my eating?'"

Ema's Evaluation (after prompt for her immediate understanding of the answer to her question). "I shouldn't waste my time with my eating."

Ema's Interpretation. "I should try to explore really the bigger picture, what I am from. . . . Just one stage of my whole life, and once I get that the eating will fall in place. What really is important."

Counselor's Comments. Some brief reminders about methodology are pertinent here. For instance, notice that Ema's question is crafted unambiguously, and she poses it as intended. The narration of this journey reports events, reflects Ema's musings, and offers one-sided conversation. The latter particularly deprives Ema (and the counselor, who is there for feedback) of the opportunity to have a spoken record of the messages from the spirits. As with Ema, the use of language when in the journey often defies grammar and has incomplete sentences, slurred speech, and changes in pace and level of loudness clearly evident in the recordings. Notable in this journey, Ema asks for clarification from the spirits as she tries to integrate ordinary and nonordinary reality in finding the answer to her question.

# Emerald Turtle

*I want to meet Turtle today and ask her, "Can you—help me to heal my eyes?"*

*Can you help me—to heal my eyes?*

*Can you help me—to heal my eyes?*

It is wet outside
and I go down to the oak tree.
I look into the hole and there is water on the path.
So I jump right in.
I seem to be baffled because
my feet feel
wet and
slightly cool.
I sort of
splash on the water. It's kind of fun to do.
I am going
deeper and deeper into the tunnel.
I feel I should go to the Turtle Cave today
because this is the healing cave.
And so I just go to the right
toward the Turtle Cave.
Today the Turtle Cave is dark. I can't see anything. It's
completely darkened.
I go to the big boulder.
It's almost in the middle of the cave.
That's where Turtle
left her big body behind.
There is no life

today in the . . .
cave at all.
So I just sit down
near the Turtle Rock.
And I just wonder whether
Turtle is coming.
Nothing is happening. I will just pose the question to the Rock,
> Turtle, can you help me to heal my eyes?
> Can you help me to heal my eyes?

My voice is
sort
of echoing through the cave. I feel I have to say it again.
> Can you help me to heal my eyes?

My voice is sort of
lingering
in the background, in the back of the
cave. At first my voice seems to be loud and then the echo
sounds and then it seems to sort of gurgle and end up at the
very end of the cave.
> Can you help me to heal my eyes?

I feel a
sort of rush of energy around
myself.
I feel I have to get up.
And I feel I have to sort of dance
slowly,
very slowly,
within the Energies. Very slowly, my arms outstretched. Sort of
in slow motion. I don't do the motions.
The Energies
seem to force me to do these motions which are really
wonderful.
I
seem to

almost *float* around that big Turtle Rock.
I am thinking back
when Turtle was still alive. I am thinking back how I met her
the very first time.
Ah, yes, it was at that little brook.
Green grass and flowers about.
I at first thought it was a black rock.
And then Turtle came
huge and
dark and black. The first thing
was that she was devouring me.
I remember my bones, everything was cracking in her
body
and I was completely in pieces in her
stomach.
And then after a while, she spit me out. And I was completely
    new. I felt light. And I felt open. My brain was not dense any
    more. It was just light and open.
Then I sort of
jump into the little brook and I
was carried away to the big ocean. Playing with other turtles
in the water.
Strange, how their memory would come back. It has been so
    many years ago.
And now she has left her body. Just the shell is remaining and
    I'm dancing around the shell. It has become stone, *beautiful*
    stone. You can see the shell,
the marks of her beautiful shell.
Dark, strong.
Seems to be completely closed up.
Because the flesh is all gone, there *must* be an opening *some*
    *where*.
*Yes*, the opening is right here. It is partly underwater
and seaweed

just had obscured the
hole. I have such an urge to go right into this rock, into this
   shell, even though it
has water in it, partly.
But still, I just feel I should go in.
So [I] just pull the seaweed aside
and *go into it.*
It has an eerie, green glow. It is like a little cave.
The hollow is a
*green cave.*
It smells very
mossy.
It smells of *earth* in here, strangely enough, even though there
   seems to be seawater, but
there is no water in here. It is dry. It is as if the seaweed has kept
   the water out.
It is wonderful.
I feel I
should not sit down. I have the feeling I want to go around
and look at the walls of this cave,
try to find out where the green glow comes from.
But it doesn't come from a certain spot. It just is there.
It is just
like a permanent
light source. Green,
not very bright, but I can see.
I can see the dark walls.
Mossy,
very mossy. I just have the feeling that I
have the urge to
eat some of the moss.
It glows so beautifully green and it has this *marvelous* smell. I'm
   taking some.
The moss seems especially thick. I take some off and I eat it.

It smells

and it tastes like earth. And, I have eaten some of the

earth with it.

Ahh! It just goes through me. I have the feeling I have to eat
  more.

It tastes so good. It tastes

comforting! Strange as it may sound but it's just

the earth. It tastes so good to eat the dark, black earth. And, I
  can almost see how it goes down my throat. All the way down
  to the stomach.

Now I have the feeling I have to sit down.

  Turtle, how can I heal my eyes?

I sort of have the feeling as if

I should not interrupt. I should just concentrate. I should
  concentrate

on my inside. I go up again and I am eating some more of the
  moss

and the earth.

Now I am forced again to sit down.

Again I see the earth travel through my body.

I just *see* how the earth

goes through every little piece of my body.

It just goes into my arms

to the *very* tip of my fingers. To my throat,

filling my mouth, my nose.

My eyes.

My brain.

And meanwhile the same is happening to my lower body. My
  abdomen.

My legs.

My knees.

My toes. All the way to the tip of my toes. Even it goes into the
  *nails.*

I now see myself from above. I look down
on my body
in a green glow. Very
subdued, green glow.
And underneath, my skin is black.
Black like the earth.
My body looks so sleek
in that black earth.
It's so moist, black,
fresh, full of life.

I have an image of
Turtle
*right on the forehead.*
She seems to go through the lobes of my brain. Sort of
like swimming.
She's green, small,
the most beautiful turtle I have ever seen, like a jewel.
Like an absolute jewel, but it is a turtle because the jewel has
    four legs
and a tail. And a tiny head. With beautiful, beautiful dark eyes.
    Soft eyes
with a loving, utterly loving expression.
She just waves in and out through the brain lobes.
In and out.
I feel so light.
Now she comes to my eyes.
She seems to nibble on them
as if there is something, a growth, and she seems to nibble it off.
My eyes feel heavy, very heavy.
Now she goes to my right eye.
And again she nibbles
on something, I can't make out.

Tears come out of my eyes.
Seeing myself from above,
it is as if
small waterfalls come out of my eyes. It looks absolutely
   splendid.
The dark body,
I almost look like a rock now.
A mossy rock.
And light blue water is coming out of my eyes
like a waterfall coming down, down the rocks. It is an *absolutely
exquisite* picture.
I am not at all human. I mean, seeing from above, myself, I seem
   to be transformed into a
rock.
A beautiful rock.
It's so peaceful.
It is so peaceful.
It is so very peaceful.
Oh, it is so very peaceful.
Now, the waterfall has stopped. And it seems as if the moss and
   the earth is breaking off.
And I see myself again.
My body. Clean, completely free of soil.
Completely naked.
I have the urge to dance.
Again, very slowly.
And suddenly, I have the turtle that was, I saw in my brain, in
   my hands.
The most beautiful turtle I have ever seen and the most
wonderful *green.*
What seems to be, I hear,
         *Don't fear, don't fear.*
   It is

echoing in this
turtle shell in that cave,
        *Don't fear. Don't fear.*
At first it was just a muffled sound but now
it seems as if
the moss
on the walls has disappeared, too.
And
the words "don't fear" seem to echo louder and louder and
    louder and louder
and louder. It almost sounds like a
sort of a chime.
I don't know really quite know how to say it, because at first, it
    started very dark.
Then louder and louder. And now it is so high I hardly can hear
    it. It seem to be very high and . . .
        *Don't fear.*
It is so high that it
forms water drops.
        *Don't fear, don't fear.*
And with the last
word, it becomes water. And is falling
on my head.
And more, and more,
        *Don't fear, don't fear.*
And more and more, water
forms
in droplets, in beautiful, silver-blue droplets.
This whole, the wording,
        *Don't fear*
suddenly
seem to be energy. And is *swirling* around me.
The drum is calling.

I have to *leave*
this place.
>      Thank you, Turtle, thank you.

So I am going through
the opening. So I am going to leave.
>      I hate to leave, Turtle. Thank you so much for helping me.

I have difficulties leaving.
It is as if
something seems to hold me back, but I really
have to go. So
I am running very fast down the tunnel, down the tunnel. And I
   am out.
Ah!

---

##  Reflections

**Ema's Quest.** "I want to meet Turtle today and ask her, 'Can you help me to heal my eyes?'"

**Ema's Evaluation.** "A very relaxing journey. I was completely gone. . . . A very, very deep journey."

**Ema's Interpretation** (after a prompt regarding whether she received an answer to her question). "I shouldn't fret too much over it, because at the very end there was this, 'Don't fear. Don't fear.'"

**Counselor's Comments.** This journey is a fine example of the importance of using care to shape the question to be exactly what you mean it to be. Ema uses excellent form in phrasing the question just as she originally states it at the outset of the journey; however, later in the journey she rephrases it, changing its meaning somewhat. It is often a surprise to the journeyer, to find that he or she has changed the actual words of the intention or question once in the journey. The issue then arises as to which question the journey answers, leaving some confusion.

It is upon reflection after the session that Ema names the green turtle "Emerald Turtle," to distinguish between this new entity and "Turtle" of old and "Sea Turtle," all manifesting Turtle Power.

# Not Alone

*What can I do—to maintain my eyesight?*

*What can I do—to maintain—my eyesight?*

*What can I do—to maintain my—eyesight?*

I am
walking toward the oak tree.
However,
I can't find the oak tree today. It is not where it used to be. And, I
   seem to be in an area
where there are no trees at all. I think I better *start again.*

The area I am at is completely barren. I don't know what this
   means.
> What can I do to maintain my eyesight? What can I do to
> maintain my eyesight? What can I do to maintain my
> eyesight? Turtle, can you help me?

I suddenly feel something embracing me. It is Vulture. I feel his
wings completely and utterly embracing me.
The area I am at is
a very
desolate area somewhere in the mountains. Nothing is growing
   here. Rather cool and so having Vulture's wings around me
brings warmth to me. And he sort of straightens me up. I was
   sitting down
and now I am standing up. He is taller than I, and
his feathers give a lightness to me. It is just wonderful.
> Vulture. Can you help me? Can you give me
> an idea

how I can maintain my
health for the eye?
I feel sort of light-headed.
A flock of ravens
seems to be coming
toward us. Black.
Black little pinpoints, but the squeaking is like that of a raven.
They are coming closer and closer. And now they
seem to encircle us.
Yes, that is exactly what they are doing. They sort of built a circle
   around us.
How beautiful the
ravens are. Their eyes are very alert.
Clean.
You can imagine that they can see very far. You can see it in
   their eyes.
I now feel energy coming from the ravens, toward us.
Before, I felt
light-headed and it was as if we were in a vacuum, sort of. A very
   strange feeling. But now with the ravens encircling us
there is a
wonderful feeling of
energy. The energy
starts from the
bottom of my feet, going slowly up
all the way to my head.
Out again.
What happens is that I seem to be like a vessel
and the energy goes
in at the bottom and go out on the top. It just goes through me.
It just goes through my whole body. Through every vein and
every muscle.
It is sort of strange but it goes in colorless. But, when it comes
   out, it seems to be sort of a gray cloud.

And the gray cloud gets darker now.
And still darker.
It's a dark gray now.
Some of the
ravens
are flying
toward my head and disperse
the dark energy that's coming out of me.
They just fly over me.
And so, what is coming out of me,
the dark energy,
is
due to their wings, due to their flying. It is just sort of
dissipating.
Now
the energy seems to be a lighter gray again.
And lighter yet. And lighter yet. And lighter yet.
And now
it is
getting toward a
light, silvery blue.

Meanwhile I am standing alone. Vulture
is
sitting
outside the circle
and I am standing on my own.
I still feel a little bit light-headed.
I feel alone.
But something is saying to me that I am not alone.
Of course I am not alone. The ravens are all there. Vulture is
   there. But I think I feel inside alone. But I feel light; I don't feel
   heavy anymore. It's a lightness within me.
      What can I do

to maintain my eyesight? What can I do
to maintain my eyesight? What can I do
to maintain my eyesight?
The ravens
that have formed the circle around me
are leaving now. They are flying away.
Vulture is coming toward me.
I look at him.
I am facing him.
He's very beautiful and very majestic.
His eyes are clear and fearless.
It is as if he is telling me that I shouldn't fear.
 What can I do?
All he seems to say is
That I should not fear.
  *Don't fear.*
I remember that is the same message I got last time. When I was
 in the Turtle Cave.
I don't fear when I'm here. I did not know that I was fearing in
 the ordinary world.
 What can I do?
Deep inside me
is a fear, I guess, which I don't know. It is I guess too deep.
 Inherent maybe.
How can I get it out of me?

I am very hot
even though
I can see the snow.
Or maybe not snow, but I see the mountains in the background.
 And yes, they do have snow on them.
It is cold but I am glowing like an oven. I can see that. It is as if
 the energy that was given to me
has

given me a
glow. Of warm,
warm energy.
I am really glowing now, like a
charcoal. I mean really, a beautiful,
beautiful glow.
Vulture is collecting twigs and things. And I put my hand out
and make a fire. I have so much
warmth within me that I
could make a fire.
I am to sit in it. I am to sit in the fire.
I have no fear to sit in there.
Now the fire
is *cold.*
The fire is cold.
I'm completely surrounded by it.
I don't feel anything.
I'm holding a crystal in my hand.
I have to hold onto the crystal. As long as I hold onto the crystal,
I will not burn. I will not burn.
I am supposed to look into Vulture's eyes.
I can see
myself
in Vulture's eyes, being a flame. I *am*
a flame.
Beautiful red. And yellow.
Beautiful red and yellow.
I have the feeling as if the flame is
trying to
reveal my inner, most-inner . . .
It seems to want to burn it out.
Past experiences are effluvial.
Burn them.
The now is important.

Just live the now. Live the now. Ema, Ema, Ema. Live the now,
    live the now.
The fire
is gone and I see myself in Vulture's eyes. It's myself again.
The whole person.
I feel light inside.
Light and airy. A wonderful feeling.
I have the feeling that I would like
to walk, but Vulture is holding me back. He wants to sit me
    down.
So I sit down. He looks at me.
He is smaller now. He's not as tall anymore. He's smaller than I.
    He wants me to feed him.
I have some
corn
with me and I am feeding it to him.
He has to open his beak really wide so I throw it into his beak.
    I can almost look down to his stomach. It's really funny. He
    wants me to give more, to feed more. So I'm having lot of corn
    and I just throw it into his beak. And more and more. Finally
    he is closing his beak. He seems to be very satisfied.
Now he wants me to *groom* him.
So I just go through his
feathers. Straighten them all out.
They were in some kind of disarray. He has *beautiful* feathers.
    They sort of glisten in the sun.
Now he wants me to
take care of his front side.
I found a little, sort of twig. It seems to be some like somewhat
    like a brush. And so I just go through his tummy feathers.
He's very pleased.
His feet. His feet are in *bad shape.*
I have to go a ways to get some water
because his feet seems to be all caked. So I go and I get the water.

I found a rock with a hollow in it. I can collect some water in
  there.
So I'm going back.
And I pour the water over his feet.
The water seem to come by itself. I don't have to go down any
  more to get the water. Seems to be endless. The water coming
  out of the rock.
And so I can really
wash all the
dirt and
particles off his feet.
He is lifting one foot now so it will be easier for me to clean it.
Oh, it takes a long time because it has caked on so badly.
Now the other foot.
Seem to have some cuts in there. I find some dried moss and put
  it on the cut.
    Oh, Vulture
    I am so happy you asked me to do this.
    I would not have seen it.
I seem to ask for help
not really looking at the
spirits that help me. I am just looking at his eyes, but not his
  whole body.
I have to pay more attention.
I guess now he is all right. Here.
Now he seems to grow again.
Now he is
taller than I, again.
Now he motions me that I can walk.
I saw in the
far distance
some rocks. And I feel I should go toward the rocks.
It is a far distance.
It will take me a long time to get there. But I don't mind because

I feel so light. I don't mind walking.
And now, the drum is calling me back. I have to go back.

I am flying . . .
And I am back.

---

 **Reflections**

Ema's Quest. "What can I do to maintain my eyesight?"

Ema's Evaluation (after prompt about whether Ema got an answer to her question). "I guess I did [get an answer] . . . I shouldn't fear. . . ."

Ema's Interpretation. "I just fear too much. I guess."

Counselor's Comments. Here Ema questions if she might start the journey again because she doesn't find her usual entry into the Lower World. Embraced by Vulture, she reconsiders, asking her question with somewhat different words than she originally planned. Ravens gather, bringing energy to fill her, gradually transforming the color of the energy from dark gray to light blue. Vulture says, as Emerald Turtle said in the previous journey, "Don't fear," and Ema says that she recognizes for the first time that deep within her is fear. Other experiences recur from prior journeys, slowly becoming part of Ema's cosmography. There is a growing sense of mutuality or partnership implicit in her recognition that, as she says, she has not given enough attention to her spirit helpers. Ema makes such discoveries from her own direct journey experiences.

# Vulture Cave

*I like to go—to the Vulture Cave today—and ask, "How many—levels
are there in the Lower World?"*

*How many levels are there in the Lower World?*

*How many levels—are there—in the Lower World?*

I am
in my garden
and go through
the dead leaves
toward the oak tree.
The hole is open and I jump right into
the tunnel.
I'm walking
in the tunnel. It is all dry.
I see mushrooms
growing out of some of the patches that have formed
on the lava rocks. Coming out of the green moss. Brownish
   mushrooms.
I have the urge to pick a few. I don't know why. But maybe I
   want to give these as a present. The mushrooms, now that I
   have picked them, have a *very strong* odor.
Very strong.
They seem to *glow*. There is a glow coming out of the mushrooms. I just
keep them however and walk with them.
It is a long way.
It is a very long way.
I am just walking forever.

I'm coming to the
dark pit.
There are some roots
hanging at the edge and
I just get myself down
these roots. It seems to be an *endless* way to go down there.
It's endless. I seem to get some light from the mushrooms that
  show me a little bit the surroundings.
It is full of roots. Somehow or other
I was right, they seem to be washed by
little
streams of water coming, oozing out of the
pit. Out of the earth.
It seems to be not lava anymore. It seems to be really earth.
  Because it has an earthy, a very earthy
smell.
Suddenly I
seem to bounce off.
I have arrived at the
*end* of the pit.
In order to get
to the Vulture Cave I will have to go one
level lower. I have to look for that
tiny spot
I can slip through.
There is the tiny spot. But I can't take the mushrooms because
  they are too big.
I, myself, seem to become sort of a . . .
I seem to be like fog.
My whole being has become
smoke or fog. And so I press myself through that little opening,
  leaving the mushrooms behind.
I really wanted to give the mushrooms as a present, but I think
  I can't

do it.
Now I'm right at
the cave.
Down here it's
warmer than it was in the Lower World. I mean in the second
areas it seems to be warmer.
I have the feeling I fell
into the cave because I sort of have to pick myself up.
And the mushrooms, for whatever reason, are suddenly also
  here.
There's Vulture,
the beautiful painting.
        Oh, Vulture. I have come here to bring you the mushrooms.
          They were so beautiful I just wanted to give you these. Also,
          I have a question
        for you.
        The question is, How many levels are there
        in the Lower World?
        How many levels are there
        in the Lower World?
I'm
sitting upright
but leaning
on the wall, on the opposite wall.
The drum is calling. I have to go back.
        I'll see you another time, Vulture.
I do become
smoke again, go up through this little
hole.
Going further up and further up. I remain smoke. So this time
  I am
much faster
to go back.

And
I am back already.

---

 **Reflections**

Ema's Quest. "I like to go to the Vulture Cave today and ask, 'How many levels are there in the Lower World?'"

Ema's Evaluation. "I don't know what to make of it."

Ema's Interpretation. "It was just endless and endless."

Counselor's Comments. This very short journey took only about ten minutes, due to Ema's desire to use most of the session discussing her recent journeys. However, in the journey she transforms into fog or smoke, attends to the journey, and completes it with discipline. Ema also makes some apt observations within the journey about her experiences and she begins to have enough experiences to build a fruitful map of her nonordinary reality cosmology.

If the HSC format is followed, a ten-minute journey will require about a half hour, or more: to make the journey, give a brief response, replay it, have a minimal statement of interpretation by Ema, discuss and further develop her interpretation, and have methodology comments by the counselor. A full thirty-minute journey requires at least an hour and a half to complete these steps. The length of time in a given journey is not as relevant as the experience. What matters is if you get helpful answers to your questions. In this case, Ema figures out the answer the spirits have given for her use.

# Turtle Cave

*I would like to go to the Turtle Cave for a healing.*

*I would like to go to the Turtle Cave for a healing.*

*I would like to go to the Turtle Cave for a healing.*

*For the healing of my eyes.*

> I,
> walk down
> the hill
> toward the oak tree. The grass is all yellow
> and lots of leaves are lying on the ground.
> I am walking slowly toward the tree
> and I look into the opening. It seems to be
> much deeper because I cannot see the path
> this time
> and I really don't feel I want to jump in.
> But I do see some roots
> on the left side of the opening
> and I just climb down,
> holding onto the roots.
> It seems to be
> quite a long way
> down.
> I have the feeling I am not at all on the
>
> right path
> to the Turtle Cave.
> I have to go up again because I would like to go to the Turtle
> Cave.

I am sort of *shut off.* I just cannot go back. The only thing I can
 do is just go down
further and further and further.
I seem to be hanging in midair
on the roots. There are no walls.
I'm just hanging and I'm just swaying back and forth, and back
 and forth. There seems to be a *warm* draft coming from down
 below.
The draft just
swings me, back and forth. It is a very nice feeling, actually. It is
 warm and
I'm swinging. It is really nice. I may as well relax if I cannot go to
 the Turtle Cave, then so be it.
But, whilst I'm hanging
I do envision
the green, Emerald Turtle. She is sitting
on my forehead. And now with just with every swing she goes
deeper and deeper into my brain.
And she seems to
*clean* out
the lobes of my brain with every swing;
I just swing back and back, and back and forth. And in this
 rhythm, she seems to
go through my brain
stretching it and
she seems to
clean it.
The bluish light is shining. It comes out of my navel area. A
 beautiful blue.
My body feels
*warm,* surrounded by a blue light.
And
this tiny little green turtle is now
in the back of my eyes.

There is a
stillness. Even though I'm swaying back and forth, but
there is a stillness. A stillness around me.
The turtle is just
*nibbling* at my eyeball
on the left side.
It seems to massage the eyeball
and the surrounding area.
The little tail is just going slowly,
slowly
all over the eyeball.
Now it goes to the right side.
It nibbles a little
growth
that has accumulated there. The little tail is just
wiping it all clean.
This is as if a weight is lifted off
my area. The upper skull seemed to be so heavy. It is all *light*
   now.
I'm
still hanging in midair. Swinging, lightly.
Turtle is now going
deeper into my body. It's going to my shoulders.
It is
just a certain massage. Massage my
muscles and
the joints. The little tail is just
going back and forth and back and forth, rather quickly.
And now . . .
The drum calling and I have to go back.
I am
trying to.
Oh, I hope somebody can lift me up!
   Snake, please, help me.

I am lifted! Somebody seems to
lift me from
above
and
I see the light. I see the sky, and I am
outside.

---

##  Reflections

Ema's Quest. "I would like to go to the Turtle Cave for a healing."

Counselor's Comments. After this journey, Ema chooses not to discuss it. The client always has this option, which she may exercise for her own reasons. Consequently, in this case, we have only the transcript of the recorded journey. As always, it is entirely inappropriate to make any interpretation of it that is not Ema's own.

It is fair to observe that some of her experiences here with Emerald Turtle echo similar experiences she had in the journey by that name and that the purpose for both journeys was similar.

In this short journey, Ema's request is clear and unambiguous. Her methodology is sound; she repeats her intention at the outset, describes her experiences in detail throughout, and calls for help when the drumbeat calls her back and she feels she needs aid in order to return.

Although the time allotted for each session is two hours, Ema spends much of it discussing her journey practice and mulling over what she wants to learn in her journey, what question she wants to ask. Time devoted to exploring what is most important at this session is well-spent. Ema uses her sessions with sincerity and discrimination.

# Advice from My Great Grandmother

*I would like to meet my Great Grandmother in the Upper World—and ask her—what my future will bring.*

*I would like to ask her what my future will bring.*

*I would like to ask her—what my future—will bring.*

I
am going down the gully
toward the oak tree. There are lots of dead leaves
and
I seem to be slipping on them.
I *am* at the oak tree. And
climb up
the sturdy branches.
I am on the very top of the oak tree
and looking up
towards the sky. It is cloudy and
foggy.
When I started to climb, the sky seemed to be
sunny and blue. But being up here on the oak tree
it is
cloudy and
foggy.
I have the feeling as if the oak tree is . . . *growing*
and
sort of pushes
toward the

sky.

I don't seem to be even at the top of the tree yet.

There's much more to climb, I see.

So I'm just climbing and climbing

up the oak tree

on the sturdy branches. Higher and higher. And higher and
  higher.

Now there seems to be

sort of a ceiling

and I have to

sort of

rip a hole

into the ceiling, but it is very easy to do.

It's like jelly. And I just sort of go through this

jelly kind of ceiling.

And here, I think I have arrived in the Upper World, because
  suddenly I am so light.

I don't have wings, but

I feel

I can float. I am floating very slowly

and I see

crystals, all the crystals.

I am floating *by*

the crystals. This time they don't beckon me at all to come to
  them. They are just

there in their cold, beautiful

splendor.

And there is this very big crystal

where the Native

used to beckon me, to come in.

But he is not there this time. I just go by. I just have to touch it.
  It is so beautiful

and so *cool.*

I am walking

toward my Great
Grandmother's
castle.
I am surrounded by
clouds. But I can see through them. It's not clouds really. It is
    just fog. And the fog is just swirling
around me. It is not cool.

I really would like to meet my great grandmother today. But I
    feel already
tightening up. Which is really sad.
I
wish I could relax, but I just
don't know whether I am tightening up just to do with my great
    grandmother or why I'm tightening up
because
I would like to know about the future but maybe I am very
    worried about the future and I don't want to know about it.
This is something I never thought about it.

I really wish I could lighten up.
I decided to go back to the crystal
and go within the crystal
and sit down
and just meditate.
My whole body
is in the white, white light. It goes through my whole body.
My whole body is
so white light. My
*everything.*
I am light. I am completely and utterly light.
I have the feeling as if I have a vision. I see *far, far, far*
in the sky.
I can see
stars,

far away.
It seems as if the stars that are supposed to be
light years away, I can see them
with my eyes. It is a
*marvelous* feeling
to be surrounded by stars
that seem to be far away, yet they seem to be
close
in my field of vision.

My [great] grandmother has arrived.
She is right opposite me.
She smiles at me.
    Thank you for coming. I really wanted to see you and wanted
      to speak with you.
She smiles and says,
        *I know.*
    I would
    like to ask you
    what my future brings.
She looks at me and smiles, and shakes her head.
She doesn't really word it, but I have the feeling
what she is saying, or what her meaning is
that I should not bother about the future.
She seems to feel that
the future is of no importance.
        *Future is.*
        *Don't worry about it.*
She has a
wheel in her hands
and she is spinning it.
        *Life comes and goes,*
she says.
        *Life comes and goes. Comes and goes. Comes and goes.*
          *Comes and goes. If you know that, you know it all.*

That's what she says. And she's spinning the wheel and spinning
   the wheel.
And now, she seems to have disappeared, but the wheel is still
   there and it is still spinning.
The wheel is still spinning
and spinning.
And suddenly it seems to become some kind of a
sky. Like a star or
like a sky body. It just spins and spins and spins and gets further
   away and further away. And further away.
And now it is just gone. Way, way, way
away.
I have the feeling I just need to get out of the crystal. I'm much
   lighter now and even though I have met my
   great grandmother I still feel I want to go
to the castle.
I see the castle, but it is
very much below me. I seem to be very high up. And so I
have the power to dive down.
And there is my great grandmother again. Smiling.
This time she asks me
to serve her tea. And so I
fill the cup
with the lavender tea, and I ask her that I could have some for
   myself.
She doesn't say anything. She just nods.
So we are both
sitting there
and drinking tea.
I always thought she was a very small
figure but
she really isn't that small.
She is light, but she is, she seems to be, at least at the moment,
she seems to be taller. And seeing myself, I seem to be also

tall.

Tall and slight. I seem to be

sitting down there with her, but I see us both

and we almost look like twins. The same

size and the same

height

and

the same features.

Strange.

My head is not at all

straight.

I wish I could ask her questions but I really don't know what to
   ask her. I just *look* at her.

She is not at all beautiful

but there's a *deep* kind of

beauty that comes from within her.

I am just sitting and studying her face. And she sits there as
   if she

wants me to *study* her face.

I can't ask her anything, I don't know why. Nothing comes into
   my mind. I am just enjoying

seeing her. Her features are so noble. Almost that of a Greek
   statue.

She looks at me and gives me the cup back. I ask her whether
   she wants some more tea. And she says,

> *No.*

Now she says to me,

> *Come back another time. Go back now.*

> *It's time for you to go back now,*

she says.

> Thank you very much for receiving me. You don't mind my
>    coming then, do you?

I don't know why, but I am crying.

She motions me to go. I am leaving.

When I look back, she is still sitting there. And she's waving. I
  wave back.
I go back
toward the Great Crystal. I think I want to sit there
and think about what just happened. I was so overcome with
  emotions, that I couldn't talk or speak.
I think she has said [it] as a person without emotion.
She didn't mind, she didn't *seem* to mind
that I became emotional. I don't know.
I sit in the crystal
and the tears seem to come out of my eyes.
Down my body.
They seem to form little crystals
all around me.
Like little tiny, crystal children. It seems to be even though they
  come from my tears, but they seem to be *so happy.* My tears are
becoming little crystal children. Happy ones. More and more.
And more and more.

The sky
has become a
*rosy pink.* Everything is
in a *rosy pink.* I don't see a sun
or moon. I just see stars. And a rosy pink
sky.
I'm getting out of the crystal.
Just the crystals.
They're standing
against the
pink sky. The crystals are silver. A beautiful, clear silver.
I wish my
brain would be as silver clear
as the crystals.
And yet I have the feeling as if my brain has opened up. I don't

feel any denseness there. I just
feel a widening.
And
I seem to dance
very slowly
clockwise.
Very slowly
around and around and around.
I see suddenly that I have the same clothes on that my great
  grandmother wore. White. The white headband. Flowing
  white
dress. Several layers of
dresses.
A slight wind is just
blowing these dresses, whilst I dance
clockwise. Always clockwise. Again and again and again.
I don't know whether I imagine it, but I have the feeling as if *I
  have the wheel* now suddenly in my hands.
>         *Don't worry about the future.*
>         *Life and death. Life and death. Life and death.*
I am spinning with the wheel
slowly.
Very slowly. It seems to be as if the wheel is sort of
driving me, around and around and around.
The *wind* and the *fog*
seem to be also
moving around me.
I seem to be in the firmament
and just swirling around.
It's like
life and death. Death. The sort of life and death just seem to
  come out of the wheel. Like birth and rebirth. It must have
  something to do with,
with the circle.

Somehow I see myself from the back again. Myself
swirling around. A *tall* figure. I can't believe it is myself because
it looks like Great Grandmother. Very regal.

The drum is calling.
I have to go back. I really thank my great grandmother.
I am very grateful for this journey.
I am running back rather quickly
and
I just sort of push the jelly aside. And am climbing down this
very tall oak tree.
And now I am back, under the blue sky.

##  Reflections

Ema's Quest. "I would like to meet my Great Grandmother in the
Upper World and ask her what my future will bring."

Ema's Response. "My goodness."

Ema's Evaluation (after prompt for initial brief answer to question). "I guess the answer is I shouldn't worry about it."

Ema's Interpretation. "What she really was saying was . . . Life just
comes and goes, comes and goes. Don't worry about it. Whatever
it brings, it's my own thinking . . . we can't really do anything about
our future. We may as well let it go."

Counselor's Comments. Once again, Ema ventures into matters of
her future. The spirit of her Great Grandmother kindly addresses
Ema's concern with humor, care, and compassion. This deeply
emotional and beautiful journey delivers a potent doorway for
Ema's future; as Ema notes above, "I shouldn't worry about it."

# Turtle at the Mossy Hillside

*I—would like to meet—Turtle—at the grassy knoll and ask her, "Why do I think about leaving my home?"*

*Why do I think about—leaving my home?*

*Why do I think about leaving my home?*

I am
walking down
toward the oak tree.
The entrance is completely blown shut by
the leaves and I have to
open it up with my hands.
Looking down at it
the lava looks somewhat moist. I'm
jumping in.
The tunnel is *very* dark and I can't even see whether it's a tunnel.
  Everything is dark.
I can't see anything.
I just feel my way
on the right side. No, on the left side. I just feel myself along the
  wall.
When I look back there is still a
little daylight coming through the stump. I don't like this at all,
  being so dark.

I'm just touching my
area beneath the navel, because that's where the light source
  seems to come from when I'm going
on other journeys, and I'm just trying to activate it.

And now a faint light is coming from that area. It's sort of
  almost like a flashlight, just coming right but it's
from that area.
But it really doesn't *show*
very much. I can see a little of it but
I wish I had a stick or something because I
do not want to walk and then fall into
some kind of a crevasse.
I just have to concentrate more to get more light.
It seems to be
the *greenish* light
is coming, but from the other side, not from me.
So, with the dim light from me and with the greenish light
that is ahead of me, I can walk.
But I am still *sort of hesitant.*
And I just
walk but very slowly. I never walked this slowly. Something
hold[s] me back. I guess it is my
fear, of falling into a crevasse or something, that is holding me
  back, because I still cannot see that well.

I have
halted. I'm just meditating again. Not meditating, but concentrating on the power source from within me.
I do walk. But very slowly. Whilst I also concentrate on the
  power,
the *light power* within me.
It sounds as if there is water
rushing beneath my feet.
OK, I just have to follow
the water source because I would like to meet
Turtle at that little
brook. When I follow the water
sound, maybe I will arrive at the meadow. It's not a meadow. It is
  really on a hillside, but it is

a grassy hillside.

And now suddenly I,
I dropped into the river, actually. That's what I really wanted to
    avoid. Just one misstep because I didn't pay attention.
So, I'm just sort of
*carried* rather
fast
by the water.
I have to dive in order not to hit my head. It is just a very, very
    small space.
I can hardly breathe.
I really should relax. I really should relax.
And suddenly I am sort of
spit out. But there seems to be a small little waterfall.
There's this little waterfall and I just kind of
go down with the waterfall and
I think I have arrived actually
at the area where I met Turtle. Where I wanted to meet her. I just
    came out a different way than I thought I would come out.

There is a big boulder
in the middle of the rivulet and I am sort of
being thrown against it.
It's Turtle.
    Hi, Turtle.
    I really came to you today, to ask you
    why I
    want to leave my home.
    Why is this going round and round in my head? As you know, I
        really love the home I live in. And yet I have the feeling
        of moving.
Turtle seems to sort of sleep. I really shouldn't have
asked her right away with this. She is sort of
moving
out of the water. And

her head is still in the shell, actually. I don't know why I rushed
into *this*.

    I am sorry, Turtle. I just . . .

I think in the ordinary world, we are rushing around and I have
brought this into the Lower World. I really shouldn't have. I
came here in a different

way. Everything was unfamiliar.

    I'm sorry.

I can see her head, but she is not about to have her head outside the shell. So I am just sitting next to her. I am lying down
on the mossy

ground. It is *so nice* and the sun is shining on us.

Oh, and the smell is *so earthy*. It's just a marvelous earthy smell.
Like after rain.

I'm sitting upright now. And I am looking Turtle's shell. It is
very intriguing.

The pattern is so beautiful, and it is really

raven black

and shiny. It is

so beautiful

and so *huge*. I see her tail

sort of

slowly,

coming out of the shell. Even though Turtle is so tremendous,
but the tail is kind of cute. And it just wiggles back and forth
and back and forth.

I feel I have to touch it. It is just so cute.

And now there is a

very kind of strange noise. And with this strong noise, her head
is coming out of the shell.

She sort of looks

sleepy. I go over to her and I just kind of

touch her face. I look into her beautiful brown eyes.

It is very, very beautiful.

Turtle, you're so beautiful.
    I rushed so much in talking to you, now I feel I don't want to
        talk at all. I feel I just want to sit with you.
The drum is calling me.
    I have to leave you. You are so beautiful.
    I will be visiting you tonight.
    Now that I know how to get to you.
    I was so hesitant. I was scared of the unknown
    and that sort of
    delayed me to come to you.

So I have to come up
the
hillside and
go into the
waterfall
and swim against the
current.
And, now I am out.

---

 ## Reflections

Ema's Quest. "I would like to meet Turtle at the grassy knoll and ask her, 'Why do I think about leaving my home?'"

Counselor's Comments. Meeting Turtle, Ema asks her question. Her concern for the well-being of Turtle is touching and their interaction consumes the rest of this journey. Again, Ema chooses not to interpret or discuss this journey. She is content to cultivate her relationship with Turtle and not to pursue her initial query. Just because we ask, we may not necessarily receive an answer, or we may not be able to interpret the answer at the moment. The answer may come to Ema later; she also has the option of journeying again for the same purpose.

# Tree of Life-Giving Water

*I would like to meet Vulture in the Kailas area—and ask him, "Why did
I have the honor—to put the human being together?"*

*Why did I have the honor—to put the human being together?*

*Why did I have the honor—to put the human being together?*

I
am walking
down the hillside.
Lots of leaves
are on the ground. Shimmering sort of golden in the sun.
And I am sliding down
right to the entrance of the oak. I am looking down
and jump into
the lava tunnel.
I'm walking.
I try to go to
the Turtle Cave.
But
I have met the fork
and I go to the right.
And,
walk right into the Turtle Cave. It is completely empty.
And it is also dry. There's no water level in there. I think I
should go right toward the East Room.

I am
going through the
caves. I call it East Room, I mean the

Eastern Cave, most eastern cave. And, I
am entering the
Eastern Cave and
am suddenly transported
up
to the Kailas area.

There is a single vulture waiting for me.
He's looking very *dark*. I mean very much darker than
the vulture I
normally
am acquainted with.
He looks at me very
sort of gravely.
I'm coming closer. I see that it is not really
a live one. It is actually a statue
of a vulture. Very dark.
He seems to be unfinished. The
feathers on the one side are
not really quite . . .
I have the feeling that I should finish
the sculpture
of the raven, [vulture]. I do not know why. I am compelled to
   do it. I'm finding a
very sharp piece of rock. It is probably
obsidian, I guess. It's just very shiny
and black and sharp. And the *wood* is very, very soft. I mean, it is
   very easy for me to
put the feather patterns,
*continue* the feather
patterns that
make up this one unfinished
wing.

For whatever reason, I do not know why, but tears from my eyes
   fall onto the wood
and
even though the wood is
black, this lightens the wood a little bit, my tears,
as if they are sort of acidy.
It just *lightens* the part of the wood I'm carving. It makes a very
   nice sort of contrast.
I'm just
doing this. I really like to carve it because it is so *easy* to do, and
the wood feels so, so beautifully soft.
And this piece
of
obsidian I have in my hand,
it's just so wonderfully sharp.
It is as if I am cutting
into something soft like flesh,
not into wood, but it is definitely wood I'm cutting
the
feather
pattern into.
I'm almost finished.
More and more tears coming from my eyes. I am not at all
   unhappy. It just comes out of me like
a spring.
Where the water lands on the,
on this
bird, on the vulture, the feathers
become lighter. I mean it is not this grave dark anymore. And so,
   patterns are formed
on the statue
and it
suddenly looks very much . . . nicer. Not as dark and
grave anymore. It just looks *cheerful* in a way.

I am
just sitting now in front of it and
now I see that the feet are also not quite finished, so I'm sitting
  down
and
I start to carve out the feet.
This is a little more difficult
because the feet are
not bigger than
the feather part, and I have to be careful that I
don't
cut through the wood so I have to be sure that I will have the
  talons all
cut out.
I am working
very fast.
I have never really done
sculpturing
with wood before, but I have the feeling
as if I have done it all my life, because it goes so very fast. One
  foot is already done. And now I'm starting with the other
foot.

I have the feeling as something behind me is watching me. So
  I'm turning around
and there is Vulture.
Of course I cannot see Vulture smile, but a, sort of
*smile* comes
from his being.
He's amused
a little bit.
He finds it sort of funny that I would *carve* this wooden statue.
And so I finally finish the other
foot also, and

Vulture is looking at it.

I *feel*

that he wants to

*peck it*

and

I think he wants to have my reaction. He isn't doing it, but I can read his mind. He wants to hack this wooden vulture with his beak, not to pieces but just slash a bit, so to see my reaction.

But, now that he understands that I can read his mind, he just turns away and tells me to follow him.

I *leave* the statue behind, but I'm taking with me that . . . piece of . . . obsidian.

It's a

beautiful

tool, and it feels very nice

to have.

Vulture is flying

closely overhead

and . . . we are walking

out into the desert.

At first I, I felt quite,

quite all right but now, it is getting warmer

and I'm getting warm.

I'm also getting very thirsty.

The rivulet is not at all

visible. We seem to be in a different area. And the lake I can't see at all.

Vulture seems to be

in good spirits. He's just flying about, but I, personally, am really starting to suffer now.

My body seems to be shriveling and

my tongue is very heavy. Everything is dried out. I find a

plant which is covered

with thorns.

And yet I have the feeling that this is a kind of plant that has water in it.

So, I'm taking the obsidian

which luckily [I] have taken with me, and I cut the thorns off. They are

*huge* thorns. I mean, very, very large. And it takes me quite a long time to cut these

off.

But I'm *very careful* not to hurt myself.

And

now I have come to a certain gnarl. I cut it off. And, the water spout is coming right out of

it and I'm just holding my mouth over it and I'm drinking. It is like *clear* water. It is

very, very refreshing.

Ah, ah.

There is still water coming out and I

feel how my

limbs are

swelling up again. They are filling up with liquid.

Ah! It is just a

grand feeling.

Amazing that a tree

like this, that looks so

prickly and forbidding on the outside,

once you have taken the

spikes off, it has life-giving water in it. I really should keep this plant in my mind.

Really.

I am very *grateful* to this plant.

> I am really very grateful to you for helping me. You really saved my life.

Vulture, meanwhile, has gone. He's nowhere to be seen.
I hesitate to go
any further, but
something just
drives me on.
I hate to part from this tree. I just hope there will be more.
I'm taking some of the spikes
of the tree as a memento because they are actually very beautiful
    spikes. They are very long,
like my small finger
and they are silvery, and very hard, almost like iron. They are
    nice to look at, and
I thought maybe I take a few.
And so
I am just walking on. I look all over, but Vulture is nowhere to be
    seen. He really has disappeared.
I should have asked him the question.
I was sort of *surprised*. I did not figure that I would
find this wooden sculpture and then when he arrived and he
was so mischievous, I really didn't feel
it was the right moment to ask him, because he had this
mischievous way about him. And now I have missed it. I should
    have asked him whilst I was working.
But it's no reason to think about things that
are in the past really.
I can always ask another time. And so I just, I really don't know.

There is a *wind* coming up.
Oh, my God!
There
is really nowhere to hide. The wind is driving all the sand
in front of it and it is
just coming toward me.
*Very* fast and

I just crouch down
onto the soil, onto the sand, and
I bore myself
into the sand as fast as I can.
There is a *terrible* noise. It must just
go
over me.
I'm getting deeper into the soil.
And deeper and deeper and deeper yet, and it starts to get sort
  of *moist* a little, which is sort of surprising to me after all. This
  is the desert but there is a *moisture.*
And the moisture seems to
be stronger toward
a certain area. And I . . .
work myself through, toward that area. I have the feeling that I
  am rather small. I feel, maybe, the size of a small lizard.
I have no difficulties getting through the soft soil. I'm using my
paws, the front,
to
get through. And, in effect, this is almost
*river-like.*
I am in an
under
ground
*water* reservoir, like a river,
and looking up, I can see daylight and I guess it is a spring,
  because suddenly I am sort of bubbling up
into a
lake.
Yes, it's an underground
well
that is emptying into the lake. I don't know what kind of lake
  it is.
I don't know. I'm still small and so

for me the lake seems to be endless. But it is
rather wavy, and I have to be sure and careful that I'm not
    drowning, so I crawl
on the
*ground.*
I sort of
*inch* myself forward
on the
floor of the
lake. And
now, waves seem to have taken me, and just throw me
onto the beach, onto the sandy
shore. Lots of boulders and I climb as fast as I can and on one of
    these boulders so that the waves will not
get me, carry me back
into the lake. And now
something is happening to me, but I . . .
I have become myself again.

There is a nest. It is Vulture's nest
and I am
losing my eggs. I had been given
four eggs
in one of the journeys. One, Turtle gave me; one Lizard, and one
    Snake, and one I got from Vulture. And I'm losing all four of
    them.
Right into the nest.
Vulture tells me to
watch over them. And they all seem to be open up now
and the little
Vulture is coming out, and the little Lizard is coming out, and
    *Turtle* is coming out. Ah,
and Snake is coming out.
I don't know.

Vulture says,

> *This is the answer.*

Vulture, what is the answer?

He says,

> *You can take life but you also can give life.*

But what does it mean? What does it make me?

> *It makes you one with us,*

he says.

> *You can take life and you can give life.*
>
> *It gives you great powers. Treat it wisely.*

Why, why did I have the honor to put this human being
together?

He says,

> *I just told you. You have the power to do that.*

What does it make me?

> *Nothing special,*

he says.

> *You are just one with us. One with Nature. Nothing special.*

I think I got it, but I . . .

I don't quite know.

The drum is calling, I have to go back.

Thank you, Vulture.

I hate to leave
those little eggs,
the little animals behind.
They are so small.
I really have to go.
Vulture says,

> *They take care of themselves.*

You have to carry me back to the
cave.

So he picks me up and
just flies with me to the cave.

And I am going down to the Eastern
Room. And I'm just racing as fast as I can. And fast and fast and
 fast and
I'm back.

---

### 🐢 Reflections

Ema's Quest. "I would like to meet Vulture in the Kailas area
and ask him, 'Why did I have the honor to put the human being
together?'"

Ema's Response. "As Vulture said to me, 'We are all one.'"

Ema's Interpretation. "I think every . . . 'Nothing special' . . . something we all can do, if we set our mind to it, and some are . . . Some
experience it and some are not, because they are not taking the
way, I guess."

Counselor's Comments. This quest derives from a journey Ema
made when journeying at her home. Myriad experiences all but
entice her from her task. Finally, close to the end of her journey
Ema asks her question of Vulture and finds an almost chastening
answer—at once simple, direct, and deep, speaking of unity and
recalling humility. She gives no summary statement at the end of
the journey, before its playback.

---

# Should I?

*Should I modernize my life?*

*Should I modernize my life?*

*Should I modernize my life?*

I am in my garden
and
the hillside is
*full*
with leaves. *Oak* leaves and leaves
from the
bay trees. And I
go down
through the leaves. They
go way to my ankles. It is so nice to go through the
rustling leaves. The air is so crisp. It is a beautiful day.
I come to the oak tree and
go through the opening.
It is very dry.
Very dry
in the
tunnel.
I don't quite know what happens.
It seems to be closed.
It seems to be blocked off.

There is something that pushes me out of the hole
and
I am climbing up the oak tree.

And
there is no ladder there but
there are strings
that come close and closer to me and seem to beckon me to hold
    onto them.
And
so, I'm holding on. And
the strings are very,
very thin, but seem to be very strong, because they just
bring me up
through clouds and so
that I think I am in the Upper World already because suddenly,
    I am
floating.

I see in the distance the crystals.
I'm going toward the crystals.
Vulture
is standing
right in front of the crystal.
I am not saying anything because I am confused a little.
Because it is
a picture of Vulture, it's not Vulture himself.
It is as if someone put [a] poster on the,
on the crystal.
And now I'm come closer, it is like a puzzle. And now the puzzle
    is just . . .
falling into a thousand pieces. It falls to the ground, so the
    poster was a puzzle.
And the puzzle
fell into thousand pieces on the ground, and there it has
    disintegrated.
And
left over is a
brownish stone.

I have the desire to pick the stone up. And so, I'm picking this
  stone up. It is a beautiful,
beautiful rock. Brown and cream colors swirling. I'm walking
  with the stone. And it is getting heavy and heavier. My God.
The rock
is about the size of a
goose egg, I would say, but it is getting so heavy. My God! I just
have to put it down.
My God, how can it be so *heavy?*
I just leave it.
I am walking.
I leave it behind, because it is too heavy.

I am walking toward the castle
where my great grandmother lives.
And she is sitting there
by the big kettle.
She offers me tea. It is lavender tea.
    Hi, Great Grandmother.
She smiles.
    I wanted to
    go to the Lower World actually and talk to Vulture. You know
      why, because
    I wonder whether I
    should modernize my life?
She looks at me, and she laughs
loud.
Her laugh is just
envelop[ping] . . .
the whole area. It is just
like thunder.
    Why are you laughing?
She says to me,
    *You should not bother*

*Vulture with silly questions like that.*
Well,
I say to her, that yes, she is right it probably is a silly question. I
  am, I know myself, but
I am still insecure, even though I *hate* to admit it.
She looks at me with
her very dark eyes.
She says to me that insecurity
is nothing to be ashamed of.

> *Once you lose your insecurity*
> *you will be defenseless. Always keep some insecurity within*
>   *yourself.*
> *From insecurity comes power.*

I was very insecure, but I have overcome that.

> *Yes,*

she says.

> *I know. But don't try to . . .*
> *Don't try to get rid of it altogether. Insecurity belongs to the*
>   *balance*
> *of life. It makes you question. That is important.*

Yes, that makes sense. Yes, that makes sense. Yes, Great
  Grandmother, that makes really sense. I am happy that . . .
that I am here talking to you. The reason I don't come up
  here is,
I seem to have difficulties at times. I try to but then I'm
not received, and so
I feel you might be busy and so that is why I am not coming. I
  am very grateful that you
allowed me to come today.
Ah!
  I feel really welcome today. It makes me feel good. I like to
    drink another cup of lavender tea.
She goes to the big pot and she gives me another cup of
  lavender tea.

We sit down and
I just look at her. It's the first time that I really study her face. I
  couldn't possibly say how old she is.
Face is sort of timeless.
She has very big, dark eyes.
She looks [at] me.
She looks at me very lovingly.
I love her, too, I really do.
    I love you, too.
She isn't saying anything but her eyes say so much.
And she must see in my eyes
what I feel for her.
It is love, but it is more respect.
I have *immense* respect for her.
I don't know what happens but she seems to . . .
I don't know how to say it but she is *disappearing*
right in front of my eyes.
She is gone.
I must admit
I was not at all prepared seeing her, so
I really
should have asked her more questions.
I do not know why I hesitate
before
asking her questions,
but I think the main
answer she has given me, and I should be grateful for that, and
  not ask for more.

The castle of course is not really a castle.
It just looks like a castle but really
you can go through
what you see 'cause it is all
*woven*

mist and
clouds.

I feel cold. I feel I should go back.
I go back and there is Vulture. Where I left the rock
is Vulture, the real Vulture.
    Hi, Vulture.
He shows me his feathers. Some of them seem to [be] broken.
    I don't have any seaweed here, Vulture. I just try to
    take care of it with . . .
There are some low plants on the ground.
The whole thing is
a porous kind of
ground, but
there seems to be
lichens. I just take some of those
mushroom-like pieces off and put it on the broken
wing. Not the whole wing is broken, but some of the stronger
    feathers. I just put it on *there*. It seems to *heal* on impact.

Vulture is tremendous.
Or
I am small, because if I have to go around him, he has to crouch,
    really, and,
he has to lie flat on his belly,
for me to look at all his feathers.
But, he is really in bad disarray.
    What happened to you?
So I'm just taking this
lichen and
putting it on the
broken parts
and then instant healing is coming about. It is so peaceful
and doing this for him
makes me feel so peaceful

within myself.

This is a wonderful moment.

Vulture is lying on the ground as if he was dead.

So now he can get up again because I have taken care of feathers
  and the wings and now I need to

take care of the

front feathers, the chest feathers.

These are not really broken. They are just in disarray.

It looked as if Vulture was in a battle, maybe with another bird.
  He isn't saying.

He looks at me with very earnest eyes.

    I met Great Grandmother. She told me I shouldn't bother you
    with my question.

He puts his wings around me.

He puts an egg into my navel.

    *Watch over it,*

he says.

    *Go back,*

he says to me,

    *Go back.*

I feel numb. I am

dislocated. I don't quite know

which way I have to go back.

Vulture is gone. And I'm lost. I'm lost.

I feel a wind coming up, and it is just blowing me in a certain
  direction.

I'm not capable of functioning at all at the moment. I don't
  quite know what happened to me.

I'm lost. I'm completely lost.

This has never happened to me

before.

Ahhh . . .

The crystals are not

inside.

It is so foggy I can't see anything.

That's not good to be lost. I'm still pushed by a

slight wind, but very slowly. Well, the drum is calling. My God, I
   cannot stay here.

I am,

Ahhh.

Uhhh!

I just got *pushed* through the sky. And I'm sitting on top of the
   oak tree.

What a scary thing! Gosh, how could I get so lost?

But I'm *back now*.

Oh . . . I am back now.

---

##  Reflections

Ema's Quest. "Should I modernize my life?"

Ema's Evaluation (after prompt about whether her question was answered). "Great Grandmother, *laughing* from all angles, like thunder. It has something to do with my deep insecurity. It all has to do with insecurity really. If I did not have that, I just probably would not care."

Ema's Interpretation. "She said, 'to be balanced, you have to have a certain amount of insecurity.' She is right! Meaning, I got my answer that I really shouldn't worry about modernizing my life. And second, I should not worry too much about being insecure at times, because one needs to be, otherwise you may just do foolish things. If you feel secure you might do things that are unwise or whatever, I think.

"I really liked what she said. I always think it's good to be secure, but when she said that in order to be fully balanced there has to be some insecurity in there, she's right, because if you feel really secure sometimes you may lose your right perspective."

Counselor's Comments. "Should" questions have special consider-ations best addressed before undertaking them. In themselves, they are well within ethical bounds when addressed to the journeyer's issues. However, there are two especially important potential pit-falls to recognize. Such questions imply a "yes" or "no" answer, potentially losing the richness of a fuller answer if the question were phrased in a more open way. Also, by asking "should I," one may fall into the habit of relinquishing the responsibility of choice and consequences of actions one then takes. To say, as a result of an answer to such a question, "the spirits told me to . . ." is irre-sponsible and disrespectful of the partnership the journeyer has with the helping spirits and does not factor in decisions based on ordinary reality considerations.

Ema's "should" question here provides an opportunity for the discussion of partnership, ethics, autonomy, integration of nonordinary reality and literal, ordinary reality in her life. Great Grandmother's humor is a powerful means to convey a deeper truth behind Ema's immediate question. It is not lost on Ema; she interprets the journey's answer as best suits her needs at the time.

As is frequently the case, Ema offers no summary response immediately after the journey.

# The Fight of My Life

*I like to meet the Green Creature today—and ask it, "What can I do to overcome the feeling of hunger?"*

*What can I do to overcome the feeling of hunger?*

*What can I do—to overcome the feeling of hunger?*

I climb over the fence and
go toward the
oak tree.
The leaves are
piled up high
and I walk through them
ankle-deep. More than ankle-deep. It is a nice feeling
to go through the beautiful leaves.
Yellow ones.
I arrive at the tree.
I see the
path is glistening with water. I jump in.
I walk and I see that the walls have moss grown
on the lava walls. And parts of
little streamlets go down. Glistening, little streamlets. Between
  the
patches of moss. It smells very earthy and very fresh in here. I
  have stopped just to see the beautiful green. I have the feeling
  that I have to
breathe it
into me, not touching it but just
seeing it and breathing the green into my body. And the smell,
  the fragrance is just so marvelous, so earthy.

Something tells me that I have to stay here a while, so that I
  myself
will take the smell
of the green. The earthen smell.
Nothing happens. I just stand there. And I seem to be pulled
  deeper
into the earth.
But part of
myself is still there.
I am stretched and stretched and stretched like rubber. I mean, I
  seem to get thinner and thinner and thinner.
And now the force lets me loose,
lets go of my feet. And I am
propelled. It's like a ball. I am now like a ball and I am rolling
  and rolling. I'm just rolling. Rather quickly,
down the path.
The
turtle is there
and she rolls me. I'm just like a moss ball. I am a ball made out
  of moss. And she rolls me into a
cave.
It is a dry cave. It's a yellow light
sort of shining, from the left.
The Green Creature is
sitting
on some kind of a throne.
It is immense.
I wonder whether it is the same creature. I have never seen it
  that large. But it is green.
It is sitting, but the whole creature is sort of quivering. I mean, it
  doesn't sit still
and the tongue is hanging out. And it
looks terribly ugly and terribly ferocious.
I have the feeling as if I am not *welcome*. But since I am not I, I
  mean

since I'm moss
I cannot quite . . .
I think I am not moss anymore, because I can't see the moss
anywhere. And,
I think I'm myself again.
I ask the creature to sit still.

I have forgotten the question. I have forgotten
what question to ask.
The big creature is
humming.

The creature has come down and is dancing around me.
  I have forgotten the question, but
  I need to know from you, what can I do
  to lose the feeling of hunger I have all the time? It is so hard
    to live with this feeling
  of hunger.
It's just dancing around me.
It just makes me completely dizzy!
  I just can't at all have you as a teacher. I just can't. I just can't
    accept it.
I just want to leave it. For me this is such an important
question, and
the creature is just dancing around completely wildly and out of
  control.
I really would like to leave.
But, when I turn around, where I came in
that part is closed. I'm completely alone
with this
creature.
It is coming closer and closer and
I just wish I was Turtle and could *kill* it with my beak.
Not Turtle, but Vulture, and just
could kill the creature.

I'm just looking around the
cave to find something to kill it. I just
have never come across something like this. It completely
unsettles me. I am completely unsettled. I just don't know at all
  what to do.
I don't want to call Turtle because I feel this is something . . .
It's probably a fight I have to fight but I don't really know how to
  fight it.
It's now ripping at my hair. And, I just can't accept
to be touched by it. I just can't accept it.
I finally see a crystal. And I run to the crystal and I take it, and I
  have the light that is coming from the left. I
have it shine on the crystal, and
I put the crystal toward the Green
Creature. And it *stops*. It stops the dancing.

It, now it seems to be like a sculpture. Standing. I lift the
  sculpture up and I put it back
to the throne
where it was sitting. It also
is not large anymore. It is now
the same size as I and it is not at all heavy. I can easily
carry it.
Since it is standing, it is sculpture, it cannot sit. I just sort of
squeeze it
where the throne is
so it will not fall.
I still do not know
the question I asked. I have forgotten it
and I don't know if it's any . . .
Now the sculpture is becoming alive and
the creature is sitting
on the throne.
It motions me to sit next to it.

It tells me that it has
understood
my question.
So I am asking him,
> What do you suggest I can do? What can I do about this? My
> life has been . . .
> spiritually, it has been so enlightening as of late, but
> physically, I mean, I just seem to be hungry all the time and
> I so badly would like to
> do the right thing, because I know
> that it is important for me.

The creature said to me that
I have just fought it out. I will be all right from now on. I won't
  have any difficulties,
living in a life-sustaining manner.
I can't quite believe it. I mean within myself.
> Thank you, if that is really the case, I am utterly grateful.
Now the cave which was completely dry
is all wet. I mean, it, it has moss on it. That's not really true.
  Actually it is really soil. I think the *light* in the cave is somewhat
  greenish and it makes it look green, but
going there and looking at it closer
it is soil. And
there is a tiny seed
in that soil. And I'm pulled into the seed. I'm pulled into the
  tiny, tiny seed.
Deeeeep in the earth, I am now.

And I suddenly feel,
light. Then I feel a warmth, hitting me. And
I'm breaking out, out of the seed, and I am sort of
going toward
the
light

and
the
warmth. And I'm getting
taller and stronger.
I'm completely
surrounded by this light. And, I am not a plant. I am I, myself.

I am looking at the throne. It is empty. Turtle
is sitting on it!
      Turtle, what are you doing here?
Turtle makes me lie down
on the soil.
          *You fought the fight*
          *for your life,*
she said.
          *You have won. It should be easy for you now to*
          *stay on the right path. The path you have chosen for*
            *yourself.*
          *Nothing comes easy.*
          *If it was easy you would not appreciate it.*
          *You would not understand. You would not know that they*
            *are opposites. The opposites are*
          *what makes our life. Light and dark. Good and bad. Hot*
            *and cold. Life and death.*
          *You have the opposites all within you.*
          *They have to be balanced out*
          *equally.*
          *That is your job. That is what you have to do.*
I seem to be so exhausted. And Turtle
is sort of hovering over me. I can see myself in her eyes. It is like
  a small
human.
Exhausted.
But, there seems to be a glow coming out of me. I see it in her
  eyes.

The glow

changes. At first it was sort of a yellow one. Then greenish. And
   now it's more white and

silver-blue. All kinds of color sources seem to surround my
   body. And she is standing in

the source.

The light sources coming from the left, she is blocking out. She's
   in her huge form. So, the light sources are coming

from within me. I mean this is what it looks like when I see
   myself in her big eyes. I seem to be an entity of light. I see
   myself, but

there is

lots of *light*

surrounding me, but it seems to be coming out of

my body.

And, it seems to be

warm. It seems to be a *warming* light.

And, I feel so hot, but I see that

water

is coming out of the pores of me. It's like

a water source. But now the drum is calling.

   Oh, Turtle, I thank you so much, for letting me understand.


I

am turning around and the cave is still closed. So, I just

run to the beam and I am sort of

sucked up by the light. And I am

back.

 **Reflections**

Ema's Quest. "I like to meet the Green Creature today and ask it, 'What can I do to overcome the feeling of hunger?'"

Ema's Evaluation (after prompt to summarize the answer to the question). "It was a fight within myself, I have to fight, in order to live this kind of life I want to live. And I was told it will not be as difficult for me anymore."

Ema's Interpretation. "So, if that is true, that would be great."

Counselor's Comments. The question, important to Ema, is answered by means and message specific to her—the most perfect for her at the time. Contents, skills, and sensitivities she develops along the way accumulate and with them familiarity and authenticity in her interactions with the spirits. Her attention, courage, and the structure of the journey method serve to keep her focused on the deep content of her journey experience. Her reservation in her interpretation speaks to her sincerity and caution, a desire not to be deceived by her own wishes.

# Ego and Harmony

*How can I live in harmony with my ego?*

*How can I live in harmony with my ego?*

*How can I live in harmony with my ego?*

I am going down the hillside toward the oak tree
and the air is very clean and has a fragrance of
flowering trees around. It is sort of crystal clear. The sky is
 beautiful!
I am going to the oak tree. I don't want to go to darkness.
I don't know what's the matter with me.
I am jumping in and I am going down the tunnel.
I still have this fragrance in my nostrils.
Now being down here, I smell mossy ground.
I am walking toward the cave. The cave is empty. Not even the
 rock is there.
The Turtle rock.
I am going to some of the other chambers. Everything is dry
 and clean. Seaweed is dried out and shriveled up.
As if there has not been any water for quite some time.
I really need to see Turtle. Now I am in the chamber where I am
 normally propelled up.
Up to the desert region.
I think it is my own fault.
This is just not working.
I hear water rushing, above me actually. I have the feeling I am
 to follow the rushing of the water.
It is flowing in the opposite direction
I am now going.

I have never been here before.
There is a narrow tunnel,
really a crawling space.
It is a very shiny dark tunnel I go through.
Obsidian.
Polished. Gosh!
I have never seen something like it. But it is very small and I
  seem to get smaller.
I can walk very fast, as if I am sort of a,
like a lizard.
It is a beautiful obsidian tunnel. Now we are at the end. No, we
  are not.
It seems to go upwards.
I have these, don't know,
these little feet.
Up and up and up, really very quickly.
Now I am in a hall.
That looks pretty much like the hall where I met that green
  creature.
I am not 100 percent sure.
Yes, it is, because the light source is on the left side there and
  the altar . . .
> Turtle, I really need to ask you, How can I live in harmony with
> my ego, Turtle? How can I live in harmony with my ego,
> Turtle? How can I live in harmony with my ego, Turtle?

Nothing happens. I have the strange feelings.
The left side of my brain is not at all with me.
It is the right side. The left side is sort of floating.
> Turtle,
> Turtle, how can I live in harmony with my ego?
> How can I live in harmony with my ego?
> How can I live in harmony with my ego?

Whilst I'm saying these words, the whole cave is filled with the
  spoken word,

"How can I live in harmony with my ego? How can I live
in harmony with my ego? How can I live in harmony with
my ego?" as if they are layered, like a mist. "How can I live in
harmony with my ego?" And it seems to fill the cave. "How can
I live in harmony with my ego? How can I live in harmony
with my ego?" It seems to envelop everything. "How can I live
in harmony with my ego? How can I live in harmony with my
ego? How can I live in harmony with my ego?" The whole cave
is in a mist now, the mist of my spoken word.

The beam that comes from the left side and it's sort of shining
on me. The light is shining on me.
Under the navel.
Not painful at all. Just sort of a light source.

> How can I live in harmony with my ego? How can I live in
> harmony with my ego?

It is a beam of light that is shining and it seems to sort of extend
through my legs and my feet and my torso and my arms and
my hands and my chest and my chin,
that goes upward,
hits the eyes, hits the brain. It hits both sides of the brain.
Warm. I have difficulties keeping awake. It is a very *peaceful,*
very peaceful.

> How can I live in harmony with my ego? How can I live in
> harmony with my ego? How can I live in harmony with
> my ego?
>> *Ignore it. Ignore it, ignore it.*
> How can I do it? It is there beside me all the time.
>> *Embrace it,*

I don't know what says.
I am not sure I hear it. It seems to come out of nowhere. It's
coming out of the mist. It's not Turtle, definitely.

> How can I live in harmony with my ego?
>> *Embrace it, don't fight it, ignore it.*

This is what seems to come out of the mist. It seems to form in
my brain.

I don't really know. I am in a very strange state. I seem to float in
fog, which came from my spoken words.

The light beam is still on me. I am held in place. I cannot move
at all.

How?

How?

I'm so tired.

How?

How?

I can't even *speak* anymore, but I'm thinking it like a mantra.

How can I live in harmony with my ego?

The words seem to form into a ball.

Round and round and round and round.

Turtle, I have just to get out of it. I need your help.

How can I live in harmony with my ego?

*You can only live in harmony with something if you em
brace it. Don't see it as your enemy.*

*Ema!*

Turtle.

I have such a rush of energy coming through me. I am crying. I
don't know why.

It was Turtle's voice all along.

Oh, Turtle.

Now the whole of mist is just dissipating.

The light

seems to go up the beam, the mist I mean. The hall gets clearer
and clearer.

I am crying.

My tears are making the cave wet.

A lot of water is coming out of me.

An inch or two and I am sitting in the water.

Oh, Turtle, thank you.

Drum calls me back.

Let me be a lizard.

Obsidian tunnel.

Oh, how beautiful. I am running rather quickly.

I don't want to leave it.

Turtle Cave and going back in the tunnel toward the ordinary
world.

 **Reflections**

Ema's Quest. "How can I live in harmony with my ego?"

Counselor's Comments. As she sometimes does, Ema addresses
her question to a helping spirit, Turtle, who is apparently not present. And "Nothing happens," according to Ema in her narration.
Persisting in her questions, a searching conversation ensues with
an unknown spirit. Finally Turtle reveals herself. While Ema main-
tains the discipline of returning to ordinary reality with the drumbeat when it sounds the return, she does not state that she is back,
which is unlike her usual practice. As a matter of information, the
announcement that she is back is for the convenience of managing the electronics and so the counselor knows that the journey is
over. She offers no evaluation or interpretation. Curiously, after
reviewing the recording of this journey outside of the session,
Ema discards it as "not helpful." It is her property and this is her
choice; the transcript remains for her to review should she later
choose to do so.

# Vulture's Gift

*How can I maintain calm within myself?*

*How can I maintain calm within myself?*

*How can I maintain calm within myself?*

I am in a completely different area today. There is a stone
formation at Point Reyes and it means a lot to me.
Point Reyes.
There is a small entrance there that I saw last time. For whatever
reason, I feel I have to go through this little entrance.
It's earthy but the walls are grown with lichen.
And, so, I'm going
straight into this small space.
It seems to be built. It looks as if it is built by humans.
The walkway is built in a triangle. It is very pointed on the top.
When I walk it sounds hollow.
I have walked, not very far actually. When I am out
it's like a terrace. I'm out in a terrace. It's like
an old ruin where I am right now and the sun is shining. It's a
bright day and *Vulture*
is sitting a little bit ways away from the terrace on a boulder. It is
a fallen column.

> Vulture, I haven't seen you for so long. I've seen you in
> ordinary life, but not here for such a long time. I just have a
> question for you, that is,
> How can I maintain my calm?

Vulture is staring at his feet and I see his feet seem to be sort of
crusted and bloody. I don't know whether they are bloody
but they are crusty.

I have the feeling I should take the mud off his feet.

I have the feeling he can't move. He's just on that column. I'm just going to get some water. There is a pool that belonged to this building. It is cracked, but it's an area where water has accumulated. I am just taking the water in my hand. I am looking around whether I can find some kind of container.

I find a stone which is hollowed out, so I put some water in there, and I am going back to Vulture. I see some lichen.

I take some of that and put it in the water. And tried to get the caked

mud off his feet.

And underneath it is as if someone had slashed his talons. Because there are sort of slashes in there.

Vulture, I wish I had some seaweed to put in around it.

I am going back to the pool and there is quite some algae at the sides so I am taking some of the algae off and put it on his feet.

He seems to be sort of frozen.

This is very strange. He used to be such a strong bird, but he seems to

need so much care. I have the feeling I have to put something warm around his whole body because

there is a cold coming from him. That is not right. He should be warm. So I look around. There is some grass.

I feel I should weave the grass together. I am just weaving. It goes rather quickly.

I have sort of a blanket, which I put around Vulture.

Oh, Vulture, what happened to you?

I think I should put some more seaweed on his feet. So I am going back to the pond, I get some more seaweed.

I put it around his feet.

I cannot possibly ask him anything. He's in such a sad state.

What happened to you?

I look in his eyes. His eyes are still sort of glassed over. Normally, they are very piercing and bright and I can see myself in it, but they are still sort of milky. I have fixed Vulture before when he had a broken wing, but I have never encountered him in such a state.

He is, I don't know,

dying. He is just

so far gone.

What else can I do, I wonder?

I don't quite know what to do, however. I see his eyes and the milky film that is over his eyes seems to vanish.

Slowly, and slowly, and more and more.

And he looks at me.

I don't believe it! Uh!

He has killed me. With one sharp crack, I see myself on the ground.

He's trampling on me. His feet are all healed and he's just trampling on me to make me real flat and the blood and everything goes right into the earth. He is trampling on me and my bones and my skin and my flesh. It seems to be sort of pulverized. It's unbelievable but now he's urinating on this whole area where I am, and so I'm completely flushed into the earth.

Deep, deep down and everything seems to come into a ball. It's a round . . .

It's a mushroom!

This whole me is accumulating in a little mushroom ball.

And now I am deep, deep in the earth, I feel it.

And now

something is picking me up. I think Vulture has dug a hole with his talons.

And now he has this little mushroom in his beak. He puts me on a bed of moss.

And now, whilst he first killed me with this horrible beak of his, now he opens the mushroom very tenderly with his beak.

Very, very tenderly and there is a *new me* coming out.

He's feeding me. He puts some nourishment into me. I don't
know what it is. But my mouth is wide open and he just puts
nourishment into me.

And whilst the nourishment is going through my body

I was a complete entity coming out of the mushroom and I was
very, very tiny of course. Now the nourishment was put into
me, I seem to grow rather fast. Strong. I see how my feet are
growing. And look into my hands. They are already grown to
the right size.

And he's still feeding me.

I'm lying on the moss. He's just looking at me with his beautiful
eyes.

He isn't saying anything but he . . .

> *I have made you*
> *anew. I have made you anew.*
> *Not to worry about the old you. Change is ahead. A bright*
> *future.*

I feel cold and he puts me upright and spreads his wings around
me. Slowly I am getting warm.

I feel new life within me. I feel suddenly that my blood is
running in the veins. And everything seems to be functioning
again.

My brain. I see sort of clear ahead. I seem to be able to look *way*
ahead.

As Vulture said, "A bright future!"

Crisp and clear. Light.

Vulture is taking an egg and put it through my navel within me.
Nothing is being said, but

> *Take good care of it. Watch over it.*

Yes, yes, I will. Of course I will.

A sort of *light* seems to shine from that area.

A beam
coming from there and it just shines
the way ahead.
And it makes the future even brighter.
It is a very strange thing, but I see way, way ahead.
Infinitely. I see so far. I had no idea I could see that far.
Light. It is all light. I see far. Far. In the future. The future is light.
Crisp, clean
light. Oohhh! I am so fascinated with it I can't think anything
 else. It is so marvelous.
The future is light and bright.

The drum is calling.
  I have to leave, Vulture.
  Take care of yourself. Thank you for helping me, making me a
    new person.
I am sort of turned around.
There I see the terrace, and I go to the terrace, and through the
  ruins
Go back through the triangle walkway, tunnel, and now I am
  back at Point Reyes. The rocks.

---

##  Reflections

Ema's Quest. "How can I maintain calm within myself?"

Ema's Evaluation. "I am not sure I got an answer, but it was just
such a gift today. . . . Altogether, it was just a marvelous journey."

Ema's Interpretation. "Of course. I then realized it was a dismemberment . . . but at first I was really . . . I was shocked. 'A bright
future' . . . light, all beautiful light; I don't know what it meant. But
Vulture said, 'I have made you anew . . . and don't worry about the
old you. You will have a bright future.'"

Counselor's Comments. Ema starts this journey from a new place in the Middle World's ordinary reality. She asks her question and immediately places priority on Vulture's needs, only to be astonished by what ensues. Upon further review, Ema may determine how this answered her question or she may seek further clarifications from Vulture, or a "second opinion" from a different helping spirit. She is gradually developing her singular approach to nonordinary reality, the Worlds, and the spirits. In this journey she experiences her own dismemberment, a classic shamanic experience. Although shamanic dismemberments are known cross-culturally with each with their own culture-specific meanings, its meaning for her is for her to interpret herself.

# To Go Back in Time

*I like to go back in time to the Cyclades.*

*I like to go back in time to the Cyclades.*

*I like to go back in time to the Cyclades.*

I feel I should go through the rock formation at Point Reyes.
And I'm
there right now.
And I walk toward the big rock.
And
walk right through
the crack. It is
just big enough for me to slide through.
It's a very narrow walkway. It is
like a triangle. It's pointed toward the ceiling, and when I walk
my steps sound hollow.
The stones
seem to have
some writings on it.
Colored writings but it is washed away by time.
I'm still walking. It is a very, very long *tunnel*.
I'm through walking but I see at the very end
far, far away. I see
a little bit of light
shining.
I *do* walk a little faster. I do not know why, but my legs suddenly
want to go fast, and I am almost running
toward the light.

And I am outside
on the terrace
of that old
temple ruin.
The grass is all yellow. It is warm.
Cicadas are singing. Otherwise it's very still.
The smell of heat, but also of dry grass. The sky is blue. Oh, it is
    wonderful. I'm
walking around to look for Turtle. There was a
pool, a huge sort of
water basin, but it was, of course, cracked by time. Yet there was
one area that had
water and I wonder whether Turtle might be there.

And Turtle *is* there. It is interesting. She is
so huge and she blends in, her shield looks like the,
like the rocks. A light color, light gray,
eaten
by time. She really looks like a rock herself.
I see the tiny, shiny spot. Strangely enough.
    Turtle, I'd like to go back in time and visit the Cyclades. I want
        to look at the
    little figurines I have seen in my dreams
    and I have made, as you know.
    Turtle. . .
I don't really know whether she heard me. I can't even see her.
Oh, yes, I can. Her head is
just . . .
I just can see her
mouth
a little bit
and the eyes are like little slits. She just
peeking out of her huge
shell.

She must have just eaten algae, because
her mouth is still
wet and green with algae.
   Turtle, do you think
   we can go together
   way, way back?
Before my eyes,
it is absolutely incredible. Turtle is changing right before my
   eyes.
The huge shield is sort of crumbling
and
it all seems to
fall off her, and
the powdery substance is
in the air. My mouth
is full of
this *powdered* substance. And suddenly, there
is this small turtle, a young turtle, I assume,
with a
nice shiny
black shield. It is *so* beautiful.
And she is walking
ahead of me.
I follow her.
For whatever reason, we are suddenly at an ocean. Or, well, at
   least
an ocean or maybe a very big lake. I'm not sure
because the water is endless.
The water is salty. I've just tasted it. So I assume
it's the ocean. And, she motions me to
come in
and swim with her.
We are swimming.
I personally have, in ordinary reality, never

done any diving. But, I seem to be able to
go underwater without any equipment. I am still
myself, because I still have my arms and legs, but I *am capable* of
*breathing* under water.
It is really very beautiful.
I see the corals are just absolutely magnificent. I seem to get lost
  in wonder about all this beauty.

Ohhh!
Turtle is coming back and, and she is coming from behind and
  *pushing* me. I guess she doesn't want me to stay.
And so, we both are swimming into
where the *corals* were. There was still sunlight, sort of filtering
through the water. But now we seem to go into a really dark,
  dark
ocean. I mean, I don't think we are diving *down* but
suddenly, there is really no visibility.
But Turtle is *behind* me
and she is poking me, and pushing me ahead. So I don't feel
  *alone.* I guess if I were here
in this big ocean by myself, I . . .

And I suddenly
seem to be by myself. I wish I didn't have that thought of *fear*
  within me.
Now, Turtle, I can't see.
I can't see anything but I can't *feel* her anymore.
And here I am in the water and
I just
don't need to breathe. I don't have to go up to get air, but
I don't really know quite where I am.
And I just sort of paddle around.
Suddenly there is a *force*
that *draws* me. It is like a
whirl, a
waterwhirl.

And it sort of,
like a magnet, just draws me and it pushes me.
I was going round and round and round and round very fast
    and it
pushes me out
and I'm
thrown onto rocks.
I can see
I seem to be on an island, because I can see
in the distance
other little islets.
This island is
almost bare. I mean, very few
plants are growing on it. They are all yellow. It looks as if there
    has not been any rain for a long time.
But, my walking it
makes me, as if I have,
not wings,
that is not the right word.
When I walk, my whole gait
bounces. I feel so free and so
unburdened.
The
*air* is so . . .
It smells of
perfume. Like
flowers I
don't recognize. But I don't see them.
I feel like dancing.
I have never
been a dancer, but I
am dancing. I am
baffled. But the stones are not too hard for me. And it doesn't
    hurt me at all to dance
on the rocks.

I see a

sort of a building, made out of rocks.

It's partly in the earth. It's like a manmade

cave.

And the fragrance comes from there it seems, because

I'm sort of drawn to it.

Oh!

There are the

little goddess figures.

They are all stuck in the ground.

Several of them.

Five. All made out of, it seems to be, it's not the rock I see.

It is such a sacred place I don't dare to touch them but it could
   be marble.

There's nobody here. Even though somebody had to

light the fire, because the fire is sort of a smoldering fire.

And a lot of

not flowers

are in there. They seem to be herbs, rather, in a green. Not like
   pine. Maybe like cedar, or, it is a plant I don't know really
   because it gives a wonderful fragrance.

I feel I have to sit down. And there is a cup

with liquid. I just feel I have to drink it.

I'm looking at the figures. They are about the size of my hand,
   not very big

but very *ex*quisite. Exquisitely carved.

It's not water.

No, I think it is meant for drinking. I am

taking a sip

and it tastes sort of

sweet.

I have this desire to drink more. Even though

I, without wanting it, I emptied the whole bowl.

It burns like fire within me. Like fire. Like fire. And the
herbs are . . .
The fragrance is so strong that it does something to my brain.
I feel faint. Oh, my God, what did I do? I feel faint.

    Oh, Turtle, I should not have.

I feel I have to
stand up.
And I'm getting out of this cave
to get some fresh air.
And, suddenly, I can see so far.
Oh! Oh! Ah!
I try to
breathe
deeply to get some fresh air into my lungs.
Why did I drink this? I should not have.
I just feel I need to get some fresh water. And I am just walking
  away.
I'm walking away, and I hear some
bubbling
like a spring maybe. And there is a *tiny*
bubble coming out of the earth.
Oh, my God, and I just
lie down and drink.
And drink, and drink. Ahhhhh!

I'm completely in the nude, I see. And I'm walking.
I don't believe it! There is some kind of a quarry.
I wonder whether this is
the quarry where they
get the materials, for the
figures.
Nobody's here, I am all alone. But I see some primitive tools
  lying around
and indeed some

figures.
Oh. I think I must have left it there. I forgot.
I really should finish this one. How could I
ever have forgotten? Of course. I was supposed to make
  another one.
I'm just using another
rock. And I just kind of
hammer out
this little figurine I had started.
It is almost finished. I just have to get the nose right.
There is sand
and I put the sand onto a
very strong kind of leaf. And I am
polishing it.
I am polishing the little figurine.
I have the feeling that I have to hurry. It has to be done by a
  certain time, because I have to go back.
I'm working on it
rather quickly, and the nose is coming more and more.
It's really getting dark. But I know the way, very well. Down.
The quarry was sort of
on a hill, and now I have to go down.
Yes, there is an empty place between the other figurines
and the one I just made,
I have to put in that empty spot.
Now that it is put in its place, I feel as if a
great burden is lifted
off me.
I'm starting a new fire.
I am putting
these beautiful
branches of this
wonderful-smelling plant
on the fire.

I feel incredible. I feel
so empowered and the . . .
drum is calling. I have to go back.

And I just jump into the ocean
and I am
sucked right down into it. And I am swimming as fast as I can
to a tiny green light, that's guiding me
toward the
area where the
corals are.
    I am getting lost, Turtle.
The turtle is there
in its
old form. The drum doesn't call anymore. It stopped but I . . .
I hope I still be back. I didn't make it. It's the first time I didn't
  make it back!
Turtle is waiting for me, and, she is bringing me back to the
  ruins. I am going through that long, long hall.
Really fast. I'm really running. And now I'm out
at Point Reyes.
    Thank you!

---

 **Reflections**

Ema's Quest. "I like to go back in time to the Cyclades."

Ema's Evaluation. "I don't know what to say. It was a very pleasing journey, though what I thought was so interesting . . . I came there as a stranger and I left as if I belonged there."

Ema's Interpretation. "The drink and the fragrance that came from the fire . . . changed me. That was strange."

Counselor's Comments. Ema's fascination with time reveals itself in the purpose of this journey of exploration. As is often the case,

Ema derives more richness and novel information than her intention implies. Much of it is around a deepening friendship and trust with her spirit helper Turtle. It becomes apparent here when Ema speaks of Turtle "in its old form," that Ema understands that the various forms of Turtle are manifestations of Turtle Power.

# Visiting Turtle for Healing

*I like to visit Turtle today and—ask her for a healing of my whole body.*

*I like to ask her for a healing of my whole body.*

*I like to ask her for a healing—of my whole body.*

I am
standing on the hillside.
The grass is all yellow. And it is
an area that is sort of flat, I think where the deer have been lying.
I seem to be in a different area because there are no trees
    around.
Oh, no, that's not true. There *is* a tree in the far distance. I think
    I have to go to that tree.
I am walking toward the tree and
suddenly I'm swallowed by . . .
There must have been a big sinkhole or something like this
    because I am falling into the sinkhole.
I seem to be at the lava tunnel. But I do not know whether that
    is the same one, however, it sort of
looks the same. I mean, it's the same
size. I can walk in there easily. And, it is very dry in here.
I feel sort of lost at the moment 'cause I don't quite know which
    way to go.
I think I just walk.
I think I just walk
toward the *left.* But this probably was the wrong way, because
it seems to be all closed.
I'm touching it just to feel
whether it is really lava. It is *very* dimly lit, and

the light comes from within me. So, I'm the light source.
Now that I've put my hand on it, what looked to me like the wall
wasn't, because I walked right through it.
It is still very dark
in here. And I see little specks on the walls.
Little light sources.
Green.
They make a noise like crickets, but they are very much smaller
    than crickets. I mean, they are really
very small light sources. Like needle heads. But many,
many, many.

Some kind of voice is saying to me,
        *Watch where you walk.*
And so, I see now that these little light sources are
on the ground. And indeed there is a *huge hole* that stops me to
    go any further.
I look into it and
I, of course, can't see anything. It is just all dark.

Now I see on the
right side to this
hole, I see a path. And so I use that path. And the path seems
    to go
*up.* So I'm going up
as if I go *up* the wall, but there is a path.
It is so steep that I have to go all four. I have to use my arms and
    so I walk like an animal, because it is too steep to
go up there otherwise.
Oh! I just came a completely different way, but
now I see down below, I see the cave, because I see
Turtle's rock there.
So I just climb. From the ceiling of the cave I climb down. And,
    the cave is all dry. I thought that the cave might be
wet so I could lie in the

seaweed, but
of course I
always
think ahead which I shouldn't. So this is
really all dry.
I just walk around Turtle Rock. And I go through the little
   opening.
Turtle Rock has this
nice little
cave within itself
with the greenish light.
>   Oh, Turtle, I need a whole healing. Please give me a whole
>      healing today.
>   Especially
>   my lower part.
>   The kidney area.

I am supposed to lie down.
I am lying down on the floor with outstretched
arms and legs.
It gets very warm in
the belly of the
rock. Very warm.
It's not steam. It's still very clear
in here, but it gets
*very warm.*
And, it seems to be that lots of water is coming out of me.
Out of every
pore of my body, it seems. I mean,
I'm like a water source.
And it's just running and running and running.
and the
floor I am lying on seems to be porous, because
there is no water around me. It sucks the water that comes
   out of me

up. It goes through the
bottom, like a sponge. And I mean
this is not
sweating, what I'm doing.
It is like, the water comes out like coming from a little waterfall.
  I mean, it's really running.
The water that comes out of me,
I don't know if whether it is green or the light makes it look
  green. It doesn't look clear, what's coming out me. It seems to
  be greenish.
I'm still not as relaxed as I would like to be.
    Turtle, please let me relax.

Something opens
up
and the wind is coming.
Hard to describe, but
something is opening up
on top of
me. And, a wind
is pressed through that little hole
and it is aimed right at my body. And so the wind seems to dry
  me off.
It has a nice smell. It is a fragrance, there. Sort of like rose petals.
The
wind
seems to be pink. I see myself in a pink
glow.
The most beautiful pink I have ever seen in my life.
I'm completely
surrounded by pink light.
Oh, my God, it just goes right through me.
I can see myself from above, lying on the ground. And, I can see
through my skin. I can see my skeleton. And the skeleton is

in a pink
glow.
It is *very* beautiful. And now I can see the innards
and they also take on a pink glow. The most *beautiful* pink you
  can imagine.
I want them to concentrate on my lower part, the lower part of
  the body, and I just have
all my might of the brain
to concentrate on that lower part, what needs healing.

Water.
The pink
light becomes.
It is very dense at the lower part of my body, and it swirls
  around and becomes liquid, and it seems to wash out the parts
  of my body.
It just swirls, through all the
parts and the veins and
it mixes the blood. Now it goes to my left leg, all the way
  through to my toes. It goes like a spiral. But it is pink liquid.
  And now it goes through my *right* leg. All the way to my toes. It
  sort of
tickles a little. And meanwhile, it has been doing
this my hip, and now it goes to my stomach, and
now it goes to my chest. And now it goes to my left arm
and shoulder, elbow, thumb,
and all the fingers. And now it goes to right side to the
  shoulders, and
to the elbow, to the thumb, and
to the fingers.
And now it goes to my *throat*. It's *really* swishing around in my
  throat. That beautiful pink. I can feel it.
This going around and round, and now it makes its way toward
  my ears. The left ear, the left part of my

face and
and my brain, and then it
goes up the right side to my ears and my nose and
my eyes.
Just goes round and round and round and round. And
to the brain.
And now,
a piece of my brain opens, to let the
light out.

Where the wind came in through that hole, it, it now seems to
   be sort of a suction, because now it, it is sucking
the pink.
The pink light goes out though that opening. Very slowly. It's
   wafting out.
I feel *so* comfortable. It's as if
I had a massage, but not outside my body but inside my body. A
   marvelous massage.
There is still some liquid coming out of my body.
Syrupy. Brownish. And it is immediately
swallowed, not swallowed, but I mean it just goes
at the bottom, where I'm lying on it. It's just like a sponge. It is
   just sucked
in there, inside.
There is still this wonderful rose smell in the air.
I myself smell
like
a rose petal. My whole body.
Now a voice tells me to get out. To get out. So I am crawling out
   through the
opening.
Someone says to me I should go to the
chamber on the right.
To the very last chamber. I feel

unsteady on my legs, so I have to hold on the wall. And I'm
  walking toward it.
There is this spring coming out
of the earth
and I'm to go there.
There is a
natural . . .
it looks,
I mean, it's not a bathtub, but the rock is formed, so that water
  has accumulated and I can lie in it. The water is refreshingly
  cool. Oh, it is really lovely to lie in there.
I have the feeling that the water is just going into me
and is filling me up. It is just giving me life again.
Oh, it's a wonderful feeling.
Ohhh.
I can feel how the water goes through my legs, and fills every
  thing.
Fills everything out.
On both sides. It's just *rushing* in there. And it feels, I cannot
  describe, it just goes so fast. It has filled up my whole body
  already. In quite
speed. Speed.
My arms and my
upper body and my
my head and my brain and everything.
I just like to lie here and not think of anything; it feels so good.
  So relaxed.
My brain is relaxed. The first time
in a long time.
And my eyes feel so
relaxed.
And my throat, and my chest. My lower body.
    Oh, Turtle, thank you. It feels so wonderful.
I haven't seen Turtle yet, but I'm sure it was Turtle who
  helped me.

I can't say anything at the moment because I'm just lying and
   enjoy the water
still
filling out my body. It goes into *every* little pore in my skin.
I cannot leave
it.
I have no power to leave. I'm just lying in here. I cannot move.
Now a voice says to me,
         *Get up Ema, get up.*
I
*can't* get up.
Okay, now I'm out.
I wish I don't have to leave.
Something is pushing me
toward the chamber
where
*I'm sucked up!*
Ahhhhh! And now I'm
in that desolate area.
It's nice and warm here. The sun is shining. It is just lovely.
I am on the high plateau and overlooking the river down below.
It looks like a little silver band. How beautiful.

Something tells me
to breathe, to breathe deep. So I get my lungs full of air.
         *Don't hesitate,*
something says.
         *Breathe, breathe. That is your life. You have to get air in*
            *your body*
            *to live.*
They tell me I should breathe deeper.
         *Get the air*
            *into your body till it hurts,*
some voice says.

They do say it with some urgency.

Now I am capable of doing it. I breathe and I can see my breath filling my whole body all the way down through my toes.

My whole skin is changing color. It was sort of grayish and now it becomes

my old

skin again.

Ahhhhh!

The drum is calling. I have to go back.

Oh, thank you, Turtle, thank you so much for helping me.

So, I have to go down. So I will

go through the sucking

hole. And then

Oh, I do not know . . .

Turtle, I don't know the way back I came.

I have to go back the old way.

I am climbing up to the wall.

I have to go that way, not the old way. And so I'm just racing

quite quickly. And I'm outside on the field.

---

 **Reflections**

Ema's Quest. "I would like to visit Turtle today and ask her for a healing of my whole body."

Ema's Response. "It was so interesting . . . I don't understand it."

Counselor's Comments. In stating her intention, Ema develops the practice of stating which spirit she intends to visit and where, followed by her request, as here. She does not always understand her journey and how it may answer her question or request and may feel she does not get exactly what she requests, yet she engages with the experience she has. Her vivid, in-the-moment experience is available, recorded for her continuing review. Ema frequently works with her helping spirits, in addition to conventional medicine, when she needs healing help. In such journeys, she is often successful and filled with great humility and awe.

# The Yellow One

*What must I do to be less sensitive?*

*What must I do to be less sensitive?*

*What must I do to be less sensitive?*

I am walking in Rodeo Beach toward the oak tree right at the
bend. I see that some sand has fallen into the opening. I push
the sand aside with my hands.

I am sliding down on my belly right into the cave. The Yellow
One is sitting right there.

> Yellow One, I am coming to you to ask you, What can I do to be
> less sensitive?

He was in a sitting position, and now he is getting up.

He has thrust his sword through my body. It has no pain.

It just happened to go through my body.

Now he motions me to follow him.

I am taking the sword out.

He's floating in front of me. I am afraid to follow him because
after all the area I am in is very high above the ground. I
mean the lower area he is floating toward.

I am just going down the path. It's rather steep.

It is really very steep.

I don't want to hurt my hip.

I have a branch in my left hand and the sword in my right.

I feel I am surrounded by a yellow light.

I am happy I didn't jump.

I am happy I didn't follow him.

The cave is very high up and

of course it is dry.
I can see sort of a river bed
where the water would come down.
I am so *scared* that I will fall and break my hip.
Now there is some overgrowth.
I have to make a path and I use the sword.
Yellow sheen around it.
I'm shaking. My whole body is shaking.
I just can't walk anymore. I just have to sit down again.
It is very still.
I just take some of the plants and I suddenly have the desire to
    wrap this all over my body.
Over my whole body and this
gives me strength. Now I just seem to roll down the hillside.
Floating.
I'm just sort of above the shrubbery. Finally, I am down
in the valley.
The valley is just huge, of course.
I can look far ahead. I see the Yellow One far, far away.
I'm running. Now I seem to have clothes on again and sturdy
    shoes.

The more I run, the farther he seems to be away.
I still have the sword. I can't run anymore. I just have to sit
    down. He's so far away.

Why did he run away?
    Oh, Turtle, what do I do wrong? What do I do wrong? What did
        I do wrong?

I am taking a closer look at the sword.
And fire is coming out of where you grip it.
Now that I see it I wouldn't dare to touch it.
Oh, but it is a cool fire. I can touch it.
I am taking the sword in my hands

Just bring me to the Yellow One.

Well, the Yellow One has come back. I am handing him the
  sword.
He looks at me deep.
Deep in my eyes.
It goes all the way into my chest, the way he looks at me.
  *You are above it all.*
  *Why do you worry?*
What do you mean "above it all"! I mean you talk about the
  ordinary . . .
have more worth than I.
  *That is not true.*
That I am equal. I am equal to every human being.
Every single one,
other,
I guess, more educated.
  *So, and if they are?*
  *They have not any more rights than you.*
  *Well,*
he says. He told me that I am and I should not slide back. He
  says he can feel that I still hesitate.
I have to bring the Lower World and the Ordinary World
  together.
That is something I have been taught before. Have I forgotten it?
I am crying and he says,
  *Don't show me your tears.*
That it would only harden him, seeing me cry.
He suddenly takes the sword high in the air.
  *Why do you fear I will hurt you?*
  *Why the fear in you?*
  *You are scared in the deepness.*
No, I am not scared. The drum is calling.
I have to leave you. I have to go back. Thank you.

I am lifted up toward the cave and I am looking back and I see the Yellow One waving.

I wave back

and now I go and step out of the oak tree.

 ## Reflections

Ema's Quest. "What must I do to be less sensitive?"

Ema's Evaluation. "What I understood . . . I seem to feel that other people have more worth than I, and . . . that they are better trained and better schooled. And so, I feel sort of . . . I'm a different person when I am down there. I talk differently, I think. . . . I do put people above me in a way. What he said was, I am equal to everybody else. . . . 'Every human being, every single one.'"

Ema's Interpretation. "And that's probably why I act the way I do. Maybe also I don't speak up enough and later on I think, well, I could have said this, or . . . *I don't know. I will have to go to him again.* I think he got to the core of my unhappiness . . . shyness. He got something very important there. He really did."

Counselor's Comments. This journey centers around personal growth, foreshadowed in the second HSC journey, hinted by the spirits again in Journeys 5, 6, 7, and 10, and raised directly by Ema in Journey 23. Challenged by the Yellow One, Ema confronts his analysis, recognizing value there, as well as her need to return for further understanding. We see her willingness to confront herself and to hear the words of the spirit, acknowledge her limited understanding, and return for deeper knowledge.

# Healing in the Turtle Cave

*I—would like to meet Turtle in the Turtle Cave to give me a healing.*

*I would like to meet Turtle in the Turtle Cave—to give me a healing.*

*I would like—to go to the Turtle Cave—to—meet Turtle to give me a healing.*

I try to go to the area where the oak tree is, but I can't find it.

I have to, in order to go to the oak tree.
This time I have to climb over a fence. So I'm climbing over that
   fence, and slide down
the gully, which is filled with autumn leaves, and I just kind of
slide down rather quickly.
I land
at the base of the oak tree. And I have to look whether
the opening is completely filled with leaves.
So I have to open
the hole and
I try to get all the leaves out.
And, so now I see the
path down below and I jump into the oak tree.
I'm walking
down the path. And leaves
came into
the path.
There seems to be a slight wind and the leaves seem to be blown
around me, which is very unusual because there has never been
   wind before.

I am now coming to the fork and I go to the

right side, where at the
end of that trail the
Turtle Cave is located.
And, I have arrived at the Turtle Cave. Today it is
wet and lots of turtles are
in the cave today.
The water is pretty high. You only see a little
of the turtles and they all have their heads up in order to
breathe.
They are entangled with seaweed. I mean, seaweed is all over the
    place, in all colors. It's not only green this time. They are sort
    of
brownish, and white, and I see also jellies, jellies in-between.
It's just a mass of
creatures.
Yeah, because I even see little fish.
It's very different.
Suddenly I am called
by my name. And I am walking
toward the
area where the call came from.
And, there's Turtle.
    Hi, Turtle.
Turtle motions me to lie down.
This is a small antechamber
and, it also has water in it. But, no turtles, but also it has seaweed
    in it. Lots of seaweed. And so, she motions me to lie down.
She tells me to relax.
She tells me to really relax.
    *Let all your thoughts go,*
she says.
    *Just be limp.*
I'm lying in the
water

and
the seaweed seems, to
completely and utterly envelop me. Oh, it is really *a very nice
feeling, actually.*
The seaweed is slimy, but
it feels like silk
on my body. I am
in the nude. And it is *so nice.* I feel I don't have to tell Turtle
where it pains me
because
Turtle knows what's going on with me in the ordinary world.
Now Turtle is above me and she regurgitates
over my face and over my body, over the part that
is still a little bit
not quite
in the water.
It's ice-cold. It really feels
strange but it feels so nice.
She's sliding over my body. Even though Turtle is very
big, but there is no heaviness
when she slides over me.
But with her sliding over me, she seems to press
some of my bones
and my muscles into place. Because I hear sort of
clicking and
cracking, within my body. And when she has left that part of the
body, it seems to be all sort of aligned.
Ahh. Now she is at my stomach area.
And now she goes
lower. I have my legs close together and she is sliding down my
legs.
I wish she could get to my heel. And I'm lifting my right foot, to
motion to her
that I would like to have some of

the regurgitating
seaweed or whatever it is,
it looks green, to put on my heel.

She says to me,
*You have*
*so much seaweed at home, why don't you use it?*
Which is right of course. Yes,
How do I
use it then?
She says it has to be ice-cold.
I have to
put the seaweed in water and soften it. Put it on my heel and
  then
put ice
on it.
My *whole*
foot.
She regurgitated over my foot.
It has
hardened around my foot. Around the heel. It is as if I'm
sort of a cast.
And,
it is very cold.
Oh,
it seems to break.
With my inner eye or what I do not know, even though I am
  lying down and normally I really couldn't see
my foot but, for whatever reason I can *see* the *bones*
and a little crystal there. There seem to be little crystals on it and
  they, they seem to dissolve
there.
The seaweed, the *juice* of the seaweed
must have gone

into it, because the whole part looks sort of dark green, and the
little crystals seem to dissolve into this

*green mass.*

Now I'm supposed to push my foot into the water.

Back into the water.

I think my foot was

higher, out of the water, with this ice around it and

now

I'm back in the water and the ice

dissolves. And

Turtle again

motions me to relax.

I want to be relaxed.

She tells me I am too tense.

*You are always too tense,*

she says.

What can I do not to be tense? I realize I am tense. I don't
want to be tense!

She just strokes me with her flippers.

*Don't be tense,*

she says.

*Don't be tense. Let your muscles rest. Let your eyes rest. Let
your brain rest. Your eyes*

*Your mouth*

*Your shoulders*

*Your arms*

*Your hands*

*Your heart muscles*

*All your inner organs*

*Just relax them. You don't have to hold onto them. They
be right there. They will be right there. You don't have to
hold onto them.*

*Your legs*

*Your knees*

*Your feet. Just feel light. Just make yourself feel light. Let all*
*the heaviness go out of you.*
*Relax your brain. Don't think so much. Just relax*
*Your eyes. Relax.*

Now that I'm relaxed
I think I
swim on top of the water.
I mean, I am not in the water anymore; I'm above
but the seaweed is still
around me. It's like a dress. It's like a second skin really. It's slimy
and it glistens.
There is a light source. I do not know where the light source
comes from. It's sort of greenish
and
especially there
seems to be some seaweed.
White seaweed, that has such a beautiful, in effect, in the light it
has rainbow colors. It is a nice play
of colors on my body. And it seems to
penetrate. Oh!
This light *penetrates* my whole body.
Oh, how nice.
Oh, yes,
light.
Colored light. Goes through my, my whole body.
It *really* relaxes me. My brain. All the colored mass.

The light goes through my whole body.
It started at the top and now it goes slowly down. To my very
toes.
I don't
really like to talk.
Oh!
The whole chamber

is colored light. It's white and
purple, lots of purple, and *lavender*
and silver-white
and a bit of green.
It's
the light of pearl mortar. It's the light
of the inside of an abalone shell. That is exactly it! Ahhhh.
I could lie
in this light forever.
Even Turtle
who is black normally
has taken on the color
of the pearl mortar.
  Ah, Turtle.
Turtle seems to enjoy it, too.
Her eyes are closed.
Her flippers
are on my legs.
There's no heaviness in there.
It seems to be as if we are penetrated by the light in such a way
 that, even though when I see myself from above, I still have the
 shape of a human.
But it is all *light*. I mean it is all this
beautiful, purplish light. Purplish-silver.
I can't think of anything else but just
lying there.
Turtle also.
I don't dare to do anything else, because Turtle seems to be
 enjoying herself, too. I just want to be like this forever.
I can't really talk.

Now the water seems to leave us. It's like
it was flooding, and now, the water goes away.
The seaweed has slipped off my body

and
Turtle is black again.
I'm so sad
because it was such a,
I don't know,
being in that light
was such a . . .
great moment. I hoped it would last forever.
Now Turtle is going with me.
She's walking into another chamber. I don't know whether she
wants me to follow her.
I just follow her.
But when I come into the chamber, Turtle is gone. I'm all by
myself.
I'm sitting down
toward the right, because this is where I seem to have the pain
in my right knee, in my right heel and my right hand, so I go
toward the right
and sit.
I'm still so . . .
so relaxed, I guess, that I don't want to do anything else. I'm just
sitting and
I'm supposed to take a rock and
and carve.
They want me, something wants me to carve
a human body, on the wall. It should be I! And they want me to
mark the
places on the body.
They want me to put signs, where I have the pain, so I'm making
the marks on the body I had carved. The drum is calling.

So I am walking back.
The Turtles have all gone.
Come to the fork and I'm walking rather quickly.
And I am outside now.

### Reflections

Ema's Quest. "I would like to meet Turtle in the Turtle Cave to give me a healing."

Ema's Response (after prompt for her observations about her journey). "Well, I think I got my healing (very affirmative) and I was reminded I should use seaweed, myself, which is, of course, something I do not know why, I am not doing it."

Counselor's Comments. Ema continues to be deliberate in her entry into nonordinary reality, carefully describing her in-the-present-moment experiences. Instead of requesting the healing she intended, she follows Turtle's directions, stating, "Turtle knows what's going on with [me] in the ordinary world," including why she is making this journey. In addition to direct healing, Turtle also encourages Ema with suggestions for her healthy behavior in ordinary reality. Upon reflection, Ema is clear that her request was honored, and more.

# Ancestry

*I like to meet Turtle to ask her what she thinks about the method, my questioning the rock.*

*I like to meet Turtle to ask her about, my method—the asking the rock—the method, to ask the rock.*

*I like to meet Turtle to—ask her about the method to—ask the rock.*

I think I
do something very different in this
journey because I have been at Rodeo Beach for quite some time
   and I see a tree there with three entrances, and for whatever
   reason I seem to stand
right in front of this oak tree. And, it is the middle entrance that
   sort of beckons me, for me to get in. So I'm just going to
slide into this opening.

I seem to be in a very big hall
with a *very musty*
fragrance.
It's very dark
yet I have the feeling, even though I can't see it, it seems to be
   very
huge.
I really have to figure out why I think it is huge because it is so
   dark. I am the only light source. It's this light coming from me.
   But, I have the feeling that I can see in the dark.
And also when I walk, the sound is such
that it is
huge.

Huge.

I don't know whether it is a cave, but it is a huge room.

My name is called

from

very far away. And I'm going towards

the sound.

My steps

give a hollow sound.

I can definitely see in the dark because my light source really
  isn't that great. But I can see the moss on the high, high ceiling.

It's a beautiful green.

The voice is still calling me and I have still not reached it.

Oh, my goodness. The voice that is calling me is not at all Turtle,
  what I thought. It looks like a grasshopper.

    Why are you calling me, then?

The grasshopper just beckons me to follow. What a strange
  thing.

Guess I made a mistake. I should have

not done this journey.

Well, never mind.

I really should concentrate on the journey.

All right. What Grasshopper is saying to me is this. I wanted to
  go to Turtle but I also

wanted to find out what was behind

the entrance in the oak tree.

And since I went into it, I came to the

World of

Grasshoppers. I would not meet Turtle here, because this is just
  very strange, the whole thing.

    Yes, I understand.

I wanted to ask Turtle about a

ritual I had done with a rock, and I wanted to ask Turtle what
  she thought about the method of

questioning the rock.

So, the grasshopper is just, sort of *very obliging*. It just beckons
  me into another hall, which is
lit.
And I *see*
a big rock, in the middle of the
hall
and it seems to be somewhat familiar to the rock I have been
  questioning.
    Yes, this is the rock.
Grasshopper asked me whether this is the rock and I,
with sort of a smile, and I have to admit, yes, it is, but it is so
  much larger than the rock I questioned. And, Grasshopper
  said,
      *That is because you are the size of a grasshopper.*
Ooooohhh. Yes, of course! This is why everything is so . . .
I was still thinking.
Yes. Yes, *now* I understand.
Yes, I was still thinking, yes, my being my size.
    Of course. Oh, yes. So, what do you think about . . .
    the method, then?
I ask Grasshopper. And, he just says to me, What do I remember
  the most
of the whole journey I made on this rock? What comes to mind
  immediately is the shell
and, with Turtle coming out. And Grasshopper is just sitting on
  the rock, and now he looks like an old, wise grasshopper. I
  mean, it's just very strange but it just has this *very*
wise appearance, I mean, the head, and the big eyes.
It's just amazing. And so, Grasshopper asks,
      *What else comes into your mind?*
    The lava fields.
      *And what else comes into your mind?*
    The waterfall.
      *And what else comes into your mind?*

The waves.

*And what else comes into your mind?*

Nothing . . .

*Ah,*

Grasshopper says.

*Turtle*

*The lava fields*

*The waterfall*

*And the waves.*

What does it mean?

I ask.

Grasshopper looks at me, and says,

*What do you think?*

Well, if you ask me that way,

the lava fields, of course, I mean. I think my answers . . .

Aaaaaaahh!

If I think way back and I want to know about my ancestors,

they are not really from . . .

Now it really gets interesting.

My ancestors are from

way back. They are from an area from where lava flows was.

And fires. I do remember.

So my ancestry in Europe, it would be

not really going very far, is it? No.

*Right!*

At the moment there is so much in my head I cannot quite
bring it out.

This is just so much deeper.

Ah. Grasshopper suddenly says that

I will not find at all find in Europe what I really wanted to
find.

If I want to find my roots,

ancestry,

*Rivers and waters are all the same, Ema. For that you don't*
*have to go*
*far away.*
I know, I know, because I really like the water here. It's just . . .
Are you telling me that I shouldn't go?
Oh, no. I'm sorry, yes, you're just interpreting. Yes, I under
stand. I'm sorry. I'm completely confused.
Grasshopper says I should just relax. I should not be flustered
because I am on a journey I did not expect.
Yes, that's
right, I asked quite differently, did I? I always jump to other
things.
*Yes.*

I am, I am in this big rock. And I am at the area where
I was thinking about going into the Lower World. And I'm
looking at this, and it is
really inviting to go into it
And I look at the grasshopper and she just
motions me I should go in if I wanted to. So I just
go into this
area.
It is
cold
in there.
Uhhh, the drum is calling and I have to go back. I came out.
Oh, it was really interesting coming to you, Grasshopper. I sure
will come back if I may.
I just have to go rather quickly. I cannot get lost in here.
So, I'm just running as fast as I can.
And, something is calling me, and so I go to that direction.
I think there is some light and
I'm out.

### Reflections

Ema's Quest. "I like to meet Turtle to ask her what she thinks about the method, my questioning the rock."

Ema's Response. "[laughing] It serves me right, doesn't it? . . . [laughing] Oh. God. . . . How obliging he was . . . I didn't realize I was a grasshopper, too."

Counselor's Comments. Again, choosing a new entrance to the Lower World, Ema embarks upon her journey. Having committed to her decision, she continues. Astonishing to Ema in former journeys, such events as conversing with a grasshopper and experiencing radical changes in size, she now takes in a very matter-of-fact way. Grasshopper tutors her in working with the question underlying her purpose for this journey; Ema comes to an answer herself, at which point Grasshopper elaborates an interpretation. Just as she merges with a rock, the drum calls Ema to return, at which point she disengages with discipline from the rock and returns. In her subsequent discussion, Ema is laughing and grateful. She offers no further interpretation of the journey as an answer to her question.

# Dismemberment in Water

*I would like to meet Turtle today—and ask her what can I do to be happier in my home.*

*What can I do to be happier in my home?*

*What can I do to be happier in my home?*

I find myself
at Rodeo Beach
And I'm sort of drawn toward that bay tree with the
opening.
But the opening is closed.
Completely closed.
I go back to my house
and I slide down the hill.

Toward the oak tree.
There is a big opening
but I can see water rushing.
I'm afraid to jump in.
The water is rushing both ways. I don't understand it.
That really
scares me.
    Turtle, I would like to go, get to you. Please help me.
It seems to me as if,
when I look now on the right side, it's as if something
has stopped the water flow. And I can go
and walk now.
I am, however, very apprehensive
that the water might come again. I'm not as

carefree as I used to be when I
walk this road, walk this path. And yet I cannot walk fast.
My legs are like lead. I can hardly get one foot
front of the other. And here I am scared
that the water might rush in again, and yet I have no ability to
move.

> Oh, Turtle, what is the matter with me?
> I'd like to meet you in the Turtle Cave.
> Not for a healing but to talk about my
> unhappiness at home, at the moment.

I am breaking!
It seems to be as if I was
made out of lead and I'm just breaking into pieces. And,
the water is back.
It is exactly what I was afraid of
happened. I broke into pieces and the water is just
rushing
and I'm carried.
But a certain peace has come over my spirit, I guess. I do not
know.
I don't really know. There seems to be a core that still makes me
think.
But my body
is gone.
But it's very peaceful. I'm not scared at all anymore. I just seem
to float.
I don't know,
when I look from above, I don't see my body
and yet I can think.

I am in a complete different area.
Oh! Yes. Yes, now I understand.
Or maybe I don't.
I see my body now, in

many, many pieces.
And this well-lit cave.

I don't know, my spirit I guess, I feel just so sorry for that heap
    of human being that is lying there. And yet I can't do any
    thing.
        Turtle, this is something completely
        unexpected.
Turtle is not even there.
Someone has to put my
body together.
I'm completely helpless. I can't do it myself.

Nothing comes to me.
Nothing comes to me.
Now, in looking closer, I see,
I think they are lizards
working over
the body.
There are just so many; they have completely covered the body. I
    cannot quite make out what they are doing.

I hear Turtle call me,
        *Ema, take care of your body first, don't worry about your*
            *home.*
I don't quite understand what it means, but . . .
        What do you mean, "Take care of body first?" I mean, how?
She tells me I have not been treating my body well
in the last month.
        *You have to adhere [to a]*
        *stricter diet.*
I guess that is more important than . . .
        *Once you are healthy*
        *you . . .*

She says that once I am healthy
I will see things very different.
I have become narrow-minded. I am too
obsessed with
little things.

Yes, maybe you are right. I probably am.
What exactly should I do?

*Be sure how to sustain your body. Be sure what you eat.*
She stresses *so much* that I should be sure what I am eating.
It seems to be so vital.

What am I supposed to eat then?
Turtle shows me a field. I cannot explain this now. But, in front
of my eyes is a field with lots of green and lots of
fruits and
salads, and ferns. And there is a pond with fresh fish
and birds are flying.
Birds I have never seen in my life. Very beautiful feathered birds.
Turtle says,

*Take from it, but very cautiously.*

It's my spirit that is there, because I don't have my body back.
I don't know. I really shouldn't have said it; it probably was
stupid.
She repeats
about my being narrow-minded.
It is like a song.

*Get rid of your narrow-mindedness.*
The whole air is filled with this. The whole air is filled with this.
Now I am back in the cave and
I see my body is completely healed
and the lizards have all gone.
Now Turtle is there. Turtle is
on my
chest and she's sort of

pressing, with her front
feet. Pressing at the chest area. And now, I seem to be inside my
   body again because I now look exactly into her eyes, while she
   is still pounding
on my chest.
  Oh, Turtle, what have you done to me?
She says she has given me a new body
for a fresh start.
   *You have to open up.*
Turtle says.
   *Talk to someone you trust.*
  Yes, I know.
   *Don't make life so difficult for yourself.*
I'm very peaceful and very tired. She talks to me
and I
take it all in. And the more she talks, it seems, the stream of
words that come from her seem to
go into my body
and bring warmth. I cannot quite explain
but it seems to me that I was really *cold*
and now I'm getting warmer and warmer.
The more she talks, I get
warmth and life back into my body.
She tells me things I knew
but I had forgotten.
She does things to me I know
but
had left me for a while.
It is just like a completely new awakening in a way.

I see again a meadow. Actually there are also lots of trees and a
   small house.
What does the house mean? Is that the house I should move
   into?

What does this mean?
Where is this house?

Now that house looks like my house
but in a different area.
And now it looks again
*small.*
It's like a film. It goes back and forth and back and forth. A small
  house and then my house.
    What is it supposed to mean, Turtle?
Turtle says I won't be any happier
in another home.

I should
look at the core
of myself.
        *You won't be happy*
        *in another home,*
she says.
        *There is no difference.*
I should
change the core
of myself. She has given me a start, a new beginning.
        *Don't be afraid.*
        *Live a life in peace.*
        *Don't be afraid.*
        *Live a life in peace.*
And my body is getting warmer and warmer whenever she
  speaks. These words seem to bring warmth into me.

She's just talking to me and I can't say all the words she's saying.
  But it makes me . . . warmer and warmer. It seems to make
  me more alive whilst, at first, I was really still. Now I seem
  to be able to move, I mean, my toes and my feet, and every
  thing, I can move again.

Now I see my house
where it is *really,* on the hill.
The . . .
The drum is calling. And I have to go back.
Ah, God, I don't know where I am.
    Turtle, you have to help me to go back.
So I'm going out of the cave. Turtle has me on her back actually,
  and she is swimming with me through the pathways.
And now, I am out.

---

##  Reflections

Ema's Quest. "I would like to meet Turtle today and ask her what I can do to be happier in my home."

Ema's Summary. "Oh, I really can't make a summary. I really don't know."

Ema's Evaluation and Interpretation (after prompt for her understanding of the journey as an answer to her question). "My question was answered. I wouldn't find happiness in any other house. That obviously is really within myself. And, the house has nothing to do with it . . . that's what I understand she said.

"The very last thing I saw was my house on the hill, which makes me think that as far as Turtle is concerned, that is the house I should stay in. Turtle said it's whatever it is. Turtle made me understand, being in another house, it will not go away. It's not the house. I got that one. It can't be any plainer."

Counselor's Comments. Failing to gain entry to the Lower World through a recently discovered portal, Ema returns to start her journey with the opening she has most frequently found reliable. She carries her question to Turtle with her as she ventures alone and helpless and her body breaks apart.

Turtle's message appears to place a priority on the issue of Ema's health and growth rather than on Ema's intended concern, finally integrating the whole journey into an answer, which Ema states clearly in her interpretation. Notice, too, how Ema describes her physical response to the power of Turtle's words. With further consideration, Ema indicates this journey is very significant to her.

# Dancing with the Energies

*I like to meet the Yellow One today and ask him, "How can I use the Energies in daily life?"*

*How can I use the Energies in daily life?*

*How can I use the Energies in daily life?*

I have to walk to Rodeo Beach because that is where the bay tree
   is located with the hole in the trunk.
I just slip into the opening. This time I am right at the opening
landscape. Ah.

It is evening and I see the moon rising out of the bay.
Carried up to the mountain cave.
The cave is empty. But a yellow cloud is coming near.
It seems to be solid. I step onto the cloud. And the cloud,
floating slowly
toward the north.
I see the landscape
with people fighting. Blood everywhere.
And fires burning. Now, suddenly I am floating.

I see people working.
Tilling the land. Everything is green.
Just the river
silvery blue.
I am very high up.
My eyes are just like eagle's eyes, I guess.

Now I come to an area. Oh. I have seen this all before.
This is an area . . .

It has thousands of Buddhas.
Everything has a blue hue.
Hue, tint. A blue tint.
It's very calming. And now
something is giving me a white mask.

The cloud is still floating. Now I am coming into
a desert area.
The smell of sulfur is in the air. It is so strong!
    Yellow One, what are you doing to me?
I am on the ground. The cloud has left and I am in the desert.
I have to take the mask off. Yellow mask.
I cannot take it off.
    *Dance, Ema, dance.*
Hot here. I guess I try to get up and dance, but the sulfur smell is
  so pungent, I can't do anything.
Voice and dance, dance. I keep moving. I'm dancing and I keep
  moving. Unfortunately, the air is glimmering with heat.
I see that I am completely in the nude. And I see I am
  completely shriveling up by the heat.
It is an immense heat! Gosh!
I try to get into the sand.
It is hard as concrete.
    Yellow One, why do you make me suffer so?
I am still moving, even though
it is I who is burning, by the heat, not by the fire.
By the heat.
My skin is completely brown.
Yet I am still moving. I am still moving.
I am *still* moving.
Now I see the Yellow One in its pure form, motioning me.
My eyesight is inhuman.
And so I just
try to run to him, but I don't have the . . .

Ahhhhh

Oh

Something comes into me that says "Get the Energies."

All my fright is out of my body now.
I was terribly scared. Now I am working with the Energies.
It is not rain.
The Energies.
I am still dancing.
I see that he is in the middle of a lake
but he is on the lake and I am on the beach. The sand,
no softness to it.
I go into the water.
Now I am in the water.
Very quickly my body soaked up all the water and ah
    . . . to ask you, "How can I use the Energies in my daily life?"
    Uh!!
He threw something at me and it hit me right at the front of my
    hand. . . .
He said that the suffering, that is the suffering I seem to do to
    myself in ordinary life.
    Yes, but how can I overcome?
. . . sword at me.
I am catching it with my right hand.
It is very hot. I am very happy I am in the water.
Ah, God! I am taking the sword and throw it back to him.
How do you say electrocuted? Something happened to me there,
   right then.
    *You think clearly here,*
he says to me.
    *Why don't you go?*
    *Why do you seem to forget it? Why not take it with you?*
The gift.
    Oh, Yellow One, I'm so sorry.

My world seems to be so consuming. I don't know why, I honor
you so much and I know you give me the gift. I just . . .

He is coming closer to me. I am still
but I feel his presence very near.
I feel a heaviness on my head.

> *I'm giving you a yellow crown. I am giving it again to you.
> Take it with you and be reminded. That crown will help
> you to collect the Energies that you need.*

I feel terribly hot, as if I'm overcharged with heat.
Not dancing, it is a floating motion.
It is a very nice quieting feeling.
Pores blown away.

A voice says to me that I should go back.
Now it is soft and I am walking on the sand.
I myself seem to be a source of heat.
There are some plants.
I was bending down in order to take the flower and it wilted.
I must be very hot yet. I am just walking. I see the mountains I
came from.
I am told to walk and so I am just walking. And I am still
walking.
And now I seem to come to the valley. The Buddhas.
Ah! I don't seem to be hot.
The stream just seems to wash over me.
It is not a big stream.
And I put my head on a soft stone.
I see the Buddha,
the very mild face.
Statue
with a very mild face.
I am now floating.
Very strange.
I am floating *against* the current of the water

to the part that is green.
I am so hungry.
Wonderful watermelons. So I am just eating watermelon.
I am eating watermelon and the drum calls me back.

Something carries me to the cave in the mountains.
I bow very deeply and say,
> Thank you, so much, Yellow One.
And now I am out in Rodeo Beach again.

 ## Reflections

Ema's Quest. "How can I use the Energies in daily life?"

Counselor's Comments. This time Ema is able to access the Lower World through the opening at Rodeo Beach, which was closed to her in the last journey. Among the images in passing, she recognizes Buddhas. The Yellow One gives her a gift to help her in the quest she poses. Masked, she dances to "get the Energies," and declares, "Now I am working with the Energies." This journey is also one she designates as important.

Ema's Response, Evaluation, and Interpretation are missing; due to a technical problem, they were not recorded. Technical challenges do occur. This is another reason it is useful to take handwritten notes of the narration, in addition to the recording of the journey. It provides an additional record as a backup for the journeyer to consult afterward. Behavioral notes and the counselor's observations add to the information not available on the recording.

# Help Me to Get Back
# My Peace of Mind

*I like to go to the—like to meet the Yellow One today and ask him—I forgot what I want to ask him, not my day today—to help me, help me to get back my peace of mind.*

*To help me—to get back my peace of mind*

*To help me get back my peace of mind.*

> I am walking
> down the path in Rodeo Beach.
> The grass is already yellow. There's
> the smell of the water,
> sort of brackish. I'm getting around the bend where the bay tree
>   is and I
> swing myself up through that hole.
> I have no momentum
> and I just have to crawl
> down to the cave of the Yellow One.
> I'm not really there. I have to
> sort of concentrate to get there.
> Suddenly
> something is just tugging at my feet and
> now I am just swished with *immense* speed
> into the cave.
>
> The cave has
> the familiar fog-like substance in it.
> I feel in an instant completely calm.
> I feel the fog is just

going through

my skin, and it's going through my bones.

It is as if my whole

body is exposed, and the pores are open

so wide that the

fog, which is energy, is just

absolutely gobbling up the energy.

Ahhh, it just feels so good!

The cave is suddenly completely empty

and clear. It is as if the

energy has all gone into me. Oh, my God, I really needed a lot of
    energy. And I can now see.

I go to the edge of the cave and I can see the

landscape.

But I hear a voice and

I have to go back. And the way I am now I can go through the
    wall. Because the cave is completely

encapsulated. And, I have to go in order to go to

where the voice is.

I just go through the, through the rock.

I cannot explain it. But

I am just walking through it.

I'm in [a] big hall.

> Oh, Yellow One, I have tried so often to come to you, but
> I just couldn't make it. My brain was just split right in the
>    middle, and I just did not have the strength to
> go to the other side. I
> would very much like you to
> give me my peace of mind. Please give me the peace of mind I
>    need to continue
> with the problems or the business deals I have at the moment.
> Make me strong. You helped me so much three months ago,
>    and now

it has all

waned again.

The Yellow One is there; he doesn't really look alive today,

just like a statue.

He's all the way up there, which means to me I am really small

again.

Yellow One, don't be up there, just come to me.

I seem to be the seed again.

*We have to start again from the beginning,*

he says.

Yes.

I feel that the cave that I thought was dry, really

has a moist floor. And

I feel that my feet

are getting wet.

And with the wetness, I seem to grow. The wetness just goes into

my body

and it makes me grow.

I hear a strange noise. I cannot quite pinpoint the noise.

It's like a bell.

It's a very high-pitched sound of a bell, I think.

This high-pitched sound of the bell seems to be very vital to my

growing.

I have the feeling as if the tone of the bell

is going into my bones, and holding the bones together.

The bell seems to be like glue.

There is a fire in front of me and I'm supposed to go into the

fire.

It is cold fire. It is

really fire.

It has flames

but

it does not burn me.

The rocks at the one wall
are sort of shiny and I can see the fire and I can see myself
in those rocks.
They *are* shiny
and, and I see myself growing.
But the high-pitched
ring
it's still around.
Still surrounds me.
I am still growing. It's a very slow process, I must say.

The Yellow One
tells me I should look at him. And
he's still way up, almost on the ceiling of that huge cave. He is
   now starting to float
toward me.
He suddenly
reminds me
that he had given me a crown. And I must admit I sort of . . .
it all comes back to me now.
He says to me that
> *The moment that you forget*
> *about the crown, it is gone.*
> *You have to keep it with you every time, every day, even at*
>    *night.*
   Well, I don't know,
   I didn't
   realize that I had forgotten about it.
He puts the crown on me again.
It is a beautiful crown actually.

I'm completely exhausted.
I can hardly talk.
The fire just . . .
Together with the . . .

I'm still getting nourishment from the
ground
because I still feel that
moisture is coming into me.
Moisture is coming into me very slowly and it has filled up my
whole body now.
The beautiful
golden flames around me.
I feel like lying down but
I am not supposed to lie down.
Somehow I've got a hole
in the top of my skull.
Something seems to come out of there but I don't know what
it is.
The flames are so bright now
that I cannot see.
I only see brightness
in the shiny wall. I cannot see myself anymore in there. So I
don't really quite know what happened, but there is a opening
in my skull and something comes out of it. It sounds as if air is
swishing out; it makes a swishing sound as if one has
let air come out of a balloon. This is exactly what it sounds like.
It makes my brain feel, my *head* feel . . . what can I say?
Before it seemed to be tight
but now it's not tight anymore. It seems as if something has
been released
from
my brain.
Some pressure.
That is a very wonderful feeling.
I can't see the Yellow One at the moment. But I feel his energy.
Suddenly
there is no fire anymore. And, the room is dark again and I can
not see

the shiny walls. So, I really don't know
what I look like now. But, I feel I am my own size.
And I can feel the crown on me.
I feel
very sticky, like honey.
And, suddenly, the Yellow One
calls me
to a corner. And, there's
water coming out
like a well.
And I'm to stand under it.
The water is taking the sticky stuff with it.
It's not only sticky as honey, it is also golden as honey.
It is a nice feeling
being under the water, it's not really a waterfall.
Or maybe it *is* a waterfall, but it is a very small one. It's as wide
   as my body really and
also goes not very fast. It's not a trickle, but it is just sort of . . .
not painful. What I mean, it's not painful when it comes onto
   me and it is just washing
me
clean.
The
cave is so dark, I can't see anything. Normally, I have a light.
Oh, the light is shining out of me again.
I always seem to have a light source
around my navel. And for a moment it wasn't there, but now it
   is. It is there again.
      Oh, thank you, Yellow One,
      for helping me.
There is a *path*
where I go out
again. This time it shows me
where I should go out.
It is like a vein

in the rocks, and I just sort of
go through this vein. It looks shiny. I do not know what it is.
And so, I just sort of
go through there
very simply.
Now I'm back in
the cave I arrived in.
Ah,
it is so nice to see daylight. I see the valley underneath me, and
the little river. I have so much a desire to go down there, I don't
know why. I sort of start crying right now, I don't know why.
Maybe because it is familiar to me
going there. But of course I'm high up. The
cave is high up. And, in order to get down there, it is a very
hazardous kind of way to go down there.
But I see now that there *are* roots, from trees, that go by the cave,
and I just wonder maybe I should climb down.
No, because the drum is calling me. And I have to go back.
Oh, thank you, Yellow One. I am so grateful. Please receive me
next time when I am at home I just need to be with you.

I seem to be sort of . . .
I have to go back. I don't want to go back. I just don't want to go.
Something is just pushing me
to go back and
I am just pulled up by something, and I'm,
Yes. Now I am back in Rodeo Beach.

---

 **Reflections**

Ema's Quest. "I like to go to the Yellow One today and ask him to
help me get back my peace of mind."

Ema's Evaluation (after prompt about whether her request was
answered). "Yes, I think it was honored . . . that I was helped quite
a bit."

Ema's Interpretation. "I had the feeling that the sound came into my body and my bones, which were sort of soft, the tone glued my bones together. I don't know whether it was a healing but it obviously stabilized my skeleton. The tightness of the skull was relieved and my head felt very light, as if I was renewed and the tightness was released. I was completely and utterly renewed."

Counselor's Comments. Again using the entry at Rodeo Beach, Ema goes to the Yellow One with her request. Along the way, she makes new discoveries about powers in journeying and experiences reminders of aspects and themes of former journeys, all refreshing and emotional. Gratefully, she concludes, as we see in her interpretation above, "I was completely and utterly renewed." To remain in the journey is often very tempting; Ema makes that clear. This journey, too, she declares "important."

# Healing by Snake

*I would like to go to the Lower World to the Turtle Cave and ask Snake to heal my body.*

*I would like to go to the Lower World to the Turtle Cave and ask Snake to heal my body.*

*I would like to go to the Lower World to the Turtle Cave and ask Snake to heal my body.*

*Start again.*

*I would like to go to the Lower World and meet Snake in the Turtle Cave and ask her to heal my body.*

*To ask Snake to heal my body.*

*To ask Snake to heal my body.*

> I am in my garden
> and I walk toward the oak tree.
> I jump into the hole, the trunk.
> I am in the lava tube.
> It is dry.
> I can hear water rushing under me, but it seems to be very far
>   away.
> I'm
> walking.
> It is nice.
> It's warm in here, but pleasant. It is really pleasantly warm.
> It is well-lit by my own
> light that is shining from my navel area.
> Now I come to the fork and I go to the right

toward the cave.

The cave is empty. Nobody there. No water, completely dry also.

I see the big turtle shell.

It is all matte.

I don't know, I'd like to go in, but on the other hand I have the feeling I should put water on the shell. But I don't really know.

Oh, yes, there is in the

right corner,

there seems to be some water coming out of the earth. And I find another shell, but not a turtle shell, a shell like an abalone shell or something like that. And, I just fill the shell with water and go to the

big turtle shell, and put water over it.

I go back

to the little spring and

fill the shell, and

put water over it. And

something says to me

I should put water over myself. So I'm at the spring and I fill the shell

and I pour it over my body.

I felt, because the whole area was,

is,

just very dry, I felt

also

dried, dry. Not really. I mean, how can I say this? I was thirsty. My whole body seemed to be thirsty. And so, now

I feel really good again and

I feel strong again. But I still have to

put more water over the turtle shell, because the turtle shell is rather large.

And it is interesting, because

the shell, the turtle shell,

is all black. But it seemed to be grayish. And now that I put the

water on it, it seems to get black again, also, and it seems to fill
*up.* And I just feel I have to do the job and
put water over all of the *whole* turtle shell, so that it will
fill up. Fill the
shell
and make it beautiful again.
I'm just going back and forth. And back and forth. Filling the
abalone shell and
pouring it over the beautiful turtle shell. It makes me really feel
good to do this for Turtle.
Now a voice is calling me
to come inside. For whatever reason I feel I should go back, and
fill the shell, and so I go
into the turtle shell now
with some water. And I go in the middle of the shell and put the
water right in front of me.

Whenever I am in the turtle shell, it is like a little cave, and I
feel completely relaxed and happy in here. This is the most
magical place
I have ever known.
And
the light that comes from me
vanishes. And I am completely dark.
But, within the turtle shell, there is a greenish light, which is very
soothing,
and
I can make out
my surroundings.
I suddenly see
Snake.
Snake wound around, wound itself around the
abalone shell.

Oh, hi, Snake. Please heal my body. Please heal my body.
Please heal my body.

The abalone shell, when *I* brought it in, was relatively small, but
   now, it has grown rather large and the water has left and
   Snake has,
is lying
*within* the
abalone shell.
I don't really know what happened
to the water. It's *very beautiful*
in that abalone shell.
I'd
like to touch it but, on the other hand, I
hesitate.

I have much admiration, for Snake.
      Oh, Snake.
Snake is hissing and between the hissing
I have the feeling
that I should empty my brain of all thoughts.
Snake says to me
I should drink *lots* of water.
I should drink so much water that it pains me.
To get the toxins out of me.

Snake says that I internalize
everything.
      Yes, that is true, I do. And I really
      try so hard not to.
The only thing Snake says is that
I have to flush it out.
But Snake says,
      *I will help you.*

Ah, she has entered my body.
She is
at the

opposite side
where I am sitting there.
There seems to be sort of a
mirror. And, suddenly, I see my skeleton in the mirror. And I see
Snake!
Snake is
crawling.
I think now
I don't feel anything but I see it in the mirror. That
she is just going through my right leg. All the way down to
   the toes.
She's just crawling, very slowly. And her tongue is just
*feeling* all the bones.
And, she is coming up again, the right leg.
She is crawling toward the left side, toward the left leg.
Ah. It doesn't hurt at all, but I feel so odd. I see it in the mirror,
what she is doing.
She's just winding around
all the bones
and also, she's coming now to the toes. And, her tongue is
   touching it all, sort of very delicately.
And now she's coming up
the left leg again. But *very strange* motion,
she's going through the left upper leg, where I have the pain.
   As if she is scraping out things.
She's going round and round and round and round with her
   body. Scraping things.
Pieces that stick to her.
To her body and go right inside her body.
Now she's coming out and she's going to the lower part of my
   body. She's going faster this time, back and forth and back and
   forth, and her tongue is touching everything.
She is working herself up my body. Back and forth and back and
   forth between my ribs, and

her tongue is going so fast. Touching everything but *very*
  delicately!
All my ribs and my back
and my *spine*!
Now she is working at my right arm. I don't really feel anything
  but I can see her in the mirror.
I feel lightness.
I feel as if I weren't there.
I feel so light but I can see my skeleton
in the mirror.
Now she is working herself toward the left side.
Now she is back and she's
working around my neck. Back and forth and back and forth
  and round and round, and round and round. And now she
  stops.
And now she goes within.
Into my skull.
I suddenly feel a heaviness in my brain.
Snake, who has been
rather large, suddenly
is small. Very delicate. And she is picking
through my brain.
I have the feeling as
her mouth is open and closed, as if she is picking things and
  eat it,
eats things.
She goes through all the lobes of the brain.
I *feel* it suddenly.
I feel her going through the lobes.
And I see
in the mirror, her mouth, still
picking. Open
and closing and open and closing, as if she is eating lots of
stuff. She does not eat my whole brain, but she eats

*things* as if
she's cleaning it off.

She is picking also now behind my eyes. Very tenderly. She's very
    tender. Yes, indeed. *Very* tender. And my nose, and
now she's going to the ears.
And now she's coming out of my mouth.
She is
drawing, very slowly down my body, and she ends up in the
abalone shell again.
I feel so guilty because
she has all that poison in her now.
I just feel I have to go out
and I find another shell. And there is lots of seaweed in the cave,
    even though it is all dry. But I just pick it up and put it into the
    shell, and I go back and
Turtle isn't . . . Snake is not there anymore.
        Oh, Snake, I just wanted to put some seaweed over you. Oh,
            Snake, I'm so sorry. I didn't even say thank you. I just . . .
I suddenly feel something on the crown of my head.
It is Snake.
And now she is coming into my hands and I touch her.
Oh, God, how beautiful she is.
Unbelievably beautiful. Her
body is shining
like silver.
        I forgot that you can heal yourself. That was stupid to leave.
        But I was so worried about you. Because you looked so pitiful,
            I thought
        you were so full of the poison you took out of me.
        I just wanted to . . .
My whole brain is scrambling because I just feel so ridiculous.
Now Snake is going down
and she just places herself right in the middle of the abalone
    shell. And the seaweed that was in there, sort of

disappeared within her body, I think. And now,
the silver just
has a green
hue. It's
*very* beautiful. *Very beautiful.* It's a greenish
silver.
Now I don't feel as stupid anymore.
Snake is saying I should not doubt myself so much. I do the
  right things, instinctively. And yet afterwards I always doubt
  myself.
    I know.
That is sickening my body,
Snake *says.*
I should not doubt myself.

I can't say anything at the moment.

Many thoughts go through me
but I can't
grasp them.
It is like a scramble in my brain. The words
I want to say,
they're all scrambled up
or they all tumble down.
I don't know what it is.

I'm taking the abalone shell with Snake and put on my lap.
And, quiet is setting again, within me.
    Oh, Snake, what should I do? How can I be the way you want
      me to be?

The whole
area where I am seems
to say
that I should not doubt myself. It's like an echo. The whole space
  is filled with the echo, "Don't doubt yourself."

The air, the energy, is full
of the word, "Don't doubt yourself."
I try to hold onto
my thought. But
I am dissolving. I'm dissolving like a waterfall.
Ah, the drum is calling.
    Thank you, Snake! Oh, thank you ever so much.
The Snake is just
going ahead of me.
She's leading the way.
And suddenly she is standing in front of me and
hits my forehead. And I am
back, and I'm running.
I'm running and I'm still running
And I'm out.

## Reflections

Ema's Quest. "I would like to go to the Lower World to the Turtle Cave and ask Snake to heal my body."

Ema's Evaluation (after prompt about whether she received a response to her request). "I was going to ask you the same question."

Ema's Interpretation (after prompt, "Think about your purpose. What was your purpose?"). "The purpose was for Snake to heal my body, and most certainly she did."

Counselor's Comments. Restarting her journey and repeating her intention again gained Ema access to the Lower World, where she seeks Snake. With advice to Ema, Snake enters her body, this healing carefully described in detail as Ema narrates. As she frequently does, Ema marvels at the beauty she finds. Staying with the journey until the drumming calls her to return, Ema pursues her relationship with Snake.

Initially, she appears not to understand her journey as containing a healing. When urged to return to her purpose, Ema consolidates her experience and purpose and then clearly affirms her healing by Snake. I suggest that Ema's immersion in the journey may preclude her rapidly switching to the ordinary state of consciousness required to analyze her journey in the context of her stated purpose. An aspect of HSC training is to develop the discipline to work in two realities and to move from the one to the other with intention and discipline. The presence of the counselor and access to the recording and the transcript serve to support the client's understanding on her own terms.

# Visit to the Light Place

*I would like to go to the Upper World and visit the light place.*

*I would like to go to the Upper World and visit the light place.*

*I would like to go to the Upper World and visit the light place.*

I am walking down the hill
knee-deep in leaves. It's surprising
how deep they are. I'm sort of sliding down.
Now I've landed.

The branches are very low
and it is very easy
to climb.

I am on top of the oak tree. And
behind me
and I am already in mist and fog.
The fog is heavy with moisture.
There is this ladder.
Turquoise color.
But the ladder is a little higher. I cannot quite reach it.
I don't usually, but I jump and get the
ladder. I am already light. I just sort of *float* to the ladder.
  I could have just floated up. But I just hold onto the ladder and
  walk up.

The ladder feels
*cold*
like made out of ice. The tone is very
strange, as if there was life within

the ladder.

A voice asks,

> *Why are you here?*
>> I would like to visit the light place I was allowed to see. I went
>> to my grandmother's castle,
>>> Great Grandmother's.

Something says to me I should be seated on the ladder

and the ladder seems to be like a flying entity.

I am being transported on this ladder.

Everything is foggy.

It is cool. The fog is still *heavy* with moisture. The moisture
seems to get right into my body structure. And my skin is
*so soft.*

I am still on the ladder,

sitting on the ladder. The dark sky and the sky is lit with light
bodies. Millions.

It's day, but the spaces in between are dark.

There is a dark layer, then a little bit

in the far distance are the stars.

We stopped. I have stopped. What I mean by "we" is the ladder
and I. The ladder seems to be not a "thing."

Ladder.

A friend. I have a feeling to Ladder as if it is a living thing.

Ladder has stopped. It is so quiet here and the lights.

Nothing is moving. It's still.

No movement. It's like being in a vacuum.

I should just quiet my brain and enjoy this. It is *so wonderful.*

Suddenly,

Ladder is swirling around so fast

I have to hold onto Ladder.

Shooting so fast, toward the stars, and

I am transported right through the stars and I see only darkness.
Not black, it is dark blue.

Stars are fading.
I am incomplete; it is
not complete. I can see
space.
Endless space.
Again, this peacefulness.
This time I suddenly became dark blue.
It presses out the liquid I seem to have had in me from the fog. I
am dark.
A beautiful blue,
very crisp and clean. My hair is long, dark blue. My toenails, my
fingernails,
dark blue,
everything.
I just became a blue entity.
I feel completely at one with the area I am in.
Faster and faster and faster. I have to hold on to Ladder.
We are still shooting
fast.
My God!

The light source! I have to close my eyes. It blinds me. I make
myself as small as possible.
Frightened.
I suddenly feel so vulnerable.
Something says
> *Why do you want to come here?*
I am not capable of speaking.
> *You have to tell the truth.*
Out of curiosity.
Oh, God! What did I do?
Not just curiosity, I was here before
and it was so beautiful I wanted to come back.
> *You have no right to be here!*

Why? Why Not?

*This is an area for after life.*

What do you mean, "after life"?

I fear that if I open my eyes I will be struck down. I am at a loss.
I don't know what to do. I do open my eyes suddenly.

*Everything* is light. Like waterfall coming from
nowhere and ended nowhere.

Oh, God.

My skin is getting lighter. I have to leave.

I turn Ladder around and we are leaving as fast as I can.

Ladder, what happened?

*What is there to explain?*

*You were told that this is a place for after life.*

It was so light and this time I saw water that brings lightness.

I look back and the light source is gone.

My body has become a light blue.

It is really like a friend

Ladder.

We are back at the area with the moist fog. It feels really good. It
feels as if I have come back home.

I would die there if I would linger. I'm really grateful that they
let me live. I am very grateful. Now I know.

I feel I am lying on Ladder. My whole body is.

I feel my heart beating again.

The rushing of blood through my veins.

I was scared, I guess, but more so because I knew I didn't belong
there.

I can't help thinking back.

I am still filled with this beautiful water
just being there.

The light source was all over.

I just feel like sleeping. Oh gosh. I am *so exhausted.*

Let's go to her. Let's go to her castle.

I feel so tired.

Ugh!

Ladder

just

was

sitting me on the ground. But she isn't here. But the big
cauldron is there. I am taking some lavender tea and
drinking it.

They let me live. I am so grateful. I am so grateful they let me
live.

Then I am taking another cup of lavender tea. It tastes so good
and it warms me inside.

I am still tired.

I see a woman coming out of the mist.

>*Who are you?*

She asks me who I am.

>I am coming to visit Great Grandmother.
>
>Not sure I'm in the right place!

>*You are at the right place.*
>
>*I have never seen you before.*

She's Great Grandmother's sister! I didn't know Great
Grandmother had a sister.

Met her in the Upper World. She seems to know all about it.
She's a very pleasant woman, I think.

She's giving me more tea.

Great Grandmother's sister.

She's dissolving in fog.

Just fog, and I thought it was a woman? I do taste the lavender
tea. The drum is calling me back!

Ladder

floating *slowly* through the fog. *Very slowly.*

>I be back by the end of the drum,
>
>by the end of the drumbeat.

Branches of the oak tree, and so I am back.

##  Reflections

Ema's Quest. "I would like to go to the Upper World and visit the Light Place."

Ema's Response (after prompt about whether she was successful in meeting her purpose). "Yes! I definitely was successful, and I never go there again, because . . . now I know. . . . It is obviously not something for the living to visit, I guess. It's hard to say."

Counselor's Comments. With "Ladder," Ema discovers the truth of the saying, "Everything that is, is alive." She, herself, becomes "a blue entity." Coming to the Light Place, she learns a strong lesson for her personal cosmography.

# Go to Kailas to Thank the Spirits

*I like to go today to the Kailas area—to thank—the spirits.*

*I like to go today to the Kailas area—to thank the spirits.*

*I like to go today to the Kailas area—to thank—the spirits.*

I am outside at my
house and I go down the hillside.
Sliding down
because it is just littered with leaves.
I arrive at the opening.
This time I try to see whether there are some
roots. But I can't see any roots at the entrance.
And in effect it looks to me as if
the trunk of the
oak tree
underneath the earth is also like a trunk or like a *shaft* more.
I'm staying there
and
in my brain I see
how the tree is constructed.
It's a shaft going down
and then
the shaft is opening up to the
path I use.
And underneath the path this is all lava.
There runs a river. And I *do see* now
that
some roots are *swimming* in the river.
Not swimming away. I mean, they are attached to the tree. But
   they are just bobbing

in the water.
They look like hair.
*Very thin* roots.
Not very thick.
Nevertheless, I'm not there. I am still at the entrance
of the tree. And I now just jump down
the shaft.

But now to my great amazement I see
also roots, but they are
at the walls. And they are not loose. They just are in the earth.
They
came through the lava.
The roots are very *intertwined* with the lava. I really should
  go but
this is the first time I pay any attention to the roots of the oak
  tree here.
Looks like a net.
I really should go.
I have to go.
The roots are going for miles
along the walls.
I'm now at the fork where I have to go to the right, in order to
  get to the Turtle Cave.
The Turtle Cave is all dry and empty
and I go through the
chambers to the north, and now I am at the
Northern Chamber,
where
I am
sucked up by a
*strong force.*
And now I'm thrown out
at the
area.

It, the area, the Kailas area
where I come out is like a
cave
but it is
in the mountains. Because I can see down below
the
silver
of the river. Very small and beautiful.
There are trees,
oak trees
in a semicircle.
No one is here. I am all alone.
Snake is coming out of my body. And she slithers
to a spot.
It is a round stone
I always have to sit on. She just slithers to that stone. And, I just
    know that she wants me to sit there.
        Oh, Snake, I don't know whether the others will come, but I
            just want to say to you, Thank you
        for taking the pain away in my hip.
I am suddenly lifted up. To my amazement,
the rock, what I thought was a rock, was Turtle sitting
like a rock.
Amazing.
I want to climb down but
something is holding me.
        Oh, Turtle. Turtle.
It's the big turtle
and I have
ample space to sit on comfortably,
on Turtle's back.
I hear swishing sounds above me.
But I cannot look up because
there is

such a
light.
It's not the sun, I don't know
what it is, but
I have to keep my
head
to the earth.
To the ground,
because
sky
is just so light.
I seem to be frozen
and the light is penetrating my whole body. And, I do not know
     whether it's Vulture but
something is swishing over me, back and forth, and back and
     forth,
I think, because it is
stillness around me. And, whilst the heat, whilst the *light*, is
     penetrating me. Oh, I hope I make this clear.
The light is penetrating me and it is not hot. Yet I have the
     feeling if I was in stillness, my body would break into pieces. I
     don't know why I think that. And so, whatever is swishing
over me
is
making some
air current that holds me together.
The stillness is coming over me.
This light is penetrating my body. My bones.
I'm not allowed to think.

Someone
has opened my skull
and is taking something out.
My inner eye sees that it is

silk, like a silk thread,
taken out of me.
It gets longer and longer.
More, more.
I get weaker and weaker.
>  Don't let me go crazy. You have to leave something for my
>  brain.
Oh, God.
Oh, God.
>  Turtle, you can't allow it.

Snake has come back
Or maybe it was always in my body.
And, she's pushing
that thread. So, I guess it is supposed . . .
I don't really know what is. I was just so afraid that
I don't know what's happening to me.
Something says, it goes through my whole body,
>  *You are on me, you are sitting on me. Nothing will happen*
>  *to you. Be strong.*
A warmth is coming through me,
through my head. I don't know what.
It feels as if it's *raining*
slightly.
I open my eyes and the whole area
Is in *fog*. Oh, how wonderful it feels, the fog!
It's caressing me.
Ahhh. It puts moisture into my body.
>  Ohhh, thank you!
Ahhhh. Ahhh.
A wonderful fragrance in the air.
I don't know what kind of fragrance.
A flowery fragrance.
It makes me

sort of
very tired and relaxed. I have the feeling that
something important is happening
to my body right now and
I should sort of
not be there in my waking. I should be there
while sleeping.
Ahhh.
I just can't talk.
  Turtle, what is happening to me?
It is like a *weaving* in my body. Things are taking out and
  putting in. Taking out and putting in. Taking out and putting
  in. Taking out and putting in. Like a weaving, like a net, I am
  surrounded by
fine,
like spider webs, threads that go in and out. Go in and out.
Something says to me,
    *Concentrate.*
  Concentrate on what?
  Yes.
Something says I should,
with my thoughts,
I have to direct the webs
in the areas where I have pain.
I direct them through my
brain, around my eyes, around the arms, the joints in my
  shoulders, my breast, and
my left hip and my right hip and my knees and
my heels and . . .
    *Float.*
Something just tells me I should float.
And, suddenly I am
released from Turtle's back. And though
I am

floating, just in the lying position, just above Turtle. And so,
I am completely
and utterly
enveloped
by fog and mist. It's very moist and yet
the moisture that's is within me doesn't make me heavy at all.
This is the first time that
I had the sense of
*fear* within me. Because things were so strange I did not know
   how to
act, or how to react. Now I'm really relaxed.
The fog is so thick I can't even see
my hand.
It is almost as if
it's also now without air. It's
choking me and I have the feeling I
will lose my . . .

I am in water. Oh, how nice, and I am swimming. The sun is
   out and
I just come out of the water.
I'm walking to the beach. It is not sand; it is rocks all over.
The drum is calling me.
   I have to go back. I don't quite know how I got to the beach,
      but please help me go back.
And I am just lifted by
a wind
and I am landed, on the platform of that cave, and
I go down
to the Turtle Cave and
I am just running as fast as I can through the tunnel. And now I
   am back.
Now I am
back in my garden.

## Reflections

Ema's Quest. "I like to go today to the Kailas area to thank the spirits."

Ema's Evaluation. "Didn't say much, or did I?"

Counselor's Comments. In this journey specifically to give thanks, Ema finds Snake to be the surrogate for the other spirits as well. What follows is for Ema to interpret. Seeking help for her return, as Ema does from time to time, she arrives back where she began in the Middle World. Once again, Ema offers no feedback on the content or meaning of her journey. I offered no prompt, in order to give Ema the opportunity to choose to make a statement on her own. Since she does not, the counselor's reminder serves as gentle methodological feedback.

# Fire Healing and Resurrection in Beautiful Light

*I—like to go to the Kailas area today, and ask for a healing of my body.*

*I—like to ask for a healing, of my body.*

*I like to ask for a healing, of my body.*

> I am at Rodeo Beach and walking down the path, toward the
> bay tree. I think it must have been
> freezing because it's not slippery but it looks very hard
> and grass is sort of frosty.
> And it is cold.
> It is not windy but it is cold.
> So I am
> walking a little bit faster, in order to get warm.
> And, now I'm standing in front of the trees and
> a slight wind is lifting me
> up
> to the opening, and I am sliding right
> through
> the earth tunnel.
>
> And now I am out
> at the cave. The cave that is high up in the hills, and so I have an
>   overview
> of the landscape below.
> Something . . .
> It's the Yellow One.
>> Oh, Yellow One, I haven't seen you for so long.
> The Yellow One is

all

mist and fog, but yellow, moving back and forth around me.

    I actually came here for a healing.

He says he is here to heal me.

He roars with laughter.

He understands my confusion because I thought I would

  see Turtle

and

Vulture. But he says,

        *You haven't asked for them, have you?*

And so, I said,

    No, I haven't. But I'm so happy to see you, I think I didn't . . .

He says,

        *Yes, you have forgotten me, have you?*

    No, no, no I haven't forgotten you, I just

    know you have healed me before.

He sort of sweeps me up

and

he's just

bringing me somewhere.

The pressure in my ears is so tremendous that I'm

actually in pain.

Ohhh.

There is a huge fire. And he pushes me right into the fire.

It is real fire; the flames go very high. But, it is a cold fire.

Now the Yellow One

is opposite me

in his form,

in his *beautiful, golden*

form.

He lifts his sword again.

And oh, my God, oh, my God. I had no *idea* that I was again so

bound.

So many

threads are coming out of me. And I thought I had
overcome all this.
Oh, my God!
They are just coming *out* by the thousands. And he just cuts it
    with his sword.
All the red threads are coming out of me. Out of my brain. Oh,
    my God, it just doesn't end; and it just comes.
Oh, God, I am back to my old ways. Oh, I had no idea.
I was so sure I had learned.
He's just
dancing around me. And his golden . . .
The sword is just . . .
Oh, God, it just . . .
It is just . . .
He says to me,
            *Lighten up, lighten up.*
And,
I also feel like dancing in the fire. So I am dancing
And he is dancing. And
he is cutting *all* the threads
that have come out of my body.
He is cutting them all off, every single one. And now I am
    dancing and
I feel so *light*! And now I feel so good. I feel so much lighter! I
    mean, those threads have been immensely weighing my whole
    body and my whole soul down.

I have collapsed within
the fire.
Water is coming out of my eyes.
They are running like waterfalls.
The fire is gone and I am
like a little heap of
human, sitting there

and it is dark.

I am full of remorse.

Not listening to the Yellow One. I was so sure I had gotten his
message. Many months ago. But I think,
Oh, what will become of me now?

I feel so desperate.

I suddenly feel

a beautiful . . .

A beautiful orange light

is surrounding me.

I don't quite know how to explain this now, but it is as if where
I am sitting

the sun, or something like the sun, is coming right from that
spot. Like the sun is

coming out

and

I am just sort of *part* of it.

It just . . .

starts with a

little sliver and I didn't really quite know what to make of it but
now it's getting bigger and bigger.

It *has* gotten bigger and bigger. I'm sort of

beyond,

behind, time. I mean, I want to describe it, but it is already there.

Oh, my God, how absolutely beautiful, the color. Ohhh. It is the
most beautiful orange, red, and pur . . .

It's even *purple* in it. It's just *absolutely gorgeous.* And I

am just one of it. I am just part of it. I am absolutely *part* of this
beautiful . . .

It must be the sun, it can't be any . . .

Whatever it is it is, it is like the sun, and I am *part* of it.

The Yellow One is standing opposite me. He is in shining gold
and I see *myself* now.

It is as if *I* am *holding* . . .

My arms are stretched and it is as if I am holding
part of the sun.
Ahhh.
I'm *almost* blending in with the sun. Not quite. I still can make
  out my
features.
Oh, I don't want to think earthly at all.
I just want to be here. Where I am right now. And not
think about anything. Oh, God
the colors are doing something to my brain.
A wonderful warmth is coming through me. Through my whole
  being.
The Yellow One is
sitting down. And he takes his sword
and puts it across his knees.
He said to me that I had lost the crown he had given me.
But that was then and this is now.

> *I will give the crown back to you.*
> *But remember it is part of you. You forgot.*

  Yes, I forgot.
I am stepping out
of the sun.
Very strange. I mean, I'm stepping out toward
the Yellow One. And so the light, and the beauty, is left behind.
  It seems to be sort of restricted.
It doesn't
shine everywhere. It is like a sphere, but it is restricted.
  Because now
I am
turning back
and the light is actually gone. So I don't really know what
  happened; it just disappeared
with my
going toward the Yellow One.

He dangles
a small crown on his sword
and looks at me
just a sort of
wild
sly . . .
One cannot look at his eyes for a long time because
it would blind you.
I don't know what
the meaning is. But I'm taking the crown from the his sword.
  It is [a] small one. Like a band.
I am looking at it. It is [a] very simple one
made of gold.
Like a band. But a very intricate
front
like a cross. No, not a cross.
It's rounded.
It bends. I'm touching it and it bends.
It is like liquid gold.
The band is stable.
I can move my finger on the way.
This is how the gold
just
works.
I make a circle.
I do make a spiral.
But
then I undo the spiral because it makes me sort of claustro`
  phobic. No, I don't want a spiral. I want
open. I want openness.
So whilst I am still working to make the perfect round, it is
  suddenly
hard. It is not liquid anymore.
Yes! That's what I want. A complete, round

circle. And I can see through it. And I can see the world,
   through it.
Suddenly it is taken out of my hands, it's like a wind. No, it's
   not like a wind.
It is
the Yellow One
who has become again, like fog, and is *weaving*
in and out, all around me.
And
something that has taken the crown
and put it on my head.
It is so light I hardly feel it.

I am supposed to
bow to the East. Ah! And now to the South. Ah! And now to
   the West. Ah. And now to the North. Ahhh.
Whenever I
bow to the
corners, it was as if a clamp . . .
something . . .
There was a crack and sort of pain
as if something was holding the crown
in place. I'd like to *feel*
my head because I wonder whether I'm bleeding or not.
   But I cannot move
at all.
Don't touch anything. Don't touch anything. Don't touch it.
Dance.
Something just makes me
weave.
I feel as if I am now also clouds
and I just do the movements the clouds do.
Very slowly,
in and out I am dancing.
Breathing deep.

The air is so crisp
and so clean. It almost hurts when I breathe
deeply. It almost hurts. This is how clear the earth, the air, is.
I want to pay attention to what happens to my body, but
   I am not allowed to.
There is so much
movement
within my body that I cannot really concentrate on anything.
   I think I'm not supposed to concentrate, I'm just to let go
and dance
with the movements
of the
clouds, or the mist, or
of the Energies, I think. Those are Energies.
*I just let go and dance.*
*I am just to let go and dance with the clouds and the movement*
   *of the Energies, I think.*
Through the Energies
I sometimes
glimpse
the Yellow One. He looks very pleased. Oh, God, I hope
   he's pleased with me!
At times I see him in his
human form. All golden. But then at times I see him just partly,
completely and utterly
surrounded by Energies
that make it look like clouds.
I never have a real
close, long look at him.
I'm dancing. Very slowly. Feeling the Energies surrounding me,
   and going through me. It has hit
my whole system. My skeleton. And the veins, and the flesh.
I see my brain. My inner eyes can see the brain. How it expands
   with the movement. How *pleased* it is. My hair is growing long.

Black. Strong. And now it starts to curl.
Tiny little dewdrops, forming at my hair, which is
tiny little locks.
The *crown* is still in place.
A *very deep* voice is coming out of my body.
It is sort of singing.
I feel I am dancing a primeval dance.
A dark voice is forming. Deep, deep.
Coming out of my stomach,
but very softly, very dark; very softly, very dark; *very softly*
   and very dark.
I am suddenly having a sword in my hand.
I am dancing with the sword. Cutting through the Energies.
Cutting through the Energies.
The drum is calling. I have to go back.

I leave the sword behind and I'm scooped up by a cloud.
Brings me back to the cave.
And I am climbing up.
   Yellow One, I am still not back. Help me.
And
suddenly I'm getting sort of a push.
And now
I'm back at Rodeo Beach.

---

 ## Reflections

Ema's Quest. "I like to go to the Kailas area today and ask for a healing of my body."

Ema's Interpretation (after prompt, "Do you think you got a healing?"). "Yes, I think so. one hundred percent. Well, it was a big surprise to me."

Counselor's Comments. As she has done over the years of journeying, Ema focuses on a particular theme or resource for several journeys. In this case, she returns to the Kailas area, making her way, as before. In her dramatic encounter with the Yellow One, she learns again his power and his teachings for her, along with new ones. In her interpretation she is even more certain and confident. Again after a healing journey, Ema provides no response or evaluation, only offering an interpretation when prompted to do so.

# Journey 37

# Healing for My Anxiety

*I like to go to the Winter Cave today for a healing for my anxiety.*

*I like to go to the Winter Cave today for a healing for my anxiety.*

*I like to go to the Winter Cave today for a healing for my anxiety.*

I am still already in front of the oak tree and jump through the
  opening.
The whole path is today wet. Not much.
I seem to be barefoot because the soles of my feet are getting
  wet.
It is very dark and I have to concentrate.
I put my hands on my
stomach. That is the area where light comes from normally.
And now I am taking my hands off and
a greenish light
surrounds me. And
I am the source of it.

Normally I could see
ahead of me, but today, I don't know,
I put the hands in front of me in order not to run into
  something, because, it
feels like smoke or
the color.
I'm at a loss how to describe it.
Oh, no actually, not at all. Smoke, the path is full of smoke
  but it has no smell. So I don't know
what it is.
I go now into the smoke

which has no
smell.
And now that I walk through it, it feels like cotton. Very soft.
It is
brushing against my skin.
Looking at myself and the way it feels, I think I am completely
   naked.
I see a yellow light
in the distance, so I follow that yellow light.
But I know I will have to go
to the right. I shouldn't follow the yellow light because in order
   to . . .
But I cannot find the
fog.
I cannot find it.
Where I am walking is completely obscured. I cannot see any
   thing with the exception of that little
yellow light.
I'm confused.

> Yellow One, I'd like to go to the Winter Cave
> and be healed
> by you,
> healed for the anxieties I still have.

There is no reply.
I just have to calm down.

Something says within me that I should walk toward the yellow
   light. So I'm just walking
toward the yellow light. And suddenly, I am out of this cotton-
   smoke. I see completely clear. But I do not know where I am, to
   be honest. So I walk toward the yellow light.
That yellow
light does not get bigger, so it seems to be far away.
And in effect, *staring* at this spot, now I can't see it anymore.

And now I do feel seaweed around my feet. Ahhh. Ahhh. The *whole* area I am at

is

full of seaweed. Ahhh.

I am still naked.

Even though the water is cold, I just feel I have to go into there and just

lie in there

and roll around. It is such a marvelous feeling, and the smell is of ocean.

Now I lie there, completely still.

Completely covered with seaweed. It is such a very nice feeling. And I feel so protected. Oh, I feel so protected.

    Turtle, please come. I'd like to go to the Yellow One. I would like to meet him.

    The Crystal Cave at the Winter Cave. Why am I here?

Something says,

> *Nothing is done without a reason where you are.*
> *Be patient.*

Yes, I really should relax. It's

ridiculous.

I am just lying

in this

clear water.

The beautiful

seaweed. I have *never* seen this kind of seaweed. It has little balls, or little pearls,

little green pearls, all over. It's very beautiful. It's very beautiful to touch.

I *press* these little balls, but they don't give.

Ah!

I hear from all kinds of

areas to relax. I thought I was relaxed but I guess my brain is not relaxed.

My body seems to disintegrate.

My body just disintegrates into the

seaweed.

The only thing I seem to see from above,

I see myself gone, but my brain is a rock. A terribly ugly rock

and I wish somebody would take it and smash it into

thousand pieces.

I hate that brain. Oh, that rock is so ugly.

But my body

has become

beautiful seaweed.

Oh, how beautiful it is.

The rock. The rock that

I assume is my brain, was at first blood-red, but now it is just

sort of fades, the color I mean. It's getting

to pink and it's

getting lighter and lighter and getting to a yellow.

And with the yellow color

*the Yellow One.*

> Yellow One. I thought I
> would meet you in the Winter Cave and
> now we are here.

The Yellow One says to me

that I should not be *so* surprised, after all he had told me that he

is everywhere.

The way

I am

everywhere.

> Where are we then?

He doesn't answer.

Doesn't seem to matter.

> I hate my brain because I think that's where the anxiety arises.
> Is that true?

No answer.

He's sitting

there, in the smaller form. Normally

when he has the start, he is large. But this time he is

small. I mean the size of a human being.

I have the feeling as if

not I myself but my thoughts are sucked into him.

And now my thoughts

become yellow liquid.

Oh, that's yellow liquid.

I am losing myself completely, now.

My thoughts are yellow liquid.

Yellow liquid.

I don't really know

what to say, because I am yellow liquid.

Rushes through my

whole being.

And now, suddenly

it is as if

a wall opened and I am in the Crystal Cave. Just as simple
   as that.

I feel heavy. I am not myself.

I have the feeling I am within the Yellow One.

I feel a certain . . .

I seem to be myself again. What I mean is, I can see

my body. But I feel

still

restricted, as if I want to get out of something.

> Yellow One, what can I do? What can I do for the anxiety
>   I have, when things get too complicated?
>> *Live with it!*
> But it is so
> stressful. It makes my life so
> unpleasant.

*That is good,*
something says.
　　That is good. How can you say? I mean, why?
He talks so fast
or *something* is talking so fast, I cannot at all comprehend.
　Because
I am within myself still so slow.
I can't accept it. I just *can't* accept it.
I suddenly
put my hands up to my head to see if whether I have the crown
still on me
and I do still have the crown. I take the crown off. And it's this
　round . . .
It's a circle on the crown and I am looking through that circle.
　I once saw Earth through the circle.
I am looking through the circle but
it is nothing to see through. It is as if
the circle is *closed.*
　　Oh, Yellow One, just help me, don't close it.
　　*You have to understand what life is all about,*
he says to me.
　　　*It is good and it is bad.*
　　　*You have to take both sides in.*
　　　*You have to live it.*
　　　*You have to balance this out, inside you.*
　　But how do I balancing ?
　　How can I balance this out? That's just . . .
　　I have to come back, because the drum is calling. I do not
　　　know how to get back; you have to bring me back. I do not
　　　know how I got here.
I am back in this room.

**Reflections**

Ema's Quest. "I like to go to the Winter Cave today for a healing for my anxiety."

Ema's Response (after prompt for a brief comment). "I don't understand it. [laugh] I don't understand anything. . . . I don't understand this journey at all."

Ema's Interpretation (after reviewing recording). "Well, it says, 'Nothing is done without a reason.' And so, I figured that belonged to the journey."

Counselor's Comments. Places and geography, such as the Winter Cave, are known only to Ema, from her journey explorations outside of sessions. They speak to her ongoing, independent journey practice. Colors, textures, emotions, size changes, cold, sense of smell, appreciation of beauty abound here. She addresses her purpose to unseen helping spirits without specifying which she hopes or expects to come to her aid. Eventually, the Yellow One engages Ema and her question, providing experiences and specific information for Ema. Her task is to discern how this journey reflects an answer to her request.

# To See the Future in a Relaxed Way

*I like to meet the Yellow One today. I like—like the Yellow One—to help me, to see the future in a relaxed way.*

*To help me to see the future in a relaxed way.*

*To help me to see the future—in a relaxed way.*

> I am
> walking the path
> in Rodeo Beach.
> I am not there yet.
> I just can't get my brain together. I'm still not there yet.
> The whole area is very foggy
> and I
> can't see the trail at all.
> But I'm looking for a stick. And so I'm taking the stick
> and sort of just use him in front of me so I will not bump into
>   anything because it is really *very foggy.* One cannot see *any
>   thing* at all.
> It must be high
> tide because I am walking through water. So, I'm just going up
>   the hill a little bit, so I won't get wet.
> I'm just sort of
> scrambling along.
> I can see
> fires.
> So I am now at the
> area

because it just goes around the bend.

And I just have walked around the bend, and so am looking up.
    Now there is a

tree. The bay tree

with the

opening. And I climb up. I'm climbing up and

go through the opening.

Normally, I am

sucked up right away, or sucked down I should say, in the Lower
    World. But this time the sucking motion is not there.

The tunnel is very small, I have to crawl; I cannot go upright
    there. So I have to go on my

knees and

I'm just crawling

along.

I don't think this is working today. I have to leave because I feel
    there is danger ahead of me. I just can't go any further. I have
    to go back.

It just doesn't work today.

I have to try another

way.

I am at my house and I go

down the hill

to the oak tree. I'm jumping right into the oak. And this is the
    path I

normally go.

This the lava tube. And I'm just walking.

I

take the right fork and go to the

Turtle Cave.

I just can't ignore Turtle calling me. I know I should go the other
    way in order to meet the Yellow One but I just can't

ignore Turtle.

Turtle is
calling me
from the Turtle Shell, and
I just crawl in now.
Something just
presses me down. And I'm lying
on the floor.
I cannot move. All my limbs are
sort of tied to the floor,
to the ground,
to the turtle shell.
I feel I'm
as flat as a sheet of paper.
I just don't understand this. But there is no fire. Well, this is
   really very
extraordinary, but I'm told by Turtle that I should *not visit the*
   *Yellow One.* I would have to go to a fire and I am
not ready for it.
I will be damaged if I go
to the Yellow One today. But fire has never . . .
I just feel I should obey. I don't know; I just feel I should obey.
    Turtle
    I wanted to ask . . .
        *Yes, yes.*
    I am just worried about the future.
    What might happen.
    And it hampers me so much. I don't know why I am this way.
Turtle says,
        *You have decided to walk alone, so you have to take the*
           *consequences.*
    Yes.
Well, in a way Turtle is right, of course. I *have* chosen to walk
   alone.
Turtle asks me whether I want to go back,

and take another route.

    No, no, I don't, I really like

    the way

    my life is now. I don't want to change.

    I just wish I weren't so sensitive toward

    changes

    I cannot control.

Turtle tells me

I should

envision

something, where I feel I have no

power over. Like I have a house and

the electricity isn't working or something

and I have no one to help me,

then what would happen. I should envision it.

    Well, I

    would

    call a lot of people.

    Yes, yes.

I don't really want to say, because I'm really ashamed

of my thoughts.

But then, this is really my problem, is it?

Turtle tells me I should go deeper yet.

To find out

at the very *core* of my being. Wow. I'm afraid I cannot quite

    explain. Today is just a very strange way of . . . the whole . . .

I can't explain it.

I just have to think what Turtle tells me, and I do not know

    whether I can say anything

because I just have to go too deep into myself.

I'm still

flat as a sheet of paper, but

I seem to have grown into Turtle shell. Which means I am sort

    of part of Turtle. And, my whole

outlook is sort of . . .

I see myself in the

ordinary world, in a scared rabbit form. Then I just feel so sorry,
    seeing that poor rabbit.

But that can't be possibly I!

But if that is the case, how can I possibly overcome it? I have
    asked for it before but I just don't know.

Turtle says I cannot go through life not trusting people.

Turtle says I have been given the gift

to sort out the good from the bad.

On the other hand, I have to go forward.

    Yes, you are quite right. Quite right.

I just want to kill that rabbit.

Turtle says to me I should not *kill* the rabbit, I just should
be kind to it.

There is a *reason* for it, and I should not beat myself up. It gets
    very complicated and I cannot express it. But I do understand
    what's going on.

I see myself as a child.

    Turtle, I don't not want to go there.

Turtle explains to me I have to go through it.

I cannot talk about it.

Turtle says I don't have to.

I see my whole childhood

going by me, very quickly. My father is looming like a huge
    mountain over me.

    Turtle, I will not . . .

    I don't want to see any more. I have forgiven him.

I refuse to look any further.

This looming, huge

figure of a man

is suddenly

going up in smoke. Not smoke, it's fog, because

there's no smell. I mean, it is just smog. No, it's
not smog, it's fog. There is no smell. No fire. No fire. It's fog.

I know it is ingrained in me and I cannot
get it out of me.
Turtle says to me,
It just
got *out* of me. I didn't realize it, but obviously something
  happened to me.

I am *still*
in the Turtle shell. And I'm getting *terribly hot.* And, I see myself.
I'm now myself, as a
form. And I'm
a dark red. I'm glowing like
coal. Dark red.
And the strange thing is that
what I had seen before,
my childhood going by,
is now coming out of my
head
as if I had a film within me and the film is just leaving me . . .
  but it is all red. It is all *hot.* And
it is just
leaving.
It just comes out of me, out of the crown of my head like a
  waterfall.
I
try hard to concentrate.
My childhood
and
my teenage years also.
And it's not only I. It's the people I remember knowing. They
  also seem to leave
my brain.

And my mother. And my relatives.
And my father. I see my father wounded
in the war. That is also leaving my
brain.
I see him suddenly as a young man
laughing and happy.
And now I see him again, in the war. Fighting
and bleeding.
Ohhhh!
Now I see myself.
I personally . . .
The
glowing red
is fading now.
Certain
images come out
in
intervals.
I see my husband. He is also leaving.
It's just pressed in intervals. And, it seems to be as if
what happens during my lifetime
has been squeezed out of me.
The red is fading more and more. And now I have my own
color again. I have a gaping
hole
in my skull.
Turtle is putting seaweed over the skull.
I am thinking
without being told
about the Yellow One. I don't know why, because I am far
  away from
where he is.

I am

completely relaxed now.

It is as if a lot has been lifted off my shoulders. I feel really
very good.

My body is filling up with liquid.

And without my wanting it, I am swaying back and forth.
  Oh! Oh!

I'm actually floating in water. I did not quite realize it.

I was thinking my body was filling with water but I'm not, I
  mean, I am actually *floating* in the water. But sitting still up.
  I'm sitting, but I'm floating also. I'm not

toppling over, I'm just

floating, and I'm just sort of being.

I just go with the waves, back and forth and back and forth
  and . . .

Yes. The drum is calling me and I do have to go back now.
    Thank you, Turtle. Thank you so much. I think I understand
        much more than I thought I ever did.

So, I'm just diving through

the opening in the

shell and I'm just running

as fast as I can

through the tunnel. And,

and I'm

out.

I'm outside now.

The drum is still calling,

but still, I'm outside already.

## 🐢 Reflections

Ema's Quest. "I like to meet the Yellow One today, to help me to
see the future in a relaxed way."

Ema's Response. "Gosh, it was so hot."

Ema's Interpretation (after prompt to make a comment). "No, I don't want to make a statement. Not today. I just don't know what . . . I think I got it, but it has been so terribly personal."

Counselor's Comments. Rejecting her progress at the start of this journey, Ema begins again, using a different entry place to the Lower World. Ema goes with the unfolding journey, accepting the disparity between her request to the Yellow One and engaging with Turtle. Faced with images from her childhood, Ema protests, then complies with Turtle's urging, knowing she has the choice to terminate the journey and return to ordinary reality if she wishes. She observes a film-like process of unfolding life events, the outcome of which is that in the journey she says she is "completely relaxed." How Ema chooses to interpret, work with, integrate, or ignore this journey is entirely her decision, not another's, no matter how tempting. Later, she labels this a significant journey.

# Healing My Inner Physical Body

*I like to—I like to visit Turtle—and I like to ask her for—the healing—of my inner, physical body.*

*I like to ask her for the healing—of my inner physical body.*

*I like to ask her—for the healing—of my inner, physical body.*

> I try to go
> down the hill from my house to the oak tree
> that has the opening
> for me to go to the Turtle Cave to meet
> Turtle.
> However, the entrance is completely blocked.
>
> I am not saying anything because at the moment I don't quite
>    know what to do.
> I look around me to
> find a spot where I might go
> to the Lower World.
> I'm going uphill. There is another
> oak tree
> in my garden that has an opening.
> Quan Yin. The statue of Quan Yin is in
> front of that opening. I have put her there
> because helps me meditate.
>
> I don't quite understand it . . .
> Quan Yin. Something is beckoning me
> into the statue.
> That must be a mistake.
> It is as if a

voice from Quan Yin,

from the statue,

says to me,

> *I know that you need a healing*
> *for your inner physical body.*

Yes, I do. I thought I should go to Turtle.

Oh, this is very strange.

Something is taking me by the hand and goes with me down the
  oak tree.

It has the shape . . .

This is very strange. The figure is of a . . .

It is a *greenish* figure, that has the shape of Quan Yin, and
  it is made out of . . .

It's not a physical form.

It's in the shape of

*fog* or

*smog* or . . .

It's just waving, in front of me.

It's leading the way.

I just follow her.

Something says to me,

> *Don't be so set on your thoughts. Don't be set on your*
>   *thoughts. Open your . . .*
>   *Open up, open up.*

Whilst I was going into the oak tree I felt so restricted.

I'm losing my determination. I'm losing myself. That can't be
  allowed.

Turtle. That can't be allowed.

Oh, my God, that can't be allowed.

I feel that

I myself

seem to go up in *smoke*. And, all that is left is

greenish,

like a greenish cloud. It's more like celadon, I have to mention that. It's a celadon.

Ahhh. And now I seem to intermingle with the shape of
the Quan Yin shape.

Oh, my God.

> *Lose your thoughts.*

Voice, very sweet, singing. It's just telling me,

> *Lose your thoughts*
> *Lose your thoughts*
> *Lose your thoughts*
> *Lose your thoughts*
> *Lose your thoughts. Don't hang on them, not now.*

It is still dark. It is the tunnel. We're surrounded by roots,
tree roots, I assume.

One is especially beautiful.

Beautiful root. Strong. Dark.

I don't want to float anymore, I fasten myself to that root.

Ohh, it makes me feel so strong.

But I can't hold onto it.

I am just floating by.

And now, I am . . .

Oh! I am outside, now. And there is *Turtle* at a little stream. And
a green meadow.

> Turtle!

Turtle seems asleep, I only see the shell, I can't see the head,
and I

just knock on the shell. Turtle is sticking her head out.

> Hi, Turtle!
> I
> come to you for healing
> of my inner and physical body. You know I am taking
>   medicines
> for high cholesterol.
> I just like

to be without these tablets.

What can I do? I need a healing. And what can I do
to help with the healing?

Turtle looks at me. I have the feeling that she was in a long sleep.
She seems to be sort of yawning.

Oh, Turtle, I'm sorry. I didn't realize that I

I only see myself, do I?

I should have waited. I should have come another time. I
should not have awakened you. I'm sorry.

Turtle is just massive. Huge.

Bigger than I.

She's getting up,

motions me to sit on her.

She goes into the water. And, what I thought was a small, little
stream suddenly

is big enough to . . .

We are floating down. It has become sort of a river now. We
floating down to the ocean.

We are not at the ocean yet, but I can

already . . .

There is an ocean smell in the air, and I can hear the waves. But I
cannot see it yet.

Again, something says to me,

*Don't think. Don't think. Keep your thoughts out
of your brain. Don't think.*

I was wrong. Actually. We are landing not at the ocean, but
it is actually a waterfall. And the noise that I thought was ocean
noise is really the thundering of
the waterfall.

It's not a very high waterfall, actually,
but it is *very broad.*

Underneath the waterfall is the cave. Turtle is swimming,
swimming with me
underneath the waterfall, into this cave.

A *huge*
Quan Yin
is in that cave.
Made out of
stone, I guess.
I am asked to wash it.
I found moss
and I'm taking moss and soak it with water
and I go and
wash *Quan Yin.*
It is a huge figure, but for whatever reason
I can climb up on her and I am starting to wash her.
Her hair. And her crown. Her eyes. Her face. It is a very
  kind face.
Her arms. Her chest. And her back. The lower part of her body.
  She has flowing clothes on.
The closest stars and moon is on it. And flowers. *Lotus* flowers.
  I have to go back and get some more moss. Put water on the
  moss.
Now I go back and
arrive at her feet.
It made me so tired to clean her that I'm
sitting at her feet and
I have a difficult time not to fall asleep.
I have the feeling as if a *rain shower,*
but it is not rain, it's
petals.
Flower petals
are showered on me.
She has this
vase-like container. And flower petals fall upon me, and my
  whole body. It's a marvelous fragrance. Of flower petals and
  water. It feels absolutely wonderful, and the fragrance is
so marvelous.

I am enjoying the moment.
*Don't think. Don't think.*
I try to be empty, and not thinking.
Suddenly Turtle is ahead,
just standing right, opposite me. And her . . .
The drum is calling. I have to go back.
Bye, Turtle. Bye, Quan Yin.
I am racing back.
I wish I could take
a piece of root with me, but I know I am not allowed to.
I can't let go of the root. I have to leave. I have to leave.
And now I am out. In the ordinary world again.

---

###  Reflections

Ema's Quest. "I like to visit Turtle to ask her for the healing of my inner, physical body."

Ema's Evaluation (after prompt for Ema to interpret her journey in terms of her purpose). "I probably got a healing . . . where these petals were just sort of thrown over me. 'Cause it was really a fantastic feeling . . . was a very beautiful fragrance of water and of a flower . . . it was just absolutely marvelous."

Counselor's Comments. In the course of this journey for healing, Ema receives new teachings about spirits, their forms, and herself. Quan Yin enters the journey toward the latter part. Of note, Ema reports that in ordinary reality, she has a statue of Quan Yin in her garden that "helps me meditate."

---

# Exploring the Windy Cave

*I like to go today, to explore—the Windy Cave.*

*I like—to explore—the Windy Cave.*

*I like to explore—the Windy Cave.*

It is strange and I do not know why, but my brain sort of waits
   for the rattle.
I sort of have to force myself to leave the house
and go down
to the oak tree.
I have to go back to the house. I think the best thing might be
   that I envision taking the rattle with me. And, so I am going
   back to the house and pick up the rattle.
I am going down
and I am sliding down toward the oak tree.
Something tells me to leave the rattle behind.
I put the rattle down and go
through the entrance, through the hole in the
oak tree.
It is pitch-dark and I can't see anything. So I'm sitting down. I
   have to get
energy
into my body so
that I will light up.
A dim light is coming from
within me now. But, I'm walking. I am walking the *path*. I have
   the strange feeling as if I don't belong here, even though I
   have done
this path for *so long*.

For all these years.
I feel
like a stranger.
I have to get deeper into
myself.
Now I'm getting to the fog and I go to the right, which heads me
   to the cave.
The cave is open.
I want to go by, but
I don't know what it is but
I have this immense desire to go into the cave.
But it seems to know where I walked last night. There is a wall.
I cannot penetrate it.
It is just closed up.
I'm pushing against it but it's . . .
no way. Because it is
just solid.
And the river,
I can hear water but it is underneath the lava bed.
I just have to go into the cave. There is just
immense desire to go into the cave. Oh, also, there is a force
   from within that just
*pulls* me into the
cave.
It is dry.
The
seaweed that is normally in
when it is wet, is worn, looks all dry and shriveled up.
I
just bend down and because I like seaweed so much, I guess I
just
take a few
and
I'm just holding it in my hand. It has a nice

smell
of ocean and
I have the desire to eat it. I'm just
putting it in my mouth. Ah, it
tastes so good.
I can feel how it goes down
to my stomach.
It makes me feel so light.
It goes to my stomach and now
I have to eat more. So I am
taking some more.
I just chip it off. And it comes in little, flaky pieces. And
I eat them again. I have so much saliva in my mouth.
I have to swallow and to swallow and to swallow because I
have so much saliva, in my mouth.
And now that the
seaweed is
in my stomach, or where it is, I don't know, but I have the
   feeling as if it is distributed from down there
to my whole body. It is just transported by . . .
The veins cannot be as big as I envision them.
I envision *huge*
veins and
the seaweed.
And my saliva is just
pushing through
my whole body. It's going to my legs, first. And then, it goes
   now . . .
I have to lie down and it goes now through my whole body.
Through the upper part of my body also.

I suddenly feel a wind
coming from that area. Uhhh, I am getting up and
the wall suddenly isn't there anymore.

I look back.

  Oh, Turtle, please protect me.

I am

scared, a little bit. But since the

lava wall has gone

I assume it is right for me to go, but it is so windy I have to . . .

Can't hardly breathe. I'm walking down the path, but

it is so dark. And I . . .

No, actually it isn't dark. Or it is dark, but

I don't quite know how to explain this now.

It is dark

and yet I can *see.*

The darkness has also light. What I mean is

I can see where I walk. It is a very strange situation. I am
 swallowed completely by the dark. And I tried to look back and
 I can't see anything, and yet

I *feel*

my way.

It is very windy still. And I'm just *clinging* through the wall.
 Luckily it has lava on it and it is very

irregular so I can

have holds there.

For whatever reason, I think I lost my scare. I am walking rather
 briskly now. And, I'm sort of lift . . .

The wind

seems to go only one way and it helps me walking faster. It is
 very strange.

And now I am going uphill. Much faster, actually, than last night.

I seem to be in tune with the wind now. The wind blows in one
 direction. And, even though it is windy, I don't *feel* the wind.

It is almost as if *I'm* the wind or what

I don't really . . .

Cannot figure this out.

I feel so light. And I'm pushed by the *wind?* Or I am pushed by my own lightness.

Oh, yes. That is quite right. I forgot all about it. I suddenly hit my head on the ceiling. And I remember last night, I forgot it. I have to *push*. And

a big

lava rock, it is like a plate. And I just push it open, and

that brought me to the cave. Yes, indeed.

Last night it was so windy. But, today it seems to be calm. At least where I am coming out, but on the other end of the cave, there seem to be

tumultuous winds. I mean it is . . . ahhhhhhh . . . ahh. Ahh. Yes. Yes. Yes!

Where I am it is very quiet; but ahead of me

and I cannot see it,

but there is so much noise and so

I can't imagine that

I'm walking toward it.

Now I am getting scared again.

Just so stupid.

I just wish I could . . .

     Oh, Turtle, should I go into this?

Something just, from the back, pushes me, and I am in

this

whirl of wind.

There is *wind* around me

and really very *strong* wind around me, all around me. But I seem to be

right in the middle of it and it is *very calm* where I am.

I don't know what to do, I'm just . . .

     *See how there's chaos around you.*

Chaos. Yes, chaos around me.

     *If you keep calm it won't affect you.*

If I keep calm it won't affect me.

Chaos around me.

Chaos around me.

If I keep calm it won't affect me. Right! Right! I am completely
   calm. I mean, I have lost

my fright.

And the wind is just so

strong. And it doesn't touch me. I seem to be right in the midst
   of the wind, and yet, I am firm

on the ground. It just doesn't touch me.

I'm getting so light. I mean I feel so light. It is amazing that I'm
   not be lifted by the wind, because I feel

like a leaf

really, or something very light. And I really,

should be

tossed around like mad, and yet I'm not.

Something says that I can

come out now. So I am turning around and go back into the
   cave, to the

quiet part.

I want to go back in. I don't know why. I go back into this part.
   And again

it doesn't touch me.

It doesn't touch me at all.

I'm stretching my arms.

It doesn't touch me. I walk out again

of that part

of the cave.

I feel so

satisfied. I feel so

like one feels when one is happy and one thinks one should
   scream and cry.

And yet I'm completely quiet

and full of happiness within me.

I am told to

leave the cave. I look back.

The wind is still raging in that corner. With immense power.
  Lots of noise.
I go through that
hole and I'm closing it again. And so now I'm just sort of
sitting on my bottom, and I am sliding down. And it is just so
  much *fun*
just to slide down. I feel
I have learned something. Or maybe not, I don't know.
Now I go.
Now the wall is there again and I cannot get out.
I have just
decided to sit in front of the wall for a while.
I am not worried.
I'm just sitting
in front of the wall, cross-legged.
    Turtle, I'd like to come and visit you
    in the cave. What can I do
    for the wall to disappear?
Something says,
        *Walk right through it.*
And I
am walking *right through* it.
Now that I am on the other side I look, and the wall isn't there.
  It must have been
imagination on my part to think that that the wall was there,
  because it really isn't. I'm going back again to the other side.
  And indeed there is no wall.
I don't quite understand this but, nevertheless I go back into
  the cave.
I'd like to go
into the Turtle Rock. I'm crawling in.
I don't know somehow I feel exhausted. I just lie down on the
  ground.
    Turtle, what just happened to me?

I think I know what happened to me.

> You have just shown me how to get rid of my anxieties, I
> guess. If that is really so, you have done me an immense,
> immense favor.
>
> I am eternally grateful. I really am. If that is what it meant.

My brain is suddenly filled with all kinds of thoughts and I just
have to lie down, and let it rest.

All kinds of lights come from this one corner. Normally when
I go

into the shell of the Turtle, it has a green light. But it changes
colors. From green

to blue

to purple.

And a white light. And also red

and yellow

and green

and blue again. All these lights sort of

seem to . . .

It's very strange because I'm lying on the ground and my eyes
are closed, but I *feel* the lights. And my body feels the colors,
even though I don't see them. But I do feel them. I feel the
colors. I feel the color red as red. And the color

yellow is yellow.

It seems to penetrate my body. These colors

coming from

the one corner of the cave.

I try to open my eyes, but it is so light that I have to close my
eyes because it hurts me.

Oh, yes. Oh, how sad. Oh, how sad. Oh. I have to go. Ah, and it
feels so good.

I

have to leave.

I am crawling out of the shell and I'm just

running as fast as I can, toward the opening of the oak tree.

And whilst I am running it seems to me as if
the colors just go with me. I am surrounded by all these colors.
And now I am out-
side.
Right. Right!
Gosh!

---

 **Reflections**

Ema's Quest. "I like to go today to explore the Windy Cave."

Ema's Initial Response. "Well, I got more than beyond my wildest dreams, I guess."

Ema's Interpretation. "The wall, that's sort of a metaphor that I build a wall or that I see things, dread things—and that's not really there. I think it was sort of showing me that in my personal life, that I sometimes dread things to do and they might not be there. When I relaxed it just was not there. It was a marvelous journey. I got so much more out of it than I thought I would."

Counselor's Comments. How vividly Ema describes her descent to the Lower World. Each time it is distinctive, yet familiar, territory that is developing over her ongoing journeys. Based on trust founded in her own journey experiences, Ema calls for Turtle's protection and advice in the dark, unknown area. Although this is ostensibly a journey of exploration, it also carries wise guidance. Ema's open self-observation allows her the opportunity to consider the meaning of this journey that actually refers back to the primary request for a healing of her anxieties in only a few journeys prior to this one. In interpreting this journey, Ema finds for herself the power of metaphor. This journey she deems significant.

# Meeting Raven

*I like to meet Raven—and ask him whether he is my power animal.*

*I like to meet Raven—and ask him—whether he is my power animal.*

*I like to meet Raven—and ask him, whether he is my power animal.*

I think I will go
down to the
oak tree. And, hopefully end up in that chamber with the vortex.
I am going down the hillside, next to my house, and
toward the oak tree.
Lots of mushrooms are
growing around the oak.
They have a nice musty smell.
I jump into the
tunnel.
It is dark.
I have to do some exercise in order to
get the light source from within.
It's really dim, but I can see very well even though the light is
    very dim.
The
light source
coming from me is very dim.
Very dry.
I have the feeling as if something is watching me, so I turn
    around but I can't see anything.
I walk deeper and deeper into the earth.
My mind doesn't concentrate at the moment.
I just will have to sit down

and concentrate.
I just envision Raven
on the black walls. It's all lava rock.
I have the urge to
find another rock.
And I try to hammer with the rock,
Raven into the lava wall.
Actually, it is just some kind of shell I found, strangely enough.
  And so, I am now at the wall and I'm starting with the beak
and the head.
Luckily the lava is very
soft material. And it goes relatively fast, that I can
sort of
sketch it.
Now I'm
taking care of the
body and
I try to do the feathers, the tail feathers.
It is very strange but, whilst I am doing it, *water* seems to come
out of the marking I have made. Water comes out but
just in
little *droplets.*
Silvery droplets.
They spread like *paint* over the area
I have chiseled out. I'm now
doing the *feet* and
the
*talons.*
And
I am afraid to put the eye in.
Besides, with the
shell the eye would be too big. I don't quite know how to . . .
am just breaking a little piece of shell off
and put it there.

I can put it there where the eye is supposed to be and
it just *sticks* there.
Raven. Ahh! That is really very nice the way I did it, actually.
It is little bigger
than the raven is.
Probably double. Or maybe three times as big, I don't know.
But it's
very nice proportions.
And
the droplets are still coming out and it goes over the whole bird.
It gives it a certain
iridescent sheen. Like the feathers
are actually. Because the raven feathers have sort of an iridescent
  sheen if one looks very closely.

>  Raven, I just
>  come out to seek you today
>  to ask you
>  whether you are my power animal and if you are, just show
>    me the way how to find you.

I am just sitting down
and look at
the raven on the wall.
Something tells me to put my hand, and go through the wall.
  I'm having my hand in front of me and
I am just walking *right through it.*
Right through it!
Darkness. Utter darkness. No source of light.

>  Raven, if you are here, you have to show yourself. Don't let
>    me sit here in the dark.

I'm sitting down again. And wonder.
I am opening my eyes and suddenly, it is as if a *dome* had
  opened
and I'm
all the way up.

I seem to see myself from above. And I see this little figure. I'm
the size of an ant. This is how far
the opening is
above me.
Seems to be sort of hopeless.

> Ah, Raven. You make it very hard for me to find you.
>
> What do you want me to do next?

I have the feeling I should
climb up the wall. It is very porous, so I can very easily climb *up*.
And actually
it goes relatively fast.
I almost have the feeling
I'm like a lizard. I just go
rather quickly up this
tall, tall wall.
Now I'm
outside, but no land. I'm in the sky.
It's very windy up here and I have to hold on
very tight
not to
be blown
into the shaft.
I assume it is in the sky
because I don't have the right vision.
It is
foggy, or maybe clouds. It is warm. Warm, windy, and I'm surrounded by clouds.

> Raven! Ah!
>
> How beautiful you are.
>
> You are much taller. Yes, you are about the size I . . . yes, yes.

I myself am very much smaller than in the ordinary world. And
Raven is the size of the raven I
incised in the wall.
I am just awed seeing him. Ahhh!

Raven,
I just wonder whether you are my power animal.
I really want to thank you
for helping me in the ordinary world, to finish the circle, and
for the feather
you dropped fourteen days ago. It was so important for me
to get a sign. Even though I didn't ask you, but I just felt it
was . . .

Raven is looking at me with great interest. His
head goes from
right to left and back and forth, and his eyes are black. Black and
beautiful and shiny, he is.
Now he comes and he walks around me. And he's just looking at
me. He picks at my hair
and he
prods me in my back. He goes with his beak up and down.
Dock tock tock tock tock tock. He wants me to stand up,
because I am sort of cowering on the ledge, since I'm afraid I
would be blown down.
The wind doesn't seem to be *there* anymore. There are just
clouds. And they are
such that
I cannot even see anymore
what I'm standing on, so actually. I think
now that I'm standing . . . I think I'm in sort of cloud formation.
It makes me feel very *light.*
He walks in front of me, back and forth and back and forth, and
he just looks at me with his
dark and penetrating eyes.
I don't really understand what . . .
If you try to tell me something, Raven, I don't understand it
at all.
It makes me uncomfortable the way he stares at me and I just . . .

Why are you staring at me like that?

And, suddenly,

he doesn't speak but his eyes seem to say,

*Well, you are staring at me too! So . . .*

That's probably true. So I'm staring at him and he

just does the same thing!

Well, I am staring at you because you are just so,

so very beautiful. Your black and the iridescence of the

feathers and your

eyes are just so alert, and so, really . . .

And he says to me,

*I'm staring at you to find out whether you are worth it*

*for me to be your power animal.*

Ahhh, right!

Now in ordinary world I would have said, "You don't have to

be. I don't want to waste your time, if you feel, you have to

think about it a lot." But since I'm not in the ordinary world

I'm not saying anything, but, of course

he knows my thoughts.

He says to me,

*Pride doesn't come into it.*

Yes, I know.

What does come into it,

Raven? What do I have to do, to be,

for you

to be my power animal?

All the power animals I have came to me. They accepted me

the way I am, but not you.

He is standing

in front of me. He doesn't answer.

He says to me

that I don't really need his help.

That my intuitions were right

when he gave me help

in the ordinary world. He is not speaking, but it is sort of, this.
It's
unspoken.
But that in future when I am really in doubt, that he will give
   me signs
in the ordinary world.

    I am very grateful. Thank you so much. That's all I'm asking
      for. I just want to know
    how to honor you.

He says that I do not have to specially honor *him*,
that I do understand that we are all related
and when I honor the others, I honor him, too.
Ahhh!

    Yes, I have never seen it that way but you are right.
    Yes, I know we are all related and I
    see it more clearly than others. That is probably true.
    Can you show me something, Raven,
    I should see? Is there anything I should know
    now? Your silver eyes. Were you really there
    in the Turtle Cave? What did your eyes do to me
    with their laser beams? You were walking all over me.

He says to me
with a
sort of
amazement that,
      *Your brain has widened.*
Months ago I would not have asked questions like this.
      *You are very alert again,*
he says to me.
But he does not answer my question.

    Should I be afraid of your eyes?
    You know that I am afraid for my eyes.

He says that

what I thought were laser
was not meant to harm me. It was
really meant to open me up. To *broaden* my mind.
   *Thank you. I'm very, very grateful.*
He taking me in his beak and he's flying down the shaft with me,
all the way down.
He says I should go back
and visit Turtle.
   Thank you, Raven, oh, thank you.
And, I just go right through the wall again.
And now I'm back. And I look around and there is
Raven.
It's still on the wall and, I must say, I don't understand that *I* did
   it because it is really so beautiful. And it is exactly the same size
   as Raven
showed himself to me. Maybe three times the normal size of a
   raven, I guess.

Ahhh! Raven said I should go and visit Turtle in the
Turtle Cave. So, I'm just walking down the shaft, and go to fork
to the right.
And here I am.
It is so hot here. Normally it is not that hot, but it is so hot in
   the cave.
   Turtle, what's going on?
I seem to be
in the nude. And I'm just supposed to sit.
It is like being in the sauna, really.
And, the water is just *pouring* out of me.
I can *feel* it, that it comes from my *hair* roots, even. It's just
   amazing.
I open my eyes and
I look like a statue where water comes out, like a little
fountain statue. Completely.

The water is just running down and running down.

Ahhh.

I really should relax and enjoy it. It is so nice.

Ahhh! Ahhh! Ahhh! Ahh! Ahhh! Ah . . .

'Tis such a nice feeling.

I don't like to think of anything. My brain is completely empty and relaxed.

I don't feel like lying down, I am just sitting here.

Water running out, coming out of me.

The water is *rising* a little bit. It's coming *higher,* and *higher.* And *higher* still. The drum is calling me back. Oh, how sad.

But it is really getting high, I have to leave. I'm walking out of the cave and

running down

the tunnel.

Then back.

I'm just looking to my right and

Raven is still there.

Incised in the wall.

 Oh, Raven, thank you so much. Oh, Raven, oh!

I have to go.

I still have to run.

And I'm out.

---

##  Reflections

Ema's Quest. "I like to meet Raven and ask him whether he is my power animal."

Ema's Response (after prompt for a brief statement about the journey's answer to her question). "Well, it was quite a surprise to me, how I met Raven. I don't quite know what to make of it, with the exception that he obviously knows all about me."

Ema's Interpretation. "He looked at me very sincerely and said it really wasn't necessary, but if there was anything and he felt it was necessary, he would give me a sign. It was definitely a cleansing. So, I got my answer, I should feel honored, even though he feels I don't need him, but whenever I am needing him he would give me signs. I think that is as good as it gets.

"It was a very, very satisfactory journey, just very different. Raven is just a very different kind of helper."

Counselor's Comments. Once more, Ema prefers to journey to the Lower World, in which she finds reliable, rich, and beautiful experiences. She becomes clearer in her partnership with Raven, while still retaining her awe and humility. Increasingly, Ema's post-journey statements combine both her response to the journey as well as her interpretation. Ema also comments on how her felt behavior differs in the Lower World from that in the ordinary reality of the Middle World. She remains open and grateful for the teachings of the spirits. This, too, she says, is an important journey.

# Asking for My Strength Back

*I—like to—meet the Yellow One today, and ask him to—restore my
power.*

*I like to meet the Yellow One and ask him to restore my power.*

*I like to meet the Yellow One, and ask him to restore—my power.*

The best way to get to the Yellow One . . .
to go through that opening at Rodeo Beach. So I am walking
   the path, toward that bay tree.
It is windy.
And I'm
walking rather quickly
toward the bend. And
jump into the
opening of the bay tree.
I'm *immediately* sucked up. Head-first this time,
normally I go feet-first, so I just
   put my hands in front of my face.

I have landed
in the big chamber
where the statue of the Yellow One
is located.
    Oh, Yellow One,
    you helped me last week
    perform on
    my friend. I
    might have made a mistake in not asking for help, because
      I feel

my anxieties have come back. I would like you to
please help me
to restore my power. I just need it
in the ordinary world; I can't do without it. I have sleepless
 nights.
I even now feel unsure,
unsure of
myself. I feel so small and so crumbly in
front of you.

The sword is flying toward me and I'm catching it with my
 right hand.
I have this glowing sword in my hands. It is all flames, but
they are cold flames. They are not hot.
I'm having it in my right hand and I just . . .
am swirling around, with it. Counter-clockwise. Very fast.
I am not earth-bound anymore. It seems as if the sword and
 I are one. And we are just spinning and spinning in
immense speed. But I am not getting dizzy. I
I just can't see anything
anymore. My surroundings are all blurred.
I'm holding the sword now with both hands, because it is so
powerful and so heavy, and it just makes me spin. So fast.
My name is called
and it echoes all around me.
My name is
like music.
It gets higher and higher. The pitch is higher and higher and
 higher. And whilst I have the feeling, in the ordinary world I
 probably would not hear it anymore, but now, I'm still
 hearing it.
It's higher and higher and suddenly, the voice,
my name, it's becoming light. Silvery light.
Speech is suddenly becoming

light.

Silvery light.

I have the feeling as if I'm screaming out. Out of my body seems to come

screams. Not of pain, but to get rid of some tension or something, to just sort of

lighten my body, which had

a heaviness in it. And the screams

become light. Silvery light.

Ahhh, God!

And now

everything slows down. I, myself.

The sword now suddenly

is just a sword again.

I feel like a feather.

The Yellow One

*now* is not a sculpture anymore. He has come

out of the sculpture

in his "wavy" form. And, I still have the sword. And I feel I have to give it back to him.

But he does not . . .

He doesn't want it. He just

points to me that I should keep it.

He says to me that I

still have a lot to learn.

He's saying things to me which I understand, but I just don't know quite how to put it.

I don't have the ability to word it. How sad.

What he says is that, I guess,

that I should not give my compassion away

because I do not have the strength yet

to give it away, freely. I still have a lot to learn.

>    *It needs years of practice,*

he says.

And then he says that I actually had never shown interest in
  healing.
I had never shown interest in healing in the
ordinary world.
I am
on a path where I cannot suddenly search my mind. It has to be
structured.
He says to me that
he sees that I do understand.
Things in the Lower World are different
from the way they are
in the ordinary world
and I have to learn that.
I have to make a distinction.

He says it differently. I just say it in the plain speak because
the way
he talks is like . . .
The Yellow One
is like energy. And the energy is talking to me. It is like
whispering wind. And so I have to be
immensely . . .
I have to *concentrate* in order to get
what he's
saying to me.

The sword
has
vanished. And I, myself,
seem to be surrounded by
the power of the Yellow One.

I am crying.
He's embracing me, as if I was a little child.
Because I feel so stupid, I think I have been told this before,

that I should keep
The Lower [World] and ordinary world apart. Mostly I do, but
  sometimes I seem to forget.
    Why do I always forget?
He's still holding me. And I feel, I don't know why,
suddenly I feel very strong again.
And whilst
the Yellow One is still cloud
energy, cloudy energy, I am suddenly . . .
I am *myself* again.
Somehow I am seeing myself from above.
My spirit, I think is above. And sees my body down below, and it
  seems to be so
clean. I mean
it is
so
full of light. *Silvery light.*
It looks as if that body
down there
is bursting with energy.
Absolute energy.
Music
seems to come out of it. Music
seems to come out of my body. Because
it has so much energy that
I have to release some
and that seems to be music.
It's a tone. It's a beautiful
sound. And that
sound comes out of me
and immediately becomes
silvery light.
Very strange. But it is happening.
It seems to me as if I am washed

with
energy and tone. And then
it comes, when it gets
too much, when it has given
what it's supposed to give, I guess,
it just comes out of my
body in
tone. Tonality. A beautiful sound. Absolutely
*beautiful*
sound.
The sound does something to my brain.
I have the feeling I have to be very careful that I don't lose my . . .
The drum is coming. The drum is calling. I have to leave.

> Oh, Yellow One, you have helped me so much. Thank you.
> I have to leave you.

I feel light as a feather. And, I am just sort of floating
back.
Sort of
slowly floating, and now I have come into a wind tunnel.
And
now I am out. Now I am back at
Rodeo Beach.

---

##  Reflections

Ema's Quest. "I like to meet the Yellow One today and ask him to restore my power."

Ema's Evaluation and Interpretation. "The Yellow One tried to give me my power back and I guess . . ."

Counselor's Comments. Learning from experience, Ema knows where in the Middle World to start this journey. From a recent Middle World attempt to heal a friend, she finds her personal power depleted and her anxiety returned. She intuits that not asking for help in the healing may be the source of her discomfort. The Yellow One, ever ready to serve, offers loving, friendly wisdom specifically for Ema, which strengthens her and gives rise to new perceptions. Her interpretation drifts off, implying some hesitance by Ema to make a strong statement at this time.

# To Ask for a Body-Soul Healing

*I would like to visit Turtle—to ask—her for a body-soul healing.*

*I would like to visit Turtle—to ask her—for a body-soul healing.*

*I would like to visit Turtle—to ask her—for a body-soul healing.*

I am
going down the embankment
toward the
big oak tree.
I can't see the opening. I guess it is probably
obscured with leaves and
I have to free the opening of
leaves
and some shrubbery that has blown by the wind, I guess. And,
   now it is open.
I jump into the
path.
It's a nice musty smell. I do like the smell
of must
and moss.
The water . . .
Glistening with water. There is a lot of moss on the water
   and water
is seeping through the walls and is
collected on the moss.
So it looks as if the walls are
like silver.
There is also some water underneath my feet. I'm going,
I guess I have no shoes on because

I can feel the water
on my feet and it feels actually very nice. And also,
some moss, on the ground.
Sometimes when I walk
it is the bare rock,
but sometimes there are patches of moss.
I just bend down and
take some moss, which is so soft
and so beautiful. I just take some moss with me.
I'm holding it between my hands.
It is such a nice feeling. It seems to do something to my body,
   actually.
There is a little river
coming from the left, out of the wall. And,
I'm just *drawn* to it, where the water comes out. And, that piece
   of wall is just . . .
I have really never seen something like it. The moss, oh, my God,
   it must be at least twenty inches thick! And it is just the size . . .
the same height as my body. And I am being drawn right into
   the moss.
It is *so* soft.

   Turtle,
   I did not expect you here.
   I am really coming to ask
   for a body and soul
   healing. As you know, I really feel well.
   I think I just wanted to see you. I tried so hard the other
      day but
   I just didn't get through.

Turtle motions to me to follow her, and I just leave and,
turning around, the moss that was
above, I don't know how many
inches thick, is completely *gone*.
Maybe I have absorbed it, I don't know, but

I feel heavy, but it is such a nice heaviness. Everything just seems
to be *so*
*right!* And I'm following Turtle.
Turtle goes *very slowly.*
We are walking toward the right, now,
in order to get to the cave.
This is something I have never seen before, but
there is lots of water coming out from the ceiling
of the cave, at least at the *entrance* to the cave. And Turtle is just
standing, right under the little waterfall, and motions me to
stand right next to her.
The water
is not at all cold. It is warm water.
It is *very refreshing.* Maybe it is cold, but I cannot feel the cold at
all. I just feel the pleasant
force of water
touching
the crown of my head, and then
it seems to penetrate my skin even, 'cause I
have the feeling that
what I absorbed
way back,
the moss,
is now
washed out of me again.
I just stay here and enjoy
the feeling of the fresh water
going through my whole body.
I look down to Turtle and Turtle also seems to enjoy it.
She's drinking the water,
so I have the feeling that,
even though I have the feeling that the water is going, into my
body. I drink water, too.
She makes very silly motions, with her head. And so, it is as if

she was saying to me,
>*Don't be so serious.*
>*Just dance under*
>*water.*
>*This is a happy occasion, that is happening to you. Just be*
>*loose.*
And so I'm just sort
of start to dance.
It loosens up my joints
and it gives such a
happy light feeling.
I'm looking at
Turtle and she seems to be very pleased, that I understood what
  she was *saying* to me. Not with words, but with,
with motions.
I'm still dancing and I'm just enjoying it, so much.
Now Turtle walks ahead of me and
she's
walking right toward the
huge, empty
turtle shell.
I have a hard time leaving
the waterfall but
I think she wants me to follow her.

Turtle is so large. And
I'm surprised that we fit into the empty turtle shell. We both.
But being
in this confinement, Turtle appears smaller now.
And also I myself, seem to be smaller.
Everything is
in *green light.*
I'm to sit upright,
putting my hands on the ground.

Turtle asks me
what I
desire, from her.
I think I just came
to her for healing
of body
and soul. I shouldn't say "and." How terrible. A body-soul
   healing. That is what I need.
I feel so good at the moment. And yet
I want it to *last*. I would like to know what I should do.
Turtle
has her eyes closed. And I just go, very close to her, and take her
   head into my lap. And I am stroking her head. It is such a
   huge . . .
I mean, not huge, but . . .
Turtle is actually
larger than I,
and her head is
the same size as my head. And I'm just stroking her.
I feel she has given so much to me over the years. And I just
   like to
be kind to her. I really like to thank her for all she has done
   to me,
for me.
And still does.
I feel so close to her at the moment.

All the
chatter in my brain
has stopped and is
completely quiet.
I feel at the moment as if she is part of me. Completely relaxed
   and quiet.
It's only now that I feel we both are sitting in water.

Just a few inches
but the water is sort of swirling around us. *Clean* water.
 No seaweed in it. No seaweed at all.
Just water.
I just take a handful of water and put it on
Turtle's head.
I don't know why I do it but I just feel she might like it.
> *You have to empty your brain of all chatter.*
> *You have to be still without thought.*

I'm still putting water onto Turtle. Onto her head.
And whilst I'm doing that, water is coming out of me,
as if I was the source of water.
> *Emptiness. No thoughts. Only emptiness. No thoughts.*
> *Only emptiness. No thoughts.*

It comes out of Turtle as if that is a lecture for me.
These words,
> *Emptiness. Utter emptiness,*
> *in the evening.*

Is that what I should do in the
ordinary world, Turtle? Or is that what you want me to do
 here? 'Cause here, it is so wonderful. Being empty.
 Just sitting still.
> *You know how to live in both worlds. Take this with you.*
> *Being empty can be very*
> *helpful. Empty your brain of all thoughts.*

Thank you, Turtle.
It feels so good already.
I almost don't feel like talking because it feels so wonderful.
I just try to explain to Turtle that I am
here with a teacher and I really
should talk more
what's happening to me. And Turtle says . . .
Turtle really doesn't say,
> *Is that how you treat*

*my message? Empty your thoughts.*
*You came to me*
*for guidance.*

Yes, I did come to you for guidance. I'm sorry.
I feel
I can't do anything else but just sit
and empty my thoughts. Because, it seems to me as if
water is also coming out of my brain, and it takes
every thought away with it.
And it is such a marvelous feeling.
Every time when I
explain, then
it seems to be interrupted. I just have to be quiet for a while. I'm
   sorry. I just have to be quiet.

     Oh, Turtle, the drum calls me back. I have to leave you. Thank
     you so much. It was a wonderful teaching you gave me. I will
     take it with me. I will take it with me. And I won't forget.

Turtle is
pushing me, toward the entrance. I am
sort of confused still.
And now, there is
water
and the water is just
bringing me toward
the opening of the oak tree. And now I'm out.

---

 **Reflections**

Ema's Quest. "I would like to visit Turtle to ask her for a body-soul healing."

Ema's Evaluation. "I enjoyed this journey very much even though I didn't talk much. Well, I did, but you know. It was very interesting."

Ema's Interpretation (after prompt about whether her request was answered). "Oh, yes. Yes. Yes. She [Turtle] said, 'Emptiness. Emptiness.' It came sort of out of her. It is obviously important that I empty my thoughts, that I do that on a daily level. Turtle said that I should take it with me into the ordinary world."

Counselor's Comments. In her efforts to follow the guideline for constructing her requests of the spirits without using the words "and" or "or," Ema uses the term "body-soul." Within the journey narration, itself, however, she inadvertently says "body and soul." This is a methodological matter for the counselor to point out and for Ema to consider. Ema emphatically acknowledges that her request for a body-soul healing was answered. Furthermore, she tags this as a journey important to her.

# Exploring the Spiral

*I like to go—to the—Spiral Room—to explore it—further.*

*I like to go to the Spiral Room to explore it further.*

*I like to go to the Spiral Room, to explore it further.*

I walk down the hill
to the
burned-out redwood tree. And I'm sitting down. I brought a
    flashlight with me, because it is so dark there
that I can't see the opening without a flashlight.
It is a tiny opening. I have to make myself really small in order
    to get into
this tiny, but intriguing, entrance.
I am still too much in the
ordinary world, I cannot quite concentrate.
I left the flashlight lying on the ground
so that the
entrance is visible for me.
There's fungus at the walls
and I don't really remember how I got in last time, whether I
    jumped, but
this time there is [a] lot of fungus and I am using them as
    stepping stones, to go down.
It is a long way down.
Maybe I should have taken my flashlight along because it is very
    dark. I don't quite see. But the fungus seems to have a glow to
    it so I, when I look down I can see
little
white spots, which is the fungus

on the walls.

It's endless. I don't really remember

it being so

long, but maybe it was.

And now I am looking down

to this huge room.

It is an underground,

one cannot really say it's a grotto.

It looks like a *huge*

room. Tomblike. Huge boulders. Never touched by human
  hands.

I have difficulties finding the passage. It was a very small
  passage. I'm surprised that last time I

found it so easily. Now that I know it's there I cannot really
  find it.

I'm on the ground

now.

I am

not quite

oriented. I do not know where north or south, or east or west is.

I wouldn't know anyhow where the passage was.

Last time everything went so fast.

There is no passage today. I just can't find it.

I just go around the boulders

and take a closer look. The rock is beautiful.

Smooth. It seems to be lighted. The rocks look sort of . . .

They have an orange glow

and even though

they look weathered, but they are very smooth, to the touch.

It is dry.

With the exception

of the fungus

that brought me, there is some fungus at the ceiling, but,
  otherwise it is a complete . . .

It is *dry.* There is no
sign of
plant growth at all.
There is no smell. It's . . . it's dry.

Oh, there it is. Right there is the passage. Yes.
Yes, it is a very small, small opening. And
I have to *squeeze*
through.
There is the opening. I wonder how I walked here last time,
  because
I have to go in *sideway[s]*
in order to go through. What a remarkable
thing.
I am
just looking into the Spiral Room. It seems such a very sacred
  place.
I dare not to go in
today. I don't know why.
In my mind I just say
that I just want to know this room
more.
I don't want to . . .
I don't know what the right word is . . .
to defile it, with my presence.
Since it was shown to me, and I was
allowed to go through, and open the passage, I feel that
it is all right that I am visiting again.

The circle is so perfect. I've never seen a perfect circle like
  this, ever.
I cannot say it was hammered
but it is
*etched* into the floor, into the ground, into the rock.
The rock here is also

sort of

rather to the yellow than to gray. Or maybe it is just lighting, I
do not know.

I do like to walk

labyrinths

in my mind. And, even though this is not a labyrinth, but it is a
spiral and

I just like to *walk* it. And I'm just starting

and

I walk it slowly.

Whilst I'm walking I look around.

This room is the same as the other one.

Smaller. But it has very, very high ceilings, if one can call it a
ceiling. I mean it is, of course, all rock. It is like a cathedral.
The height is just immense.

One has the feeling being in something

very sacred, of course. And, there are no

windows or anything. And yet there is a light that

is within.

I feel slightly faint.

I just have to sit down.

I crawl like an animal 'cause I just

feel so

faint, or I do not know what, but

I just cannot walk upright at the moment. I just

crawl on all fours. I am

smaller than

I normally am.

I feel the beautiful rock on my hands

and knees. It is soft as silk.

Even though it is

*weathered* rock, it is not like marble or something like this.
Far from it.

Or maybe, it has been washed by water, even though there is no

water now,
but maybe thousands of years back, maybe, I don't know.
I am *drawn*
toward the middle.
I remember last time.

I really shouldn't think about last time. I should think about
  now what I'm doing.
When I look up, I have the feeling as if I am the size of an ant.
  Everything is *so*
*massive.* And this room is the same as the other one. No life. I
  mean, no plants.
No water. A dry smell.
The spiral
seems to be endless. But I enjoy it. I enjoy to
crawl, because
the rocks feel *so strengthening.* It is really very hard to explain. I
  do like rocks anyhow. They represent strength and
this is exactly
what happened right now.
Now I feel I want to go upright again.
Looking back, I really haven't done that much. The spiral seems
  to be, whilst when you see it with your eye, it seems to be just
  of a normal size. But once you start it
it,
it seems to be
like a lifetime.

I don't really know how far I got last time. But I'm still so
  far away from the middle. I can't even see the beautiful
  rounding. And I don't dare go fast
or something just keeps me from going fast.
I wonder
what the meaning of this is.
I'm too apprehensive.

All the thoughts I have within me, I should really empty.
  Uhhhohh.
I should
just get rid of my anticipation. *Why* am I like this? *Why* am I
  so . . .
So why can I just not . . . ?
I'm not *afraid* but I'm apprehensive.
I am apprehensive. I don't know why.

I feel a slight wind coming up, which is sort of strange. I do not
  know where it possibly could . . .
Maybe through the passage, I don't know.
The wind.
All right, I think I have stopped because I was sort of apprehensive going any further, but now there is a slight wind that
  seems to push me ahead, *not much,* just as if, if it's guiding me.
I just
stretch my arms, and just think nothing and I just
let the wind push me.
I'm closing my eyes.
I am barefoot
and I feel the grooves. My feet just fit into the
spiral grooves. The rock is not cold at all.
I am opening my eyes again. I have come
quite closer. And I see the
middle
very clearly now.
And I see that
actually
I am right at the edge.
My God.
It is
like a big hole.
I am getting ice-cold.

I want to go steps back, but I can't. I am just
*paralyzed* to the spot. Oh, God, I don't want to go down there. It
  looks so . . .
I am thrown into the vortex. Oh, my God.
I am spiraling down
to a never-ending void. Oh, God, what have I done?

I have become very light.
I see *stars*. Thousands of stars. Ohhh!
I am in the sky, night sky, I think. It is dark. The thousand stars.
Sky bodies I have never seen before.
I myself seem to be lit like a
star. I'm not saying I'm a star, but I have this light round me.
Ohhhhh.
What does this all mean, I wonder.
I'm just floating. I cannot think at all. I wonder where I am. Oh,
  my God, and how do I get back?
I have a fright within me.
But I am still surrounded by the wind. He seems to
sort of
guide me. He, I say, I mean the wind. I don't know why I
  say "he."
You say "the wind," I guess.
Oh, it is the most beautiful sight.
I enjoyed it at the moment
but now I am not enjoying it anymore. I am getting scared.
  Not to find any way back.
I shouldn't have come.
Oh, why did I do it? But
for whatever reason
I am sucked into . . .
And I'm going up and up and up and up. I hope I will land in
  the . . .
I am sort of spit out

and I am in this
room again.
Oh, my God. I am wet with sweat. I'm just, got so terribly scared.
  I'm *shaking* all over.
I cannot walk. I'm just sitting down and shaking.
I have the feeling I did something
I shouldn't have done. I went too far.
But since I *was there,* what was the meaning of it then?
What it says to me is that,
that I went through the navel
to a place
to before I was born.
Before
I was born.
This spiral is a life path and I started at the end and I went
  toward
birth.
I'm so hot. It sort of makes sense
to me.
Why was I so scared out there?
The drum is calling. I have to go back. Actually, I'm quite
  relieved. I am just climbing up.
I can't find the passage.
There it is.
Oh, God, I did everything wrong.
I am looking for the
fungus. *There is* the fungus.
I am just flying up.
And now, I'm back.
The redwood tree.
Still hot.

**Reflections**

Ema's Quest. "I like to go to the Spiral Room to explore it further."

Ema's Response. "I'm still hot. Gosh."

Ema's Interpretation. "It [this journey] showed me how I am in ordinary life. I like to explore, and then I get scared."

Counselor's Comments. This is another journey of exploration with no other overt purpose, such as to seek an answer to a question or to receive a healing. Consequently, Ema offers no interpretation immediately. In the fluidity of time and space, she recalls lessons from earlier journeys that help her meet the anxiety she feels.

It is only in the post-journey discussion, as she considers details of her journey, that she concludes that she got the message, as she states it above. Ema gives genuine expression to her emotional and physical feelings as they are happening. She also states that she feels less fear and less questioning of herself now, since beginning HSC. At the end of her journey, Ema says, "Why was I so scared [to go] down there?" At the close of the session, she offers, "Maybe I [can] ask Turtle about it [space]," indicating her increasing use of the tools she has at her disposal.

# Healing My Back

*I would like to go—to the Lower World, to the Turtle Cave and visit Turtle for a healing, for a healing of my back.*

*I like to go to the Turtle Cave—for a healing—a healing of my back.*

*I like to go to the Turtle Cave, for a healing—a healing of my back.*

It's nothing at the moment. I am still here.

This is very strange.
I just have to go downstairs from here and go to my car.
And now I am driving with my car.
I try to get to my home.
I don't want to use the highway.
I am driving.
It seems to go much faster
than ordinary life but
I am already in Sausalito.
I'm driving by the shopping center.
I'm driving up the hill.
The gate is already open. I'm driving through the gate
and get out of the car.
I'm climbing over the fence. And now I'm really *drawn*
toward the oak tree.
The entrance seems to be larger today.
I
climb into the
entrance and
I am
walking

in the large tunnel.
My steps give a hollow sound.
Normally there is a water . . .
It's a rush of water
beneath me. It is a lava rock, but this time
I hear nothing. It is
really very quiet. And everything is dry.
I don't see any moss
on the walls. Oh, I see moss actually, but it is all dry.
All dry and shriveled.
I take the right fork toward
the
Turtle Cave.
The Turtle Cave is closed.
But I have done this before. I can walk right through the
closing, through the
whatever-it-is
rock.
But the Turtle Cave is very dark.
I have to feel my way
toward the
huge turtle shell. Everything is so dry.

    Turtle, are you in there?

I have to feel my way. It's pitch-dark and I have to stoop down
  and have to find the entrance because it is just very small.
So I have to feel my way around.
I think I'm at the other end. I have to go around.
I'm feeling my way around
and, there seem[s] to be
no opening this time.
Whenever I think things are easy, they are not. Is that my
  punishment, huh? All right, I just sit here and wait patiently.

    Turtle, I am coming here

to ask you for a healing of my back.

I do not like it that it is so dark because

I can't see anything and normally there is

light coming from

*within me,* but for whatever reason, there is no light coming
from within me. I'm just sitting and I think I just want to
concentrate and hope there will be light coming out of me.

Normally it comes from

the navel area. And so I have to just sit for a minute and not say
anything, because I have to

sort of concentrate.

Well, it's very strange. It's not that *I'm* aglow, but suddenly the
turtle shell

is aglow. Whilst normally inside it is green,

the outside *suddenly* is *red.* It is a red glow, like a coal. Ah!

And I am

at the completely different area where I thought the entrance
should be.

That's very funny! That's why I couldn't find it. So I

am now crawling through the entrance, and I am at the turtle
shell.

It is so warm in here. Ahhh. Not quite as warm as in the sauna,
but it is just right.

And, the inside light is this time not green. It is also this
*beautiful red.* I have the feeling as if I am within a
*glowing coal.*

A huge, *glowing* coal. Ahhh, it is just lovely.

Turtle . . .

There's no turtle there.

I'm sitting myself in the middle of the shell

and just let the warmth go through my body.

I am sitting upright.

Something tells me I should stand up. So I'm standing upright
now. And

I'm starting sweating. The water is just running off me.

Seeing the water, it's running down my body. It looks like
glowing lava. It's amazing. Just amazing.

My whole body is aglow and glowing lava is coming right out
of me.

It's a wonderful feeling; it really is.

The area where I have my back pain,

it seems to me, but I cannot see it. Because

I cannot move. I seem to be just completely riveted to the spot.
And, I cannot move at all. I am completely paralyzed. But I *feel*
something,

as if a spear

is

or several spears, two,

are stuck in my back

and it's getting the area exactly, I guess, where the pain is
settled.

It's not painful at all. It's just that

I have to be careful.

I don't want any scare to come up. I have the feeling that if I get
scared

it might harm me. I have to get my mind off being scared.

I really have to concentrate on the *beauty* of it all. The beautiful
*red color*

glowing. And lava is still coming out of me. I mean, I don't think
it's lava, but it just looks like it. It just sort of

oozes out. At least out of the front of my body, I can see that. I
do not really know what happened in the back.

Even my *toenails* are glowing. It's just

such a *beautiful color.*

The whole

shell is

an energy field I feel. And I see flowers.

I don't know how to explain it. I know they are not real. But,

I see

the energy field is made out of

flowers. That is, blossoms. I see

roses

and peonies.

Ah!

I don't know what happening to me. I just don't know what

happening.

Something I have never noticed before but,

the bottom is opening up

and I'm

slowly

sinking

through the ground. I'm still standing.

And with a big

sizzle, I am

in water.

Yeah, this is really hard to explain. It, it was if

I was . . .

I don't really quite know what happened, but

I am myself again.

And I am swimming in the . . .

I don't know what it really is.

The water is not

salty. I can taste it.

It is

fresh water.

It is

in a cave, I guess,

because the light is very subdued.

I'm swimming on my back.

Flowers everywhere.

It is as if the

red flowers that
were
at the turtle shell
were just
like a vision
and now they are real. They are just swimming on the water's
surface.
Mostly roses.
Red. No fragrance. Just of utter beauty.
I try to figure
out what happened to me, but I cannot figure it out now. And
   there is no one I can ask, because I am all by myself.
Something is touching me from down below.
They are leaves. The leaves look round like water lilies, but
there are no water lilies
on the water.
Those flowers are roses
but the *leaves* seem to be
the round leaves of water lilies and they
seem to be alive in such a way that they
touch me, and it
almost is like
a massage, but very
*gentle* massage.
The water is not still, I feel now. And it is the wave motion
and the
leaves are
doing the massaging. Something says,
     *Shut up and concentrate,*
not really "shut up," but "be quiet and concentrate," but, very . . .
What can I say? . . .
indignant, sort of,
     *Don't try to figure things out, just live in the moment,*
something tries to tell me. Still sort of indignant.

It *is* nice. I'm still lying on my back, and I don't have to do any
  motions in order to keep flowing.
I just float by myself. As if the leaves are holding me up. And the
  wave motions
and the roses and the flowers,
as with every wave they just wash over my body. No fragrance,
but beauty.

It is such a wonderful relaxing feeling.
I don't really know what happened,
but
suddenly it seems to be as if daylight is coming
through.
There is an opening
at the top of this
cave, or, I don't really quite know what it is.
I cannot make it out, but something has opened up
and daylight is shining
through. And now when I look around, there are really no
  flowers.
And now there is no water. It seems to me as if I had sort of
  *dreamt* being here, in all the water. Maybe just
*left.* I don't quite understand. But,
everything is dry
and I'm sitting in a
field of
. . . I don't know . . .
It's not seaweed, but it's leaves.
They are still moist.
Very curious.

> Turtle, I really would like to talk to you. Why don't you show
>   yourself? Was it a healing I have gone through, or
> what is the meaning of all this?

Ahhh.

Through that opening, at the top . . .
*Oh!* The drum is calling. I do have to leave.
> Thank you,
> Turtle,
> if you help me. I have to come another time to find what this
> means.

So I just sort of
climb up
the roots now
and, toward . . .
Now I'm
in the turtle shell. Right! And so, I climb out of the turtle shell
  and know
I have to run rather quickly
because the drum . . .
And so, I'm out now.

---

 ## Reflections

Ema's Quest. "I would like to go to the Turtle Cave for a healing of my back."

Ema's Evaluation and Interpretation (after prompt about whether she received what she requested). "I definitely think so, even though Turtle didn't show up. Yes, she probably was around, but I didn't see her . . ."

Counselor's Comments. Ema describes in detail her nonordinary reality path from the site of the session to the oak tree in her garden at home, and from there, walking into the tunnel. As has become a familiar pattern, she announces the purpose of her journey to a spirit, in this case, Turtle, even though Turtle is not yet there. While Ema has special experiences, she does not know their source. However, with the call of the drumbeats, she returns to ordinary reality, convinced that she received healing. Frequently,

Ema does not make an immediate response after just completing her journey. Here, she gives an interpretation after reviewing the journey and being asked whether her quest was successful. She is becoming more observant of her own process within the journey, as seen in her comment that she didn't see Turtle.

# Advice from Turtle

*I like to meet Turtle today and ask how to overcome my anxieties.*

*How—to overcome my—anxieties.*

*How—to overcome my anxieties.*

I'm still here in the room.
I'm still in the room; I can't get off.
I have to do something.
I have to turn that picture around.
As if I'm jumping, I want to jump into it. I do not know. Maybe
  it would have been a good idea but I don't know how to.
OK. I like to meet Turtle
and ask her, How can I overcome
my anxieties? How
can I overcome
my anxieties? How
can I overcome
my anxieties?
I'm already in front of the
oak tree, in front of the entrance, and I'm jumping right in. This
  time there seems to be water in it. And, it's just
running water. And, I have to walk against the stream. But it is
  just very little water. Only my feet . . . bare feet.
Only my feet are in
water, and I'm just
sort of splashing. It's actually very refreshing.
Ah. The water is coming out of a little opening, on the
left side.
It's in the area where

I drew once a raven,
and it is just coming out
of the raven's mouth. Out of the raven's beak.
One has to look very closely
because the wall is black lava, and I incised the raven
into the black lava, but I know where the spot is, and it just
    comes right out where the beak is. That's where the water
    comes out. And, it's just a very small kind of
stream.
I just go to the
Turtle Cave
and see whether I meet Turtle there. Now
I have gone over the
threshold and
now it is
dry. Now I'm walking on dry ground.
I have the feeling I have to go back. And, I should sort of
cleanse myself. Going to Turtle today, I just feel I'm sort of, I
    don't know . . .
I just go back and have the water
rinse over my hands.
I just wash my hands, and my face; and I drink a few sips. Just
    for spiritual reasons,
I just I feel I have to do it.
Ahhh. The water feels really good.
I just don't feel I want to go.
I'm just sitting down and have the water run
over my face, and over my body.
I don't know whether I just envision it, or I
think Turtle is coming toward me.
    Turtle, what are you doing here?
I make space
for Turtle. So I have the feeling Turtle wants a drink. Or just
    wants to do the same. And in effect, I have

water poured on my hands and I just now
wash Turtle with it. It seems to be sort of sacred water. I
cannot put my finger on it. And I'm washing Turtle.
Turtle is sort of muddy
as if she has been
on muddy ground.
I'm just
washing her.
And now her beautiful black
comes through, and I also wash her face.
Turtle is
rather huge.
I have the feeling I probably am smaller now. Because it takes
   quite some effort for me to
climb on Turtle in order to
really clean her.
But it makes me feel good.
It seems to be
sort of a
holy thing I'm doing. I *feel* so privileged.
I take
great pain to
clean
*everything.*
Her feet are so dirty, so muddy. Not really dirty, it's muddy; it is
   really earth. It is clean earth.
Turtle asks me . . .

> Yes, I wanted to clean you first. Yes, I called you because I
>    wonder,
> can you help me to overcome my anxieties?
> Oh, I should not have been so upset
> just doing things up here in the ordinary world; like buying the
>    car, or do business. Is there any way . . . ?

Turtle motions me to

sit on her back. And she walks through the lava wall
with me. It is as if she's going . . .
The lava wall feels like
running water, suddenly, and we just go right through it.
And, we are coming out, I would say it is a well.
We are coming out
of something
where the water is just bubbling out the earth. And we are just
   coming right
out with the water. It's like a spring. And I actually do know
   the area, I just have never come to it this way. It is a small
   creek and
it is a little hilly. Lots of trees, birch trees.
And beautiful wildflowers and lots of
grass. But, *boulders* also. There is grass but not meadow-
like because there are too many trees and too many
stone formations. Everything is green. The stones are full
   of moss
and the flowers are
*all* colors. Just absolutely
springlike.
*Very beautiful.*
We are still in that little
running water, which is very small.
Turtle is right in the water and so I sit on her, and the water is
   sort of
transporting us
downhill. Very slowly.
I'm getting tired. I so want to keep my eyes open because it is
   really very beautiful.
And suddenly we seem to be underground.
I saw it. It is sort of a sandy area coming up, but we are not . . .
anymore . . .
There is no

daylight. Yeah, it seems to be
sort of a
*sand.*
Yeah,
gliding through sand! But, we are not getting
sand in our faces.
I cannot explain it but
we are just gliding through sand. Everything is . . . beige.
And now we are coming out again. And we are at the
beach. I would
assume it is the ocean.
It is the ocean because I
taste salty water.
Turtle motions me to look at the ocean.
Turtle says
I should let nature come into me. When I get upset I seem to
    forget nature.
I should never forget nature.
I should just
*pull it into me,* so it will have a permanent stay
in my body.
It is true; I forget completely about
everything
when I am in that state, I remember. *How can I overcome this
    state?*

Yes, that is true. I was in complete uproar before I had to go. But
    then the day, when I went, I was completely calm.
        *Yes, I know.*
Why can't it be like that? I have the feeling I do damage to myself
being this upset.
Turtle says to me I shouldn't
worry about it. I have come today to be renewed.
        *We should not strive for perfection,*

Turtle says.

*Don't try to be perfect. Ema!*

Right! Quite right.

I have the feeling as if I'm completely grounded at the moment.
I'm sitting on the sand, but the waves are
very near. I'm very close to the water.

Ahh!

The waves just *swirl* around me. And then when the waves go
back, they seem to take something out of me, out of my body.

I have the feeling as if something is pulled out of me. When the
waves have come
and splashed on me, and then when they go back, they take
something out of me.

Something with them.

Turtle is right next to me and that same also happens to Turtle.
To *both of us.* I am not sitting on Turtle anymore. I'm sitting
right behind, right next to her. Turtle opens her mouth and so
the water goes right into her mouth, and so I'm doing the
same.

And
it is salty but it is not too salty.

And I feel the water going through my inside.

I seem to be like a statue because
I'm sort of riveted to the spot. The water
goes into me
through my mouth, and then goes out of my mouth. It's like a
spout.

I am like stone
and also Turtle seems to be like stone, because the water goes
completely through us,
like cleansing us, and then it
goes out again.

And now comes in and then *goes out again.*

I think it is probably

the tide is coming in because
whilst I was only sitting, I was sitting in the sand and the
water just
came, was coming back and forth.
Now, I am sitting in the water. The water comes higher
and higher. And still, I am not capable of moving.
Seaweed is just swishing around me. Red seaweed
and white seaweed. A beautiful combination.

And now I'm swimming.
The seaweed had
completely encapsulated me and ripped me free
from the ocean floor, from the sand, and now I can swim, and
   I'm sort of bobbing along on,
on seaweed. And Turtle is right next to me. It feels really nice,
   actually. I do like to swim anyhow, so it's, it's just
so freeing, to swim in the water.
Something is in my ears,
as if
the waves, or something is saying to me,
          *Don't be perfect. Don't try to be perfect. Don't try to be*
          *perfect. Don't try to be perfect.*
I'm just
enjoying myself at the moment; I'm just bobbing up and down.
   Being held up by the
seaweed.
We are in the midst of the ocean. We seem to be quite a ways
   away
from
land. Because I
can't really see it. We are completely
just floating
at the wide open ocean.
I'm not afraid

at all. I'm just feeling

relieved.

I'm feeling *relieved*

that I don't have to be perfect, I guess. Even though I never
  thought that

I wanted to be, but maybe that was in the back of my mind,

come to think of it.

Things are in the back of our minds and we don't really realize it
till it is made

clear by someone

we trust.

Turtle is still next to me.

Now she is diving and I don't want to lose Turtle, so I dive right
  after her. I am in the water and I don't seem to have to breathe.
  I do not know what it is, what kind of mechanism, but

I'm just following Turtle.

Turtle is not really swimming; Turtle is *walking* on the ocean
  floor

and so am I

just following Turtle.

And now

there is sort of a rock formation, in the ocean. And, she squeezes
into a little,

sort of, hollow there. And I follow her. And we seem to be
  now . . .

Yes, we are! At the Turtle Cave! What a surprise! Ahhh!

The Turtle Cave is relatively dry. There is some seaweed in there,
  and it's wet but

not much water. Turtle motions me to . . .

Oh! Oh, my God, I have to go back. I have to go back. Ahhh,
  I have to go back. I don't think I can find my way back. I have
  to go back the way I normally go.

    Bye, Turtle. Thank you so much.

I am running as fast as I can.

And I go by the spot where the raven . . .
And the water is completely dry. Everything is dry.
I'm running as fast as I can. And now I am out.
Ahhh!

 **Reflections**

Ema's Quest. "I like to meet Turtle today and ask her how to overcome my anxieties."

Ema's Response, Evaluation, and Interpretation (forthcoming only after reviewing the recording and after she is asked if she received an answer to her question). "Yes, I guess I did [said in a firm, clear voice]."

Counselor's Comments. While overcoming her anxieties is important to Ema, she does not find them disabling; she chooses to explore this theme in her journeys. Her response, although brief, is to the point, and the tone of her voice implies her conviction. Absorbed in the immediate contents of her journey, Ema has the opportunity to replay this journey and continue to learn from it after the session.

When a person is unsure of the answer to a question, it may be revealing to examine the journey recording and transcripts closely to see if the question asked at the outset is the same as the journeyer actually asks the helping spirit during the journey. Sometimes they are not the same, much to the surprise of the journeyer. This situation then poses a dilemma about what question the journey answers.

# A Very Powerful Dismemberment

*I would like to go to the Turtle Cave to meet Turtle for an overall healing.*

*I would like to go to the Turtle Cave to meet Turtle for an overall healing.*

*I would like to go to the Turtle Cave to meet Turtle for an overall healing.*

I am walking down the hillside. It is very wet. Very wet and
slippery.
A lot of leaves are around the oak tree. I [am] looking down at
the entrance and I hear water running.
I am picked up by the neck and I have the feeling it's Raven.
For whatever reason, I cannot turn around. I am paralyzed and
there is lots of picking at my neck.
Now I am sort of . . .
I'm not really pushed, but I'm suddenly
at the
tunnel.
The water seems to be under the lava, because
I'm walking and
there is no wetness there.
It is very strange. I'm still
being picked at, not only my neck, but all the way down my
back.
Right in the middle,
all the way down.
It seems to be several.
It's not only one
"pick," or however you say it. It's several.
And, I'm still paralyzed. I mean, I can walk.
I can only walk, I cannot

turn my head and

I cannot chase away

whoever does this to me because my arms are also useless.

But I'm not uncomfortable. I'm sort of

pressed by whoever is doing the picking. Actually I wanted to see

where I am. But,

I can't really

see it because the signs are to the

left and I can only go forward. I cannot see anything at the sides.

But I'm coming now to the fog

that leads to the

Turtle Cave.

The Turtle Cave is closed.

And now I see

it *is Raven*. Several actually, that are just banging with their
  beaks

at the entrance, which is closed, in order to be let in, I guess.

So it is opening up now. And the ravens are gone.

It is *very dark*. And I am not giving that much light from my

body at the moment. I was more scared by the

ravens and

knowing where I was going, it was so very dark.

So I g . . . I *know* by memory, where the huge turtle shell
  should be.

I think it is here, in the distance where it is because I just *stubbed*
  my toe on something.

And I feel

the roundness of the shell.

I'm leaning against it, because it's a huge

shell.

I do not like that it is so dark 'cause I like to see

what's going on.

And I

finally found the entrance, which is sort of down below and I
  have to kind of slide in. It is dark, and it seems to be

as if I have hardly space in there. I have the feeling lots and lots
  of spirits are
are
already arriving here
and within the shell, which is, of course, whole.

> Turtle, I thought I would like to come for an all-around
> healing for myself but
> there seem to be so many spirits here, today
> . . . maybe you want me to leave.

I feel ripped and tugged at by my body by
all kinds of . . .
it's not like hands, it's more like spiderwebs
that sort of . . .
attach my body.
Well, I just, I think I have to sit down.
What I do is I put my hands on my
navel area in order to make it light. I have light coming from
my inner
body. I just didn't think about it.

It is still dark and I'm still sitting on the ground.
Now
there, a green light seems to be.
I am surrounded by a green light,
which comes not from within me. It just is suddenly there. And I
  see I'm surrounded by . . .

> Yes, I haven't seen you for a long time.

I just happened to talk about
the masked creatures
and
here they are
surrounding me.
They hardly ever sit still. They are always in movement. And so,
  they are just

moving around me like
fog.
I just don't know what to say
at the moment.
They're attacking me all over the body.
And now they are not that friendly anymore. At first, when I
   couldn't see them, it was as if, like spiderwebs touching me, but
   now they seem to treat me . . .
They have these . . .
Their hands have these long fingernails. They look like birds'
   talons. And they just
probe me
all over the place.
I am sitting, but they just
make me stand up.
They are just so *fast*, and
they have taken my whole body.
All I can see is now, I see
myself from above, and
what I see is a skeleton. Upright. But
the flesh is all gone.
I think they *ate* it,
or I don't really know what happened to it. The tweaking that I
   thought was just probing or so, was taking
the flesh
and
everything with it.
      Oh, Turtle, what . . . ?
Now,
Turtle is now there.
      Oh, Turtle, I am so happy you are here. What did they do
         to me?
Turtle, herself, just,
she just pushed the skeleton and I am now lying on the ground.

Turtle is coming in her rather large form
this time. And she is just crawling over my skeleton and she's
  just cracking it, absolutely, into complete powder.
I just see it all from above.
Water is coming into the shell now
And, with it,
algae. It is not seaweed. It is algae. It is *very soft*. It's like *a soup*.
And it fastens itself to the skele . . .
There is no skeleton anymore, but
where the skeleton was
is
white
powdery.
Well, at least that's what I thought it was, a powdery substance.
  If it is, it does not disappear with the water coming in. And
the algae seem to anchor,
hold,
holds it all together, I guess.
The skeleton is coming back, but it is completely and utterly
overgrown or, within,
it seems to be all algae. And it has a *green* tinge. Instead of a
  white skeleton it is greenish now, but it has become a skeleton
  again.
Oh, no, the water is coming higher and higher.
The water just
uprights the skeleton.
I'm
faint.
The creatures are swirling around me. But I don't see
them anymore singly. They are all
together
like
a cloud or like fog swirling around me. And an
immense speed.

I'm getting so hot.
I'm getting so hot.

> Turtle, what is happening to me? I don't like to be out of
>   control! Ah,
> I can't hold onto anything and I'm completely
> put into the swirl with . . .
> I want to be in control!

Something tells me that I should
*let go*!
I'm just completely
falling within it, myself, and I just . . .
I just don't care.
The area *screamed* at me in such a manner that
I guess it might be for my own good if I just let *go* for a moment.

I am completely entangled in a mass
of these creatures. And now, I'm . . .
Oh. That's what it was about. I myself again. What I mean is
I am in flesh again.
I'm touching my whole body, and my hair and everything is
  back. My fingernails, and
my toenails, and everything!
It just had to be.
Ohhh, I am just too stupid to understand all this. That's why I
  was just fighting it.

> I am so sorry.

They said, whether still after all these years, I still don't trust
  them.
Well,
that's not really true. That's not really true. It's just that
I just . . .
when I'm not in control, I get scared.

> Yes, I know, I know. I'm very sorry. I do trust you. I really do. It's
>   just that . . .

I can't say more than "I'm sorry." And I'm very grateful that
you put me together again. I really am very grateful.

I am still
sitting here. Though actually I am not sitting, I am still standing
upright. I'm being held by the
creatures so. They are sort of
angry that I didn't let go.
And to be honest I,
I do be sorry I didn't trust them because
I know
they really don't
mean harm, it's just that this whole thing . . .
They say I should not
try to explain. I should just pull myself together and
enjoy
where I am at this moment.
So I'm
sitting down on something. Oh, it is Turtle. Turtle, in the small
form.

Oh, Turtle, do you mind if I sit on you?

And, so I am sitting on Turtle. And,
my body is completely
*green*! Oh, my God!
Ahhh!
It is a nice green, actually.
It is almost like . . .
Oh, yes, it is an algae, algae-green, but it is more to the turquoise
side. It is really very beautiful.
And, whilst my body was so terribly hot a while ago, now it is
just cool and it looks actually
very beautiful.

Oh, Turtle, thank you so much. I do know now, understand that
it was a healing. I just . . .

I am still very slow
to understand this.
Now the creatures are all gone and I . . .
Oh, Turtle, I feel so sorry that I didn't . . .
I just hope I didn't do any harm there.
I do trust them. It's just that
I feel so full of guilt.
Turtle says I can always go and visit them. Again. Oh, God, it
is . . .
The drum is calling. I've got to go.
Bye, Turtle. Thank you so much.
And so I'm getting out of the
shell, but
it is completely underwater and I have to swim. Ummm, ahhh.
I have to swim all the way. It is as if *everything* is under
water.
I'm still swimming.
And now, I'm
just sort of
plopping out.

 **Reflections**

Ema's Quest. "I would like to go to the Turtle Cave to meet Turtle for an overall healing."

Ema's Initial Response. "Oh, my God" [quietly].

Ema's Interpretation (after replay). "There can never be an end. It was a really amazing journey." (Then, after prompt about whether her purpose was fulfilled) "Yes, I think so. Definitely. Definitely."

Counselor's Comments. The very refined, elegant structure of this statement of intention is simple, clear, accurate, and includes who, where, and for what purpose Ema is making this journey—without using "and" or "or." In the graphic dismemberment sequence, Ema engages totally; although apparently distressed, she draws on the lessons of journeying for years to confidently interpret this journey, both within it and after. This one she regards a significant journey.

# Turtle Heals My Eyes

*I like to meet Turtle today, in the Turtle Cave, and ask her to heal my eyes.*

*I like to meet Turtle and ask her to heal my eyes.*

*I like to meet Turtle, and ask her to heal my eyes.*

*I like to meet Turtle, and ask her to heal my eyes.*

I cannot quite focus at the moment.
I am walking down the hill.

I am still not focused.
I still can't get off.
Something is pushing me from behind. Toward the oak tree.
And, I am just pushed right
into the opening.
The ground is slightly wet.
I'm still pushed.
I'm sort of *hesitant*. I don't know what's
going on, but I'm still
slightly pushed toward,
forward.
It is
very dimly light. I don't give much.
It seems to be as if I'm sort of on low power, because normally
    when I go in, it's a light coming from the navel area and it gives
    me enough light to walk in the Lower World.
It's just very, very dim. But since I know the way I don't have
    difficulties walking it.
I am still pushed

slightly.
The walls that used to be
normally black, and
sort of lava-like, they are all green. Moss is growing on the
 walls and
they look very,
very dark, but
the fragrance from the moss is very earth and
I have the feeling as if I'm not walking in a hollow tunnel, as
 the tunnel normally is, I have the feeling
as if I'm walking now through . . .
As if I am in the soil. But I am allowed to go
untouched, by the soil.
But it's very
sort of narrow.
I still can't make up my mind. I don't know what's the matter
 with me.
I am baffled by the newness of, of this.
I expected the other road and now it is a different one.
I'm hesitant to proceed, because . . .
     Turtle! Ohh! Thank you for coming; I'm completely lost.
I thought I saw Turtle but now it is all dark again. Ummm.
I just don't get anywhere. I have to turn back.

I'm outside again. I have to start it again.
And now I look down and okay,
I just jumped down again.
I must have taken the wrong turn because now I'm at the tunnel
 I know. Hollow
underneath my step.
And I am starting running.
I'm already at the Turtle Cave.
Turtle is . . .

Oh, Turtle, you are here. I would so much like you to heal my
  eyes. You know how scared I am. I don't really want the laser
  treatment.
That would be . . .
Turtle. . . .

She just ask me to lie down. She asked me why I gave up
on the first journey.

Well, I suddenly got confused, because I
  couldn't get anywhere.

Turtle says to me that I *have* to try new ways.

Yes, I'm sorry.
Nothing is being said, but
I formed flippers.
She is massaging my body. Not my head, but my body. And, I
  seem to be
sort of thinking back and forth between the two of us, which I
  am not capable of
saying.
I think what she means is that
I, for a while I was very set in my ways, then I loosened up, and
  now I seem to be getting again, setting in my ways. I should *not*
  be *that way.* I should
be open. I should listen more.

Listen, to yourself.

It feels really nice.

Thank you, Turtle,
  for massaging me.

I have the feeling as if she is pressing something out of my body,
  because
I felt, not really bloated, but
somehow, I don't know. It feels already so much nicer at the
  moment. My whole body feels comfortable.
I am told

that I have been good in eating seaweed, but [in] the last months
I did not eat any seaweed. I should start eating seaweed again.
  Yes.
Turtle
says again to me,
        *Seaweed is good for you. Why don't you believe it?*
Meanwhile,
without my realizing,
my head
is partly in the water
and
seaweed surrounds me.
It seems to be as if I personally have become porous. And water
seeps into my body.
And, I would say it
cannot be seaweed. I don't know whether seaweed . . .
It is something green. It could be algae, I guess, because it is very,
very light,
very.
It just goes through my whole . . .
It just
flows.
It just goes like water
into my body.
And I have the feeling, I cannot see myself, but I have the feeling,
  a *green feeling*. I don't know, it's just that
everything seems to be green, and I *feel* green, if that is possible.
  It is a very nice and relaxed feeling.
I also feel it to get into my skull. And also around my eyes.
  And it
is in a wave motion. It just goes very
*gently* back and forth.
Turtle is still
working on my body. My arms also. And also my legs.

Ummm.
Something is
massaging my whole body. My whole body is pressed. It is
  pressed *down* and then when it
comes up, water goes into my body.
And when it is pressed down, water seems to go out. I have the
  feeling as if I am a wave. And I just go up
and down, and up
and down and very gently.
Very gently.
And algae, I think it is
is going through my body. With every motion, with every wave
  motion. It comes in and out. I have the feeling as if I am like an
  empty shell
and I can't do anything. I'm just
rocked back and forth and back and forth.
Turtle says I should concentrate on my eyes.
      *Put seaweed on your eyes,*
Turtle says.
      *Put seaweed on your eyes.*
I just have to give myself
to this motion for a moment. I cannot speak.
I am still
rocked back and forth.
I feel Turtle nearby 'cause she is making funny noises. I think
  she's eating.
I like to take a look at Turtle, but I seem to be
paralyzed.
I'm just this
wavy motion. That I'm motion, that's all. I'm just motion. Back
  and forth, and back and forth.
And the algae, or seaweed, just goes through my body.
It is as if the inside has become
algae.

It is a very *relaxed* feeling.
Oh, I wish I had this feeling all the time,
so relaxed and so peaceful.
I just don't want to speak.
The water seems to get higher. And I
seem to go up with the water. I'm floating now
on top of the water. Because, yes, I can,
I can
move again. Because I can see that the water is going
higher and higher and higher.
Turtle motions me to follow her.
And, we are both going to this
chamber, where we go up the vortex.
I feel, now that I see myself, because we are in this cave,
which is opening up toward
the rocky landscape and I can see myself now. And it seems to
   me I have sort of a greenish tinge on me. And, Turtle tells me I
   should sit in the sun. And, so, I have a crust around . . .
and the
seaweed is *drying up* and it's just falling off me.
It peels like a skin, but by itself, I'm not touching it. It
just falls off me. I have to turn around now. First
the front, and now
I have to turn
my back towards the sun.
And looking to the floor,
to the ground, it has disappeared. It is just not there anymore.
The Yellow One appears
in smoke
and tells me that
I start to worry again. I should relax.
>    *You are the one who takes the peace away from yourself.*
>    *You are the one who's harming yourself.*
A lot of green is squeezed out of me. But it

disappears. Immediately it comes out of my body, it disappears.
It's taken by the
air.
The Yellow One is very gentle.
He speaks to me, but I don't understand him.

    I don't understand you, Yellow One.

    The drum is calling, I have to leave you. Thank you so much
       for helping me. Thank you, Turtle. I have to leave.

And yet I seem not . . .
Something is pushing me again. And I am going down the
    vortex. And I'm running as fast as I can.
I'm running, and still, I am getting a push again. And now I'm
in the ordinary world again.

---

 ## Reflections

Ema's Quest. "I like to meet Turtle today, in the Turtle Cave, and ask her to heal my eyes."

Ema's Evaluation and Interpretation. "Well, I think I did get a healing."

Counselor's Comments. Ema restarts her journey and eventually goes to Turtle in the Turtle Cave, where she makes her request. While healing Ema, Turtle also offers friendly challenges to encourage Ema in positive, healthful strategies. The Yellow One, as well, appears with additional wisdom to aid Ema. Throughout the drama, Ema continues to narrate and to be mindful of the guidelines supporting her journey outside of time, in nonordinary reality, including her return to the Middle World and ordinary reality. Ema's developing style for interpreting her journeys involves engaging in the journey, listening to the replay, and then consolidating her interpretation with her personal response to the journey and analysis of whether the journey addressed her stated purpose.

---

# Ask to Meet the Yellow One

*Okay. Today, I would just . . . like to have a visit with the Yellow One.*

*I like to have a visit with the Yellow One.*

*I like to have a visit with the Yellow One.*

I am walking down the hillside.
The
entrance to the
oak tree
has a huge spiderweb
as if
Spider doesn't want to let me in. And Spider is sitting right in
   the middle of it, a big spider. And he looks straight at me. I
   have the feeling that I am very small.

     Spider, I
     would like to go down
     the entrance
     to meet the Yellow One.
     Where is a good place for me to get in?
     Your spiderweb, I really don't want to
     take it apart; it is so beautifully done.
Spider is
black and around the eyes and the head is *green* like little
   feathers.
Spider is
going down
with speed-lightning, all the way to the ground. And is
digging with its feet. It's making a little entrance for me.
As I said, I must be already small. The entrance seems to be

large enough for me to go through there.

So, I'm crawling, however. I am crawling through underneath the net.

Thank you, Spider.

I'm looking back

and Spider has gone back, to the middle

of the spiderweb.

Nice. Nice to have it locked in a way, so nobody can follow me to the Lower World. I like that idea.

I am walking

the tunnel, the lava tunnel.

Everything is dry. You can see moss on the walls but it is all dried out. And it has the

smell of dried moss. I guess that is what I smell. It is dried.

I guess it is dried matter of plants, so I assume it's the moss.

It is a *good smell*. I do like it.

I have now landed in the

Turtle Cave.

I just walk right

by the big

turtle shell. Everything is dry here, too.

The kelp is also all shriveled up. And when I walk on it, it just breaks. It is so brittle.

I do walk to the

chamber

and

I step into the vortex, and . . .

I am in the Summer Cave.

I am looking out at the landscape.

No tree.

Everything is dry, like it always is. I just see down below the small sliver. It's like a silver band, goes that river. Like a silver band.

I smell sulfur. That's the Yellow One.

I
cannot turn around. Something is stopping me of turning
   around.
I am pushed
from the back and I am falling down. The Summer Cave is
very high up. And something is pushing me.
And I'm
falling.
It is the Yellow One, who has pushed me, on his . . .
The energy
is like a cloud
and I'm
lying on that
cloud. And, it is carrying me.
It is already going through my body.
It is a very strong sulfur smell. A very strong sulfur smell. My
   eyes begin to tear.
The Yellow One says,

> *Cry, cry. Cry all the*
> *pain*
> *you have within yourself. Cry it out.*

I can't see anything because
I'm crying so hard. The water is just coming out of my eyes like
   a waterfall.
I can't see anything. It's probably good, because
I do not know if we are high up in the air or
whether we are
low. The Yellow One
is just
*surrounding* me
with energy.
Or I should say
it looks like a cloud, but a yellow cloud. Not *bright* yellow, but
yellowish.

The smell of sulfur is still so potent. I can't see anything else. My
 God. There is so much . . .
I had no idea that so much pain was
*within me.* That's most certainly not a healthy thing. It is just all
 coming out.
Now suddenly,
I don't
cry anymore and I have been put into the
river I saw from above. But
the river,
from above it was really very small
but now, being down here, the river is relatively
wide. And I was set
right in the middle.
And so I have to swim in order not to drown. Ahhh, how
 wonderful
it feels. Gosh, it's
really ice-cold. But I must have been
also *hot.* I don't know but it feels so
refreshing
being in this river, and swimming. I'm diving all the way down
 to the
bottom of the river. And I am feeling
rocks.
Soft rocks.
And fish are swimming by me. And I can breathe
under
water.
I'm not swimming aimlessly. It's as if I have to go to a place, but
 I am . . .
I think it is the river,
the pressure of the river
just
*carries* me in one direction. It is in the direction where I saw the

sun, actually, when I looked out of the cave. The sun was
straight ahead. And I have the feeling that's what I'm pushed at.
I feel really so good in the water.
I just don't feel like a fish. Oh, no. I feel like a turtle, actually,
because I am much *broader*. I'm not fish-like at all. I'm *broader*,
I am turtle-like, because I have to stabilize myself
with my whole body.
But I'm not a turtle. Oh, no. I am not a turtle at all, no,
now I am . . .
Ahh, it seems to be that there are rocks in the river now and I
can hold onto the rocks
and I
can climb out of the river.
It is a rock formation
that blocks the river partly. If I had gone at a certain area I could
have swum through, but I'm
actually happy
I'm out now. And I feel the warm sun on my body.
The Yellow One motions me to come off the rock.

It is a
desert landscape. There is no green. Nothing. There is the river.
And then there is sand. And that's it. And lots of rocks. No
plants. Nothing. The Yellow One is
weaving in and out and weaving in and out. Ahead of me. Like a
cloud, moving ahead of me,
motioning me
to follow him.

There is some
steam coming out of . . .
of the earth. And when I get closer
it is all yellow. Sulfur.
Lots of steam coming out. He motions me to sit
where the steam . . .

The steam goes at a certain direction and he wants me to sit
right there, where the steam comes out.
The smell of the sulfur doesn't bother me at all now. It goes
right through me.
The Yellow One says,
> *Stop talking and let the . . .*
The steam is so clear, the steam is to clean me. Yes. I am again
cautioned not to talk.
The steam is burning my insides out.
My whole body is yellow crystals.
I have to leave in this state.
> Thank you, Yellow One. The drum is calling. I have to go back.
> All beautiful crystals, thank you.
He's taking me
and we are
flying back to the Summer Cave. I am going up the vortex.
I am running through
the tunnel
and out. Under the spiderweb.

---

##  Reflections

Ema's Quest. "I like to have a visit with the Yellow One."

Ema's Response. "Never in my life did I think I would have such
a marvelous journey. This was *outstanding*! Just outstanding. I
mean—gosh!"

Ema's Interpretation and Evaluation. "It was a cleansing, definitely,
more so than ever, even though I didn't ask for it. He said, 'Cry all
the pain you have within you.' Ice water cleansed me right there.
  "It was probably a gift of the Yellow One that he put something
within me to keep me strong. I do not know because nothing was
being said. I just had these yellow, these beautiful little crystals. But

I had the feeling something was taken out of me and the yellow crystals were put in.

"That was marvelous. I didn't expect much at all. I had the feeling I might not be received."

Counselor's Comments. What appears to be an innocent, benign, even social request ("a visit with the Yellow One") becomes a journey Ema calls significant in retrospect. She discovers within herself a well of pain previously unknown to her, as well as its resolution. As she remarks after the journey, this experience was a quite unexpected gift. Such journeys powerfully reach beyond preconceived notions and offer the opportunity to consider the power of a wider world than that of everyday reality.

# Middle World Lesson

*Today I would like to go—to the Middle World and talk to Spider and ask him why I was denied entrance to the—Lower World?*

*Why I was denied entrance to the Lower World?*

*Why I was denied entrance to the Lower World?*

> I am walking down
> toward the big oak tree.
> No spiderweb
> at the entrance. But I see
> some spider legs
> sticking out between the bark of the oak tree. There seems to be
>   sort of hollow, and I see some legs
> sticking out.
>> Spider, I
>> want to talk to you.
> Spider is coming out.
>> I want to ask you, Why did you deny me the entrance to the
>>   Lower World?
> He is shriveling up. And, in effect, when he came out of the hole
>   he was already sort of bedraggled. He *looked* sort of bedraggled
>   and now, he seems to shrink even more.
>> I want you to look at me in the eyes, Spider. I want you to
>>   tell me
>> what the reason was.
> I must admit
> I do, still, being here and talking to him, I still have a residue of
>   *anger* in me.
> I'm not saying that to Spider, but maybe he senses it, I do not
>   know.

I don't believe it!
Raven has come and ate him.
  Raven!
Raven has flown down, and just
ate him up.
The spider.
I wanted to ask him why he didn't let me in
the Lower World and now
I will never know, will I now?
Raven says,
   *No matter.*
He says,
   *You can be curious but you don't have to know. It's of no*
    *importance.*
  Does it mean you are
  in all three levels? I mean, I have met you in the Lower World.
   And I know you left me the feather
  in the ordinary world and we are still in the Middle World.
  What are you then? I mean how do I address you? How?
Raven says to me,
   *Don't get complicated now.*
  Well, you are right. I am confused because
  I wanted to know
  why I wasn't allowed to get
  to the Lower World. However, you are right. It has been all
  taken care of. So you think I should just leave the past be
   the past?
Raven just walks back and forth and back and forth in a way as
 if he feels sort of
*bored* by my talking.
   *Then, should I explore the Middle World?*
Raven says to follow
him
and he is going to the Lower World with me.

I am walking and he's sitting on my shoulder. He's nibbling on
my ear. And he is nibbling in my hair.
Now we are coming to the lava
wall. The whole tunnel is made of lava rock, but there is this area
where I
incised
a raven once, and that's where we are. That's where I'm standing
now and
Raven.
We are
going right
through the lava, through the other side.
We are coming to a big hall. Raven just
looks at me
and says,

> Don't concern yourself with the Middle World.
> All right, am I not ready yet?

I ask him whether I am not ready yet.
He doesn't answer me.
Something very curious. This is a cave. But in the middle of the
cave is a huge redwood tree. I think, yes, it is a redwood tree.
And, he takes me
and flies
with me up
to the very top.
The top seems to grow out of the cave, and
I can see now
an area which I, in the Lower World, have never been before. It is
blue sky; the landscape is green
and lush. No trees, however. Meadows.
Very peaceful.
Raven suddenly says to me,

> Enjoy the ordinary world, Ema. Enjoy the ordinary world.
> There is much beauty to be seen.

*Don't concern yourself with the Middle World.*
Was Spider my enemy?
Why did he want to kill me, Raven? Why?
   *It's in the past,*
Raven says.
   *It's in the past. And because*
   *Spider is dead, no reason to ask questions*
   *of the past.*
Did he want to kill me? I just got to ask.
   *No, you don't,*
Raven says.
Raven says to me,
   *I am helping you here. Don't live in the past, it's no good.*
He says I should forget the whole episode.
   Am I not ready yet for the Middle World?
   *The Middle World is of no benefit to you. Of no benefit*
   *to you,*
he says and he stares me in the eye.
   All right. I forget the whole episode.
I only now realize that we actually sit in a nest. I guess it is
  Raven's nest. It is *really nice.*
Very comfortable here.
I suddenly feel as if I am in an egg.
In a blue egg. It feels so
comfortable in here, so peaceful.
   Oh, Raven, I am sorry for being so stubborn. The drum is
    calling me. I have to go back.
And so he picked me up. I'm still in the egg, and he is flying
  down with me.
And we are going *right*
through the wall. And, the moment I went, hit the wall, the egg
split.
And now I'm on the other side, and I'm I, myself again.
And I am running very fast.

Now I have to climb some roots, in order to be in the ordinary world again.

 **Reflections**

Ema's Quest. "Today I would like to go to the Middle World and talk to Spider and ask him why I was denied entrance to the Lower World."

Ema's Response and Evaluation (after prompt regarding whether her question was answered). "I just got my answer pat, so what am I gonna say? [laughing] Can you imagine? I just . . . [more laughing] . . . I'm sort of speechless."

Ema's Interpretation. "It was a marvelous journey. I got the answer and, obviously, I'm not ready for the Middle World. He said, 'Enjoy the ordinary world. There is much beauty to be seen.'

"The egg has such a meaning. It seems he wanted to . . . as if he realized he probably was a little harsh to me, and so was a gift that I suddenly was sitting in the egg.

"Why did he [Raven] eat the spider? For me, I thought it was important, but has obviously no meaning for my benefit of any kind. I probably should . . . it's of no benefit anymore, for whatever it was, it's of no concern, so I should just forget it. It was not the answer I was expecting."

Counselor's Comments. In a solo journey outside of a session, Ema finds herself denied access to the Lower World by Spider. The present journey follows up on that previous one, stimulating Ema's curiosity and self-observation. Raven pointedly advises Ema about engaging in the Middle World's nonordinary reality aspect.

Note: In Ema's nomenclature, Middle World refers to the nonordinary reality or spiritual aspect of the Middle World, while she calls the ordinary reality aspect of the Middle World "ordinary reality" or the "ordinary world." Recall that in HSC, as is largely found throughout shamanism, there are three worlds: the Upper World, the Lower World, and the Middle World. The Upper World and the Lower World are solely spiritual (nonordinary reality), while the Middle World has both spiritual and conventional aspects (nonordinary reality and ordinary reality).

# Another Healing of My Eyes

*I like to visit Turtle and ask her to heal my eyes.*

*I like to visit Turtle and ask her to heal my eyes.*

*I like to visit Turtle and ask her to heal my eyes.*

I am walking down the hillside. The leaves are very high. The
leaves go *almost* to my knees. Ahhh, it is a very nice feeling.
The entrance to the Lower World has leaves around it.
Free the entrance.
They are not oak leaves. They are different leaves. Large ones.
I'm taking some leaves with me. I don't know why.
Now I am in the tunnel. The leaves are very dry, and brittle. I
crumble them in my hands.
They give a *very nice smell.*
My hands have the wonderful fragrance of these leaves.
I [am] nude and put my fragrant hands,
the leaves,
over my whole body so I would have the fragrance over my
body.
I cannot see myself.
I was there for a while in the nude. Now I seem to be dressed
again.
And now the fragrance is filling the tunnel and heat comes from
my body.

Raven! Raven, the last time I saw you . . .
Hi, Raven, how is your foot?
The last time I saw you, your foot was crippled.
You're not crippled anymore.
That looks really good, doesn't it?

Raven is pecking on my hair. And he is eating the leaves.

He is also surrounded

by this fragrance.

He is flying ahead of me

and we are going into the cave.

The Turtle Cave.

He is banging with his beak at the shell. He is going into the
shell.

    Oh, Turtle.

He is already picking on Turtle's shell. But Turtle doesn't mind.

    Oh, Turtle, I am worried about my eyes.

    They could not put the pressure on my eyes.

    Please help me to reduce the pressure, and the fear, and take
      the fear away from me that I have.

Raven is pecking like a mad bird.

    Please stop! I cannot concentrate when you do this.

Turtle motions me to sit down.

The whole room is perfumed with the smell of the leaves. I have
never smelled something like it before. Just marvelous. More
like tobacco, almost. It's like tobacco but has a *sweetness* to
it, but

not too sweet.

Not overwhelmingly sweet.

Turtle is coming closer to me and

she's nibbling on my feet and my legs

and she is coming closer to my face

and her breath is the same

fragrance.

Turtle also has the fragrance on her.

We are bound together

by this fragrance.

The three of us, linked together as one entity.

It is Raven who suddenly pecks at my eyes. And even though he
pecked at my eyes we were still linked. He used to be small, and

then became big. Raven's beak is immense.
I have the feeling that the fragrance has anaesthetized me
because I didn't feel anything, even though he was working on
  my eyes. On the other hand, maybe there was no brain.
I do not fear
Raven. I can only feel that he is pecking.
Mmmm.
I think that he opened up my skull, because he is not frontal.
  Umph.
He opened up my skull. Reaching all the way to my eye.
Something is very softly touching the round of my eye.
The fragrance is immensely strong now.
Almost makes me want to fall asleep. I have lost myself
  completely. I'm blending into Turtle and I am blending into
  Raven.

I'm lost.
It is a marvelous feeling
Absolutely marvelous.
I'm floating in water and I am opening my eyes and I am in
  water. They are swimming. We are swimming as one entity.
Yeah, we are the fragrance. We are not mass anymore. All three
  are the fragrance. The fragrance being surrounded by water.
I realize this is an immense gift.
      Ah, Turtle!
Floating.
Being nothing.
Being nothing but fragrance. I can't speak anymore.

Raven
is suddenly Raven again, and he's putting the pieces together.
The drum
calling me back.
I'm a tiny little human, and he flies with me
through the tunnel.

And now he just pushes me out through the opening.
And I am back.

---

 **Reflections**

Ema's Quest. "I like to visit Turtle and ask her to heal my eyes."

Ema's Evaluation. "Something very softly is touching the round of my eye."

Ema's Interpretation. "We [Raven, Turtle, and Ema] are bound together as one, by this fragrance."

Counselor's Comments. The health of her eyes is a repeating theme. This is consistent with the understanding that serious health issues often require more than one (even many) shamanic treatments of the spiritual aspects of a condition. Ema takes advantage of what she finds works; that is, both her ophthalmologist and her shamanic helping spirits. She has been diagnosed with a progressive, non-curable condition, and the prospect of losing her sight is a grave concern, compounded by living alone.

Ema asks for direct healing of her eyes and, also, she asks what she can do to maintain her eye health. She has had the experience of eye health improvement following her shamanic journeys for that purpose. In addition to her treatment by her ordinary reality physician, when her eye problems began to recur she returned to what she perceived as helpful in the past—spiritual help through her journeys.

In this important journey, her request to Turtle within the journey is more elaborate than stated in the outset intention. It also includes an additional need. The potential for misunderstanding or misinterpreting the journey is compounded where there are multiple parts to the request. Ema, Turtle, and Raven blend together, or merge, during this journey, which Ema poignantly describes, joining in unity, a classic shamanic experience.

As is her frequent wont, Ema offers no immediate response or summary at the end of the journey. Her interpretive comment is suspended by her observation of herself merging with two spirit helpers in fragrance. It is this experience that becomes her primary interest in discussion, secondary to the original intention for the journey. In this journey, Ema receives more than she requests. A reasonable direction for Ema to further consider the meaning of this journey is for her to examine how the totality of all that happened after she made her request of Turtle is an answer to her entreaty that Turtle heal her eyes.

# A Milestone Journey

*I like to go to the Lower World to the Kailas area to meet Vulture.*

*I like to go to the Lower World to the Kailas area to meet Vulture.*

*I like to go to the Lower World to the Kailas area to meet Vulture.*

I am walking down
the hillside
toward the oak tree.
The opening is *quite clean* and *clear.* And I jump right
into it.
The tunnel is
still somewhat moist. I still see
moss
at the walls.
Moist.
I am walking.
The tunnel is well-lit.
Water oozes out of the wall
where Raven
normally meets me.
I walk
through the Turtle Cave. That is the only way I know how to get
   to the area where normally meet Vulture.
The cave
is very dry. I go to another cave and then the second one
with the vortex.
It brings me up
to the Winter Cave,
which overlooks

the area.

Vulture is

hugging me from behind. I can't believe that he is already there.

But I cannot look around.

He squeezes me so tightly.

> Vulture,

> you're hurting me.

He's squeezing me so tightly.

I hear all my bones breaking

like glass.

I have the ability to see my skeleton. It is broken into

tiny fragments.

They look greenish.

A wind

or the flapping of wings. Ah, they took all the fragments with
   them,

the wind

or the wings. I don't really know where the

source of wind came from.

Oh, my God! What will happen to me?

I am flying and I have the feeling I have sort of materialized into
   Vulture.

I see

the landscape from above. It is a

typical Tibetan landscape. I see the river, like a little silver

snake

through the landscape. No sign of

plants anywhere. *Beautiful*

rocks. A very solitary landscape. Just beautiful.

I am not only

with him,

Vulture,

I feel I also have wings. And whilst I'm gliding, every so often I
   have to steer

to stay on
course, because, it seems to me as if there is a certain
area we have to fly to. Or something within me is just
*pointing me* in this direction.
Now
I'm going.
I'm made to fly down
to a . . .
Oh, *yeah*! That is the area where I got
my first
initiation! Ah.
Ahh, the Native is here.
    I haven't seen you for so long.
The Native is an Indian
I met, oh, way back
at the beginning of my journeys. And he is
there and
some other
people.
Painted.
Dark-skinned men painted with white,
having white paint on their bodies. It is the same.
It seems to be as if I am back in time, because it is the same.
Or is it?
They sent me
into the
mountain. Into the outcrop. I have to go deep, deep inside,
  which I remember I did before.
I am not Vulture anymore.
They motion me to go deep, deep, deep inside.
Ahhhh! There, I see myself sitting
within fire. And I'm motioned by my self
to go
into the fire and merge with myself.

The fire is cold.

Even though it is cold, what I now say is probably not right, but
it burns

the whole fiber of my body, but not with a

*hot* flame, but a *cold* flame.

The Native is coming. But he is dressed in Vulture

outfit and he motions me to follow him.

I still remember

when I was initiated

I sat in this cave. For months. I was dying. But this time I had to
sit only

very few minutes, it seems.

Now, the men are dancing

in a circle. They are all males.

They open the circle and let me in. And they let also the Native
in, being still

in Vulture clothes. And I myself, looking at me now, I am also in
Vulture clothes.

I am human, but it seems as if I wear sort of

an *outfit*

that resembles Vulture.

The Native now motions me.

He's dancing

and he motions me

to follow

his dancing.

The men are sitting down again

and seem to

blow on pipes

that are made out of bones. Maybe bones from Vulture, I don't
know. They look like

flutes. Very thin. Thin like a finger, but they give

beautiful sounds. So high that I guess

as a human I probably couldn't hear it, but being Vulture

I can hear it, in the back of my head.
In the back of my head, I hear
the sound
of these flutes.
Ahh, God.
I am dancing.
Tears just come down.
The *sound*
of the flutes . . .
My brain, in the back of my head. It is a *feeling*.
     Vulture, *don't*. I cannot lose myself. Don't.
I see myself on the ground. I think I collapsed.
They put white paint all over me.
     Oh! Ah. Oh, I don't want to lose myself.
Suddenly Vulture is there. Not the Native, but really Vulture. He
   makes the men to stop.
     Oh, Vulture,
     I had ignored you so long. I am so sorry. I am so sorry. Good
       Vulture.
Vulture just stares me,
stares into my eyes.
He motions me to follow him.
Vulture is walking
in a very strange manner. And we are going to the water,
to the river. He wants me to go into the cold water; it is icy-cold.
   And all the heat that was on my body, just, with a swish,
disappears. The white paint
disappears.
     Vulture, I would like to come to you ever so often. I need your
       *strength*.
     Did you send the turkey vulture to me yesterday?
The huge vulture becomes small, and
he is
like the turkey vulture I saw yesterday. Just for a second and

then, he is he himself again. The huge one
I am normally afraid of. This time I am not afraid of him.
I know it is very strange that I would say it, but I feel like I am a
  brother to him. I feel as if I'm male, even though I'm
not. I have my human form again, my female form. But toward
  him I feel sort of
a brotherly love.
I cannot explain it and I don't want to.
    What just happened to me, Vulture? Explain it to me.
He isn't saying anything; he is just looking at me.
He has this
immense, clear, beautiful eyes
and his feathers have this beautiful, sort of shiny
appearance.
He said to me,

> *Don't be afraid*
> *in any world you are living in.*
> *You have gone through something today*
> *that will give you strength,*
> *more than you ever needed. More than you ever need.*

I am completely penetrated by these eyes.
    Why is the fire *cold?*
He says it's the fire of spirituality. It's not the real fire,
the way I know in the ordinary world. The spirit has
completely and utterly engulfed me. That is his present.
For me to take wherever I go.
    Oh, Vulture.
I feel so hot again. I have to go back into the water.
And when I go in the water,
the water around me feels suddenly warm. It seems as if I have
  so much heat within myself
that I don't feel the ice,
the ice-cold water.
Ohhh!

I want to get out but

Vulture motions me to stay. He says I have to get my balance. I
    have to stay in the water till he tells me to come out.

I just have to enjoy this, I cannot talk.

Now he motions me to come out.

And he put his feathers around me like a big towel

to dry me off. Now he picks me up.

I feel completely renewed.

He flies with me

to Kailas.

I see the big crater within.

It is all under snow.

He says to me,

> *Meet me there next time.*

Then we are flying back.

The *drum* is calling. We are flying back to the
cave. And I go down the vortex. Running through Turtle Cave.
    Along the tunnel. And now I'm out.

---

###  Reflections

Ema's Quest. "I like to go to the Lower World to the Kailas area to
meet Vulture."

Ema's Initial Response and Evaluation. "That was too much. Oh,
God. What a journey that was. . . . I sort of take this one extraordinary serious. The journey today was so profound. That certainly
was a dismemberment, if there ever was one."

Ema's Interpretation. "When I asked him about the fire and he said
it was a spiritual fire and he was giving it to me, I thought, 'Oh,
my God.' Before, I was always sort of in awe for Vulture and I had
the feeling as if he just kind of didn't take me seriously, because I
still had to learn so much. This time he took me as an equal. This
time he was not talking down to me, but taking me as an equal.

That's what the whole journey was about. I guess he has accepted me as an equal, in a way."

Counselor's Comments. A simple, straightforward intention to meet Vulture in the Lower World, without an otherwise purposeful agenda, becomes for Ema a milestone journey. Transformation, reunion with a spirit long-absent from her journeys, ceremony, and renewed initiation memories made present experience culminate in ecstasy and the aid of Vulture, one of Ema's helping spirits. After listening to the replay of this journey, Ema details her further understanding of a more equal relationship with one of her helping spirits, Vulture.

# Death and Resurrection

*I want to go to the Lower World today, to meet Vulture—at the, the Kailas Crater.*

*I . . . want to go to the Lower World today to meet Vulture, at the Kailas area, Crater.*

*I want to go to the Lower World today to meet Vulture at the Kailas Crater.*

Nothing.
I'm walking down
the hill.
I see a vulture, a turkey vulture, to my right, sitting
in the grass, just looking at me. And I don't quite know what I
   should do.
I have arrived at the tree now, and I look back, and he's still
   sitting there. Like a statue.
I am hesitating.
He pays no attention to me.
Well, I jump into
the entrance
and . . . it is dark
and I have the feeling as if one or two birds
are flying ahead of me.
Okay, I can't see anything, but I am following the birds,
the sound of the wings.
'Tis swishing sound.
They're
leading me

where I think I normally go, because we haven't come to the fork
  and I'm going
to the right.
By God, it's Turkey Vulture! He's with me in the
Turtle Cave.

I'm hesitant. I don't quite know what to think.
I was thinking about the *huge vulture,* but I know that the huge
  vulture also can be Turkey Vulture.
Now he's walking ahead of me. The Turtle Cave is sort of lit. We
  go to two other caves and
he, just gets me by the neck
and we go up the vortex together.
Skeleton bones.
Skeleton bones?
In the cave.
The skull,
all kinds of bones
lying there.
I *see* in the corner. And, I see, uhhh,
*flesh.*
Vulture motions me to
take the
flesh pieces.
Ahhhhh! He wants me to put the skeleton together.
I—e-eeeee-ayeee-yiii.
Ohh.
Ahh.
Ah! Ayeee.
He and I,
we are both pulling
the flesh.
And
I have to put the veins in first. And, the heart. All the

intestines. It is all there. And I can.

It was *all*

neatly stacked in the corner. And it has no

smell. It was

fresh and clean and I just

seem to know where everything goes.

Actually, I do it

rather quickly.

Ahhh. I'm in trance, sort of.

Aeyeeee.

I have to get

the flesh now and

sort of

put it

all together.

It seems to cling

right where it is supposed to be. For whatever reason, I seem to
  take the right pieces and

I have been starting with the feet and

I . . .

It's no blood involved.

The veins are not . . .

It's empty. I just put it all together, no blood. No liquid.

No liquid.

Ahhh!

I had a moment of fear, that I could not

put the human together.

It's

the Native. Oh, God!

It's

the Native. I put him all together

and, now, how do I . . . ? How do I make him alive?

Ohhhhh.

    Oh, Native,

what happened to you?

I take him in my arms but I know that will not help.

I

take him in my arms. And I . . .

Yes. The cave is way up high and I

want to go down

and go with him to the river.

I

must be awfully strong because, I hold him in one arm and with
    the other I go down

roots. All the way down

to the valley.

Vulture is flying about me.

It's very hard work for me,

getting down.

Now, I lost the grip of the roots. And I'm just falling.

Ohh, but

I'm landing on a bush, or something, and I'm still having

the Native

in my arm.

Oh, it is so hard!

I'm carrying him now

to the water, to the river,

and I go with him into the water.

I have to *say* something.

    Oh, Vulture, what am I to do now? Teach me. How do I . . . ?

        He was my teacher. How . . . ?

For this moment I ask Vulture what I should do.

I didn't watch

and the body has disappeared. I guess the

*current*

is so strong, and

it has taken him away.

It's

floating. I can't see him anymore. I mean, it's floating
toward
the sun,
toward
the mountain,
toward Kailas.
And I myself
am now carried away by the water. I can't hold on to anything.
I am partly underwater, but I can breathe under
water.
It goes with lightning speed.
It goes so fast I can't even . . . I hope I don't bump into any
rocks. Because
I just . . .
As fast as it goes,
something seems to steer me
away from
these rocks I've just talked about.
I was so afraid I might hit them.
Mmmm.
We are at the
*foot* of the mountain, and the
Native is there
alive.

    Oh, Native, I think what I did to you, it was all a dream, was it?
He could not have been dead; I mean, could not,
I mean, this is not possible, is it?

        *Life and death. All one. Life and death. All one. All one.*
    Yes.
    Yes.
    Yes, I understand.
    Yes.
    We die
    and we are born again.

Who knows?

Yes.

Ever and ever.

Yes.

I look it up the mountain.

Oh,

Native, I cannot go up there; that is so

high up. That's where Vulture wants to meet me. How can I
possibly . . . ?

It would take me months. I'm not a good mountain climber,
you know.

The Native

motions me

to go into

there. There is a cave, and we go into the cave.

It's sort of lit. It's not a cave. I don't really know what it is but, it's
a tunnel,

sort of.

Well, Vulture is there.

Vulture, what . . . ?

I mean,

where am I?

He says I'm in the crater.

But,

ah yes, of course, the crater. Yes. Yes. Yes. Of course.

In ordinary world I would have climbed *up*

And then *down* again in the crater, and this time, I just had to
go . . .

*Very clever.*

Very clever!

Where's the Native?

What happened to me there?

With Native, I mean.

Vulture looked at me. He doesn't say anything, but

it is

relayed to me that

the vulture, that . . .

The Native just explained it to me, what happened.

 Yes, I know. And I understood it, too. Sorry for asking again. It
  seemed to be so
 unreal, I didn't know, you see.

The creatures are all within me then.

 *Always have been,*

it's related to me.

 *Always have been.*

 Yes. Yes, Yes.

I am still

sort of shaken, a little bit.

And in fact, I'm shaking.

He asks me why I am

so shaken.

 Well, it doesn't happen to
 the person every day to . . .
 to put the Native together, I mean the way I had to. It's just . . .
 It takes me a time to get used to the fact,
 what was asked of me.

He says I should not be afraid of death.

 Oh, my God. What are you trying to say? What are you trying
  to teach me?

I have my own thoughts at the moment; I cannot talk about
 them.

Vulture is,

with his huge beak, he is sort of

*hitting* me

on the head. Not a lot, just a bit as if to jog my memory, as if to

help me

digest what just happened to me.

He motions me to look.

The sun is

south, I guess. It is the opposite, it must be north. He motions
  me to look to the northern side.

> Oh, my God. What are you doing to me?

Skeletons,

ahhh, ahhh, ahhh,

as far as I can see.

Skeletons. Not only humans. Also animals. Elephants! Oh!

> What are you doing to me? What do you want to teach me?

Now, I see them all

*alive.*

Elephants!

Penguins!

Little babies.

All, all, all.

Masses. Now they are all skeletons again.

> Well, what is the meaning?

> > *Life and death. All life and death.*

Ahhh.

> Oh, I know. Why are you teaching it to me now? Oh, the drum
> is calling, I have to leave. Oh, Vulture, you have to bring me
> back. I cannot go on my own.

Something is picking me up. I don't know what . . .

but I'm carried

with lightning speed

toward the cave.

> Thank you, Vulture. Thank you for teaching me.

Oh, I am still not back; I have to run. Ohhh!

Down the vortex.

Oh, now. I'm out!

## ❧ Reflections

Ema's Quest. "I want to go to the Lower World today to meet Vulture at the Kailas crater."

Ema's Evaluation. "I don't . . . Well, I think . . . I'm always so surprised, you know. I thought I would fly there and that was it—and then I found that skeleton. What do you make of it? Me, putting it together."

Ema's Interpretation. "This seems to be about life and death this time . . . all of humanity and the animals. Life and death, it's all the same. It comes and it goes. 'Don't be afraid of death,' he [the Native] said to me."

Counselor's Comments. Here, much to her surprise and, perhaps, some dismay, in partnership with Vulture Ema becomes an instrument of putting a dismembered individual back together, re-membering, him. As she searches within her journey for the meaning of her participation, she is given powerful teachings about her spiritual relationships, which she struggles to understand. Although Ema initially does not know what to make of her journey, upon recalling it and talking it through, she gets a clear understanding of its message. In the discussion, Ema notes that she understood it then, in the journey, "but now, being here, my questioning mind comes into it again. The whole journey was about death."

Her thorough grounding in journey methods serves to keep her fully aware and functioning in each reality, at will. Ema notes that from this point onward, all of the journeys take on special significance to her.

# Asking to Heal My Need
# to Eat to Feel Good

*I want to ask Vulture—to heal my need—to eat to feel good.*

*I want to ask Vulture—to heal my need—to eat—to feel good.*

*I want to ask Vulture to heal my need to eat to feel good.*

I'm out on my porch
and in order to get to the oak tree, down the hill, I would have to
　climb down
another oak tree
that is
growing over the porch.
Vulture is already sitting there. Like a statue. I don't really know
　what I'm doing, but
he is not at all moving, so I'm just picking him up, and put him
　under my arms, and
climb down the oak tree.
I am walking down the hill with Vulture under my arm. It's a
　statue
but it has feathers and everything.
I'm not quite sure whether I should meet Vulture outside now.
　I've never brought anything with me.
I'm hesitant.
Vulture seems to come alive suddenly and he just
jumps into the
entrance, of the
oak tree, and I just follow him.
It is dark.

He's flying ahead of me. I'm following the sound of the
wing beats.
I don't know where I am going, which normally I really don't
  like, but I trust Vulture completely.
Suddenly I don't hear any more
wings. I'm all by myself in the dark.
It feels really nice
being in the dark.
I'm not frightened. Not now. Not yet.
I hear water trickling
on the walls. They must be very moist.
I do smell moss. So I'm
testing. I'm just trying to get close to the walls and
I *feel* the water.
Not much. It is just a very
little water
*oozing* out of the walls. But, it feels *moist*
and it *smells* so good. I think it's the moss. I'm touching the
  moss now. It is so soft. Ah!
I'm touching the moss.
I feel the urge to eat it. Not because I am hungry but because I
  want to
internalize the softness.
Oh, I wish I could eat it; I would like to internalize the softness.
  Should I eat it?
I'm hesitant.
I'm putting my tongue out in order to get the moisture, the
  water. And it tastes *so*
*refreshing.* I have the urge to also
eat from the
moss, not using my hands, just using my mouth. And yet, I'm
  hesitant.

    Vulture, what is this supposed to mean?
    Help me, please.

Aahh! At the
corner of my eye, I saw something
to my right.
Like a flash. Like the flash of a
light. Like the flash of a star.
Just a
source of light.
But it is not there anymore.
I'm taking the moss in my hands, and put it on my navel,
on the area of my navel.
A light
is coming now from there. Green. Very light green. Beautiful.
   And I'm holding it toward my
navel. A little bit lower than there. That's where I think the
   *tan tien* is, the chi area.
I'm walking. Toward where I thought the flash of light was.
Mmmm.
It feels really good. Even though I have the feeling I'm not
getting anywhere.
I'm not *driven*. I'm not really *driven*. No, no. Oh, no. I'm not
   driven at all. If I don't see Vulture today then
I may see him another day when he has time for me. I'm just
   walking,
surrounded by this green light.
I have come
to the light source.
I don't know what it is. It is a light
that shines from down below.
A very bright light. But it is so far down.

Ugh! Something just
pushed me down.
But I'm not
falling fast.

It is as if I am . . .

No, no, as if I am on a cloud. And it just lets me down very
    gently. To the light.

I'm right in the middle of the light.

*Flames*

surround me.

Cold flames.

    Oh, Vulture, Vulture.

Vulture once told me that

when I am surrounded by cold flames,

it means fire of spirituality.

    Are you telling me I have lost my spirituality again, after just a
        few months?

    Oh, Vulture. Why? Why?

    Why am I not strong enough to even hold on to

    the spirituality?

    I always thought I . . .

The voice says,

    *This is no time for regrets. Look forward. Look closely*
        *within yourself,*

Something says to me,

    *No regrets.*

    How should I look

    within myself? Where is the place to look at? Oh, Vulture. Oh,
        Vulture.

    Where is the place to look at?

I still have the moss in my hand. It glows such a *beautiful* green.

Life,

Life,

Oh, life.

I talk to Vulture but I can't see him. I just

feel his presence.

    Vulture,

    please heal my need

to eat.

Oh, Vulture. I feel lonely sometimes, then I eat. Oh, oh. Oh, oh.

I'm completely split open. I mean, what I'm saying is, I don't
  know quite how to explain it. I feel whole. I see myself whole.
  And yet I am split open.

My soul, my spirit is a complete disarray. Oh, no. That is the
  hardest to keep in check.

Vulture, what can I do? Oh, tell me what can I do. Heal that
    part of me. Oh, please heal that part of me. What can I do?

I'm in complete disarray. I mean my thoughts are.

I suddenly see my brain

in compartments.

Ah! Something takes

the moss out of my hands, and puts it . . .

I don't know,

I think it is pressed into my brain. Oh, my God what a
  wonderful feeling. Ah! Oh!

Ohhh!

I saw my *brain*

and myself,

sort of gray.

And now with the

*green* pressed into it,

it has this healthy sheen of

sort of

*pink.* Oh! Oh, how beautiful.

Oh, Vulture. What does this mean? You know, I have
    difficulties to understand. Tell me the meaning.

I don't really know whether I'm told this, but

what is *relayed* to me seems to be that

I have to concentrate more, now. On myself. On the happenings
  within my body. Not from the ordinary world

perspective, but from the

unordinary, unordinary world,

the nonordinary world. Where everything is.
Where everything has a purpose. Everything needs time. Where
  you have to see your insides
a different way.

> *Throw away the education you had*
> *in the ordinary world, because that's not the way the*
>   *body is*
> *in the nonordinary world. We will have to teach you,*
> *about your body*
> *here, and that is what will help you*
> *out there.*

The
drum is calling. Oh, how sad! I wish . . .
Oh. I have to go back.

   Oh, Vulture, I do not know how to get back.

I am lifted up
and I'm guided.
I'm guided all the way
toward the entrance
with lightning speed.

   Oh. Vulture, oh, thank you so much. I think I understand what
     you're saying, but when I'm in the ordinary world, I
   I have to come back. Oh, thank you.

Oh, I hate to go. I am pushed out
with an immense force. And I am out
in the ordinary world. Again.

---

### 🐢 Reflections

Ema's Quest. "I want to ask Vulture to heal my need to eat to feel
good."

Ema's Evaluation. "Well, it was a very interesting journey. A very
deep one, I think. As always, I understood completely what was

said—in the nonordinary. And then my thinking comes in when I'm in the ordinary world, which I know would happen . . . yet, I think I know what was taught to me."

Ema's Interpretation. "I think Vulture wants me to internalize more. For example, when I walked, suddenly I heard noise like water running. Very softly. Then instantly, I smelled this wonderful green of the moss. I wanted to eat, not because of hunger. I wanted to internalize the softness of the moss. As if I need some kind of softening up within me. I have to bring this all together. That's the meaning of it, to pay more attention to what goes into me, what it will do, which I have never really paid any attention before. Also, to visualize what I'm eating, where it goes in my body.

"I think the healing, probably [was] right at the beginning, when I felt the softness, when I wanted to *eat* the moss, not for my hunger, but for the softness. I think that was an instant healing, too, and I have to go deeper into that, because there is a meaning there which I haven't quite grasped. . . . The healing started then.

"One of my great journeys."

Counselor's Comments. As the journeys proceed, Ema contributes more comments and observations about them and herself, incorporating them into her interpretations. The HSC counselor, on the other hand, has less and less commentary to offer. Ema integrated basic concepts, vocabulary, and journey methods, has developed her own journey style and firmly established relationships with her spirit helpers as she continues to meet challenges, to learn and grow in ordinary reality as well as in nonordinary reality.

# Introduced to Life in a
# Buddhist Monastery

*I like to meet Vulture—for him to introduce me—to the life—in a—
Buddhist monastery.*

*I like to meet Vulture—for him to introduce me—to the life—in a—
Buddhist—monastery.*

*I like to meet Vulture—to introduce me to the life—in a—Buddhist—
monastery.*

I'm still here in the room, I can't get off.
I am
walking down the hillside.
*Beautiful* colored leaves are lying on the ground.
I'm
right at the entrance of the oak tree. I'm just *hesitant.*
Something just *pushed me*
into the opening and I'm
in the tunnel.
It is very dry. It smells of dried moss.
I don't know whether the tunnel is smaller. Normally when I
go in the tunnel
everything is
sort of free.
But now I'm walking on it, I'm hit, not hit, I mean it is just
*very soft.* The ceiling of the tunnel
has lots of moss and soft roots
that are hanging down, and, sort of
hitting
my face. Hitting is not the right word. Just

Sort of *softly*.
I am *softly*
hit by those
dried plants.
Very dry. Everything is very dry.
My step sounds hollow. It sounds very hollow in my brain,
  almost as if
my head is sort of
*empty* and
the steps I'm making sounding, resounding,
in my head.
There is a voice in my head.
I cannot quite believe it whether this is already true but it seems
  as if something is saying
"Om," in my head. I don't believe it, but
it is really true.
With each step
there is this
"Om" in my head.
And it reverberates
through my whole body. Like, "step, Om, step, Om." It just goes
  through my whole body.
I am going very slowly; I would like to go faster but it is just not
  possible.
It is as if I am already in a
meditative state.
And instead of going
where I normally meet Vulture, it seems to me as if this, the path
  I'm walking,
is leading me low, lower. With each step
I seem to go deeper and deeper
into the
earth.
I am led by instinct. I am closing my eyes.

I have my eyes closed and I seem not to be able to open my eyes.
  And yet I feel light.
I just, one step,
"Om." Another step, "Om,"
just reverberates through my whole body.

*Oh!* I think I am already in the temple.
I don't know. I don't really know what a monastery is like.
I am
in a room. It is very colorful.
Lots of red.
There is a noise, somehow.
I have to readjust something.
Something is just not right. I have an extra noise in there.
Oh, maybe that was it. Was there a lot of banging? Oh, right.
  Right. That's interesting, because something was just not right.
Let's see what happens.
I'm still in that room. Lots of carvings. The red.
Red. And gold.
Painting or lacquer,
I do not know.
The colors are just very vivid.
Beautiful. It's a beautiful room I am in.
Lots of Tibetan gods.
I see Manjusthri. But he's not alive.
I see Tara.
The Green One. And many I do not know by name.
I am very much drawn to the . . .
Yes, I am very much *drawn* to the . . .
Ah! These are the creatures
I met so many years ago, and are so kind enough to be within
  me at times when I need them. I see them
as statues.
A voice says behind me, I am not supposed to touch them.
  I turn around and

an older *man* is there but he . . .
I don't quite . . .
He has a face like a human but
he is dressed in feathers, vulture feathers.
I hear myself apologizing to him. He asks me how I got there.
I tell him I don't know. That I had asked Vulture
to introduce me to a monastery, and I don't know how I got
  here. But that
the creatures I
*touched* were familiar to me
and that they sometimes
are within me
when I need them.
I ask him whether he is the only one.
He just lifts his finger. And indeed I hear
song. Not song. It is *wording*
and song together.
I ask whether I can join
in this
song.
He says,
       *No.*
I ask him why he wears
feathers.
He isn't saying anything. I tell him that
I am not familiar
with the etiquette. I don't even know whether this is a
  monastery or a temple. I apologize again. He says to me that I
  do not belong here. And I say,
   Where do you want me to go?
He motions me
to go to a . . .
what I thought was a wall, but it turns out to be a
door. Very beautiful again, carved

with beautiful creatures on it.
The one creature is so . . .
It has *horns* and
it looks so scary, but, my God, I . . .
I'm so taken by it.
I'm just embracing it!
And, suddenly, the moment I embraced it
I am *suddenly* in the desert. As if where I was, was a dream.
But the *creature*
is still with me.
It takes me by the hand
and we
are *running as fast as* I
can hardly imagine
through the desert. It is almost like flying, but it isn't because
my feet
touch the ground,
but it is *sooo* fast.
We are stopping at a . . .
well.

It is a *lake,* a small lake, *ice-cold.* And, he motions me to look
    into the lake, and, *Oh, God!*
I'm looking exactly like the creature!
All red. With these
*magnificent* horns. These huge eyes.
And so suddenly, the creature is
putting his hand in the water
and it is all gone!
I'm still sitting at the lake. I feel sort of empty. And I still cannot
    quite comprehend what happened to me.
I'm just left alone.
I'm touching myself and my face,
I personally am still this creature, because I still can feel horns.

And I don't have really feet. My feet are like hoofs of an animal.
   And, it is as if I'm
all energy.
Even though I personally feel . . .
I really cannot quite explain this now . . .
I feel I'm surrounded and I, myself, energy. I feel it flowing
   though my veins.
      Oh, Vulture!
      Please come. I cannot make anything out of this.
I'm looking up
and there seems to be
a building
made out of . . .
chiseled out of rock.
Ah, oh, yes. Okay, so
it
is actually a cave,
I assume, but it is also
a temple, or
a building made as a temple? I go in
and it
seems to be

just
empty.
Everything is earthen.
Ah!
      Oh, Vulture, what is this?
Something says to me I should enjoy.
It is
*so old.* It is ancient! I mean, some of the statues are broken and
something says to me,
      *Then put them together!*
So, I'm still in my creature form, strangely enough. And whilst I
   have hoofs

as feet, I *do have hands.* And so,
I hardly touch the stones
when they
just, like magic, come together. And, now
the drum is calling and I have to go back. And I don't even know
  how to go back. Oh, God.
     Oh, Vulture, I have to go back.
But it seems that the creature
I am
suddenly takes over
on its own.
But, strangely enough, there is no temple. No temple.
I'm
coming up the steps. In the tunnel.
And I'm out.

---

 **Reflections**

Ema's Quest. "I like to meet Vulture, for him to introduce me to the life in a Buddhist monastery."

Ema's Response. "I was a cute little creature [laugh], otherwise, I don't understand anything."

Ema's Interpretation. "This Buddhist part is a completely new direction. One has certain ideas and then things come quite different. Maybe it just showed me a different way I should go. Maybe it wasn't even that strange after all. Maybe I'm just guided into a new thing."

Counselor's Comments. Having initiated this line of inquiry, Ema finds herself in a quite different environment that invites her to explore. With equanimity, she acknowledges "not knowing." She says this is an especially important journey.

Early in this journey, Ema adjusts her earphones and immediately continues her narration, skillfully managing both realities.

# Being Received in the Mystery Chamber

*I like to go to the Lower World—and be received at the Mystery Chamber.*

*I like to go to the Lower World to be received in the Mystery Chamber.*

*I like to go to the Lower World—and be received—in the Mystery Chamber.*

I am still here,
this room.
I am walking down the hillside.
The leaves are wet.
*Very* fresh smell.
The hole in the oak tree seems to be smaller today.
I climb right in.
I can smell the roots, this time
very fresh. Some are damp.
I take a few roots with me.
I am already in the chamber.
It's empty.
No fire.
The green light on the left side of the chamber gets
stronger.
I take some of the
roots I have and I, sort of, crumble them between my hands.
  And put it on the ground, because
the shrine is not . . .
It is like a television screen. I mean,
you

cannot touch it. It is
in this rock.
It cannot be touched. There seems to be an invisible
*force* that
keeps me at bay. And it is,
"television screen" I think was not the right word.
It is like a *painting*. But, it is not always there. Today it is there.
Whilst I cannot touch the painting, but, the force
that comes from this
mysterious
being
is immense.
And with it,
out of the depths of the earth, comes this rumble, again,
which I receive as "Ommmmm." But it is very
faint. Very faint. I can
hardly . . .
I am so mesmerized by this,
I do not like to say apparition, that's not really right. I really
  don't have *words* for it.
I have the feeling as if this being is made out of . . .
It's somewhat like
the Yellow One. It made out of,
oh,
*energy.*
I feel that there is a presence here and I turn around and
it is the Native.
He asks me,
> *You did write a list?*
Yes, I did write a list.
> *And you want it to come true?*
Yes,
but only if it doesn't interfere
with the spirits. I don't want anything forced,
not anymore.

I don't dare to ask questions.
I feel so small.
I am overwhelmed by the power
of the energy. I am starting sweating, but
no fire.
Frankly, I do not know what
question to ask. I'm confused,
not really confused, but I'm overwhelmed. I'm overwhelmed.
I have to sit down.
I couldn't stand anymore. I thought I would faint.
Oh, God!

> Why do I always feel so small in here? So terribly insignifi-
> cant?

I am told that if I want to walk
this path, I have to start all over again.
I was sort of
*pushed* into this. I don't really know how to adjust.
I was told that I don't have to worry, that I will be led.

> By whom?
> > *By the Energies.*

But I'm afraid of the Energies, because they make me so,
almost tired.
I don't feel energized
by the Energies,
*if that makes sense!*
I think I had my eyes closed. I, I don't really know, but
the whole chamber . . .
the elephants . . .
the elephant statues
are there, as if I was blind when I got in. It was as if they were
always there, because they are life-sized and *so strong*. And,
beautifully sculptured.
Ah!
I just feel I just had to go to one

and hold his trunk, so that I'm stabilized again.
The sound
from the
deepest core of the earth is coming
closer.
No fire.
I see the
back side of the creature.
*The Native*
has been a shape-shifter always.
It is like a film
that goes very quick. I see
all he is. Vulture, Snake,
some humans I don't know. It goes so fast I can't,
I can't follow it that fast, but also
the creatures,
the Yellow One . . .
Oooh, ooh!
He says to me,

> *I'm all this and so are you.*
> Yes, I know. I do understand that
> very clear.

The heat is leaving me and it is as a cool
steam.
It is not water, but it is like a wind
that is
enveloping me.
But it isn't. It's not a strong wind. *Cool.*
To cool me down.
You can see what was here once.
It is long gone.
As if
he was saying
that I would get my teachings

from the Ancient Ones.

Who are they?

I don't dare to ask again.

When the wind was

surrounding me, I felt so strong and so powerful

and now, I feel again, so small.

Am I ready?

Can I grasp it?

The Native says,

*You are here, aren't you?*

Yes, but I . . .

He has always the same . . .

It is always the same voice, but

he's always shifting; there is never a

moment that he is

stable.

He shifts and shifts and shifts.

I just would like to *grasp a piece*!

I would like to grasp a piece that makes him steady.

And suddenly the voice says,

*But you are not steady.*

*I am just showing you*

*you yourself.*

Oh, my God.

I had no idea that I was so much in uproar.

I thought I was balanced.

And I am told,

*Yes, you are. In the ordinary world, you seem to be quite*

*balanced. But on this path*

*you are not.*

I will have a long road ahead of me. This is so foreign to me. Oh,

God. This is so foreign to me.

But, on the other hand, *why not*!

It was as if the part that is

fearful and
in my brain somewhat dissolved.
And I'm sitting on the floor,
quite relaxed. The Native is sitting
opposite me.
He is a monk.
I don't know what to say. I feel intimidated.
Nothing is being said.
Nothing is supposed to be said.
I did not realize because I didn't hear the rumbling.
I'm not even sure whether this is
"Om." But it seems something coming from the core
of the earth. A very pleasant sound.
I feel so tired. But *happy*.
The
monk opposite me,
he has a very peaceful face but his eyes are closed and he smiles.
I see my list.
It cannot be.
I know it is on my mind.

> *Yes, it was written in a sacred way.*

   Ohhh, thank you. Thank you so much. I wasn't sure whether
     you could accept it.

I think I need input from both worlds,
The Lower and the ordinary.

   My brain is just very simple.
   Only at times
   there seem to be flashes.
   Then I seem to understand
   something I cannot express in words.
   And this is why I have chosen the way. And now you have
     pushed me here. As you said, you would guide me, 'cause I
     do not even know what questions to ask.

. . .

Yes.

. . .

Yes.

. . .

Yes.

Ahh! Yes!

I cannot worship him.

I cannot worship anything.

Thank you.

The

drum is calling.

"Ummm, ummmm."

Still not out.

Ah! I'm out.

---

 **Reflections**

Ema's Quest. "I like to go to the Lower World and be received in the Mystery Chamber."

Ema's Evaluation (after prompt about whether she accomplished her intention). "[quietly] I don't know. [loudly] Yes. I have this difficulty grasping it. I can't help it. [crying]"

Ema's Interpretation. "I now understand . . . it's energy. I cannot call it . . . optical illusion . . . mirage. Certain moments . . . my brain is clear and I can receive it.

"I was told I would get teachings. . . . He told me that . . . I was that. I was unsteady . . . Crying, the meaning is, I am okay in the ordinary world . . . it's only now I understand it was somewhat powerful . . . and then, that it was the beginning . . . new adventure.

"I'm stabilized here in the ordinary world, which I needed to be. . . . and now I am ready for more teachings that are going in a different way . . . so I'm at the beginning of that, which would be very interesting. . . . I also was in such a trance . . . what was taught to me was not from my brain . . . was from my . . . I cannot explain it. I all understood but cannot say it, because I am not there yet. I was very deep . . . very deeply gone."

Counselor's Comments. Ema introduces us to more details of her journey environment. Her immediate description of transformation so vivid and apt, invites clearer apprehension of the in-the-moment event. With it, the deeper spiritual message specifically for Ema, as well as a lesson of introspection: there is always more. Where early in her journeys, Ema is shy, retiring, and fearful, here she has a courageous, even joyous sense of adventure, as she accepts the challenge with, "Why not!"

Ema's ability to suspend disbelief in her journeys allows her to access wise insights, images, and experiences beyond her immediate comprehension.

# Asking Snake for a Healing

*I like to go to the Lower World to meet Turtle—and ask her to heal my gall bladder.*

*I like to go to the Lower world to meet Turtle and ask her—to heal—my gall bladder.*

*I like to go to the Lower world to meet Turtle—to ask her to heal my gall bladder.*

I am walking down the hillside.
Flowers all over.
Daffodils, lupines.
I'm afraid to go.
Something . . . sort of . . .
I cannot explain it. I feel I am asking *too much*. Nevertheless, I
   am going through the opening.
The tunnel that normally doesn't bring me to the Turtle Cave,
   but
I do not want to go back. I am just going forward.
I have landed in the Mystery Chamber. I see myself already on
   the ground.
All by myself.
It is dark
and yet I can see myself on the ground.
    Turtle, please . . .
No one there.
I am just *lying* there.
Oh, God. I should not have asked for it.
    Snake! What are you . . . ?
    I haven't seen you for so long. I thought I lost you.

Snake has come out of my navel.

I don't *know* what a gall bladder looks

like . . .

what looked like what I saw on the poster

in her mouth.

Oh, God!

She put it on the ground. I'm just so overwhelmed I couldn't say
 anything.

Her body is slimy

and the slime is just put onto my belly button. She is settling on
 my stomach.

Not heavy at all.

It warms . . .

from the insides.

Make my insides glow. It's a healing *glow*.

I can't say anything, but, I just *feel* the healing within me.

I feel very light and, I am getting up. Snake is hanging around
 my neck

and I see

herbs and

do not know what they are.

The fire pit . . .

I am told I should love it,

I mean, my gall bladder. I should pick it up

and

put it on the sacred fire

together with the herbs. Which I am doing.

I am told I have treated the gall bladder *very* badly.

> Yes, I know.

> Yes, spiritual healing. Yes, never thought of that before.

I'm very disconnected with my body.

The herbs are smoldering around me.

My gall bladder crystallizes. It is a *perfect crystal*. I am to touch it.
 I am to hold it. I'm holding it in my hands.

An absolutely gorgeous, perfect crystal.

Clear, like water.

    Turtle.

I don't know if Turtle was here all the time but

Turtle is coming out of the wall

and, she tells me to

swallow it.

        *Swallow it!*

I swallow it. Ahh!

I don't know where it is settling

but as I swallow it,

it seems to be sending

beams

out

to all my body. Especially my lower body.

    Oh, I feel so light.

    Oh, Turtle.

Meanwhile, the herbs . . .

so much . . .

I don't know how to say . . .

It's like fog. The fragrance from the herbs come like clouds

completely around me. Swirling around me. And Turtle, too.

  Where's Snake?

I want to *thank* Snake.

I haven't seen her

for so *long*. And yet she

comes

here

to heal me.

I have so many questions.

I don't dare. I don't dare to ask.

    Turtle. Can I take the healing with me into the ordinary world?

She is answering but I can't hear it.

The clouds of the herbs seem to put walls between us

and I can't hear what she is saying.

> That is all right. That is quite all right.
>
> I am so grateful.
>
> Protect me.
>
> Whatever you see fit.
>
> Here and in the ordinary world, I will take it there because I trust you.

One cannot live without trust. I have done it for so many years.
  I have
to come back to it,
to trust.

Ohhhhh. I'm all dissolved in tears. I always get weepy.

I am reminded of another journey.

I am being reminded that it is not healthy to keep tears in, that tears have nothing to do with strength.

It is good to relieve the tension.

I am getting *so hot.*

I am looking like a fireball. Energy! Spiritual energy! This is what I am at the moment. I can hardly see myself. I see *spiritual energy.* It comes from that crystal, which is lying in my *lower body.*

> How can I keep the crystal? How can I keep the crystal?
>
> > *You have to change your ways of thinking. You have to change your ways*
> >
> > *of feeding*
> >
> > *your body. Feed your body to keep it alive. You have to change your thought process.*
>
> Oh, my God. Yes!

What a fool I've been. Oh, God! I could have saved myself a lot of trouble.

Today is a new beginning. And I shall not forget
that,
that I have learned today. No matter what happens.
Apart from myself.

The drum is calling. I have to go back.
    Ah, please.
I'm still not myself. It is as if I am like a fireball
and I am just rolling through the path. And now I am myself
   again!

 **Reflections**

Ema's Quest. "I like to go to the Lower World to meet Turtle and ask her to heal my gall bladder."

Ema's Evaluation. "I can fill certain things in which I didn't say, because I learn more than I could say at the moment, actually. What was said to me was that when I eat, I should see eating as just to sustain me. . . . I have understanding of my spiritual body but not my physical body—and I have kept them apart. . . . And so, I . . . should embrace my physical body. I should put the physical and the spiritual body together. And, the main part is that . . . I should have a diet that keeps my physical body closer to my spiritual body. So that, maybe what is meant [is] that I would eat when I didn't have to eat. I would eat certain things even though I wasn't hungry or I would eat more than I should. I understood this and what I finally got it! It suddenly dawned on me that I have to change my ways completely. I should feed my body only so much that I am sustained . . . that I live. Period. That is what I understood."

Ema's Interpretation. "If I want to live the way I want to live—a spiritual way—then that's the way I have to go. I've been taught this before. I just was not ready for it."

Counselor's Comments. Clear and to the specific point, Ema phrases her purpose, accepts the journey as it presents itself, and receives Snake's ministrations and messages. The trust bond between Ema and Turtle further establish Ema's responsibility to her ordinary reality self.

# Meeting Turtle in the Abalone Cave

*I like—to go to the Lower World—and I would like to go—to the— Abalone Shell Cave to meet Turtle.*

*I like to go to the Abalone Shell Cave to meet Turtle.*

*I like to go to the Abalone Shell Cave to meet Turtle.*

I am walking
down the path
at Rodeo Beach.
It is hot.
I have reached that little bridge.
The poison oak is already
changing color.
I have arrived at the
bay tree. I have to take away some sticks and some
debris
in order to find that little
entrance.
I am
sliding down the entrance.
It's dark.
That's not good. Because I really don't know the
path that well. I don't have any inner light. I'm afraid to go. I
   have to sit down.
Something is pushing me
from behind
very gently. I just can't see anything. I'm not afraid, but

something is just
nudging me.
I still can't see. I'm still *pushed*
gently.

    Turtle, it is you?

I turn around
and I can't see anything, but I can feel it's Turtle.

    Oh, Turtle!

Turtle is pushing me
gently,
not saying anything.
Oh!
Ah.

I am in the Turtle Cave. I frankly don't quite know what
  happened to me. It was as if I was just for a minute, I lost my
  conscious or something. I don't know, because I am suddenly
  in the Turtle Cave.
The Turtle Cave,
ah, it has water in it and
the seaweed is just
moving back and forth.
Ah, it's really nice. I'm lying already in it. Mmmmm. That feels
  really good.
I have the feeling as if I don't want to do anything,
it is so lovely in here.
The water is
getting higher, a little bit. I just have my head sticking out.
Turtle says,

    *You have stopped eating seaweeds.*

I should start eating seaweeds again.

    Yes. You are right.

Turtle tells me I should be relaxed
with my eating habits. As of late

I'm so terribly scared that I will gain
the weight back, that I'm making myself completely crazy.
Turtle tells me that I should relax. The more I obsess about, the
   worse it will get. I should know this by now.
   I really wanted to thank you
   for helping me along. And also Snake. I just do not know
      where to find Snake anymore, since I had not seen her for so
      long, and I was so grateful that
   she helped me.

Turtle says to me that I seem to have forgotten
that Snake has been within me
for many years now.
That she is sleeping within me.
And that she,
when she is needed, she just
will help.
   I want to thank her properly. What should I do?
      *She is you and you are she.*
      *She knows all your feelings. All your thoughts.*
I am told that Snake is actually the closest to me.
That's why I don't seem to realize it, because Snake is so much
   part of me.
   I don't quite understand,
   I don't understand what you are saying.
What Turtle says is that
if I would *see*
with the eyes of my guiding spirits, I would see myself
as Snake quite frequently.
      *You have become a shaper-shifter,*
Turtle is telling me.
      *But Snake is more than that.*
   I know. I have
   been told in the Mystery Chamber. I mean,

I know that
shaping,
that everything goes through me
shifting.
I must admit I took it as
something
but I guess
maybe I really didn't quite understand and appreciate it.
    Yes, yes.
Turtle says that, now I know, I should not forget.
It is important
for me to know that I am not only the one, that I am the many!

I'm still in the water.
It is as if the seaweed is massaging my body. It feels really
  absolutely gorgeous.
    Turtle, I want to ask you something. About the
    abalone shell. Is it real? I mean,
    I wasn't sure.
    . . .
    Yes, I know, I know, I know, I know. I know.
    It was utterly gorgeous there.
    No. No. I don't want to be there.
    I was just thinking,
    Did I make it up?
        *No, not really.*
    I know.
Turtle says to me . . .
We have some
talk back and forth, but Turtle says I don't have to relay it.
Turtle says,
    *Don't wrack your brain*
    *in order to*
    *explain this.*

And now Turtle
just puts my head *underwater,* and
I can breathe underwater.
And when I see the *ground,* which normally I have never seen
   the ground actually because even
when it's dry, it has
seaweed on it. But now that the seaweed is waving
I can see the bottom
and, it seems to me that it has an abalone shell bottom.
I don't know where the light source comes from but
with each stroke of the
*seaweed,* it just opens little spots and I can see these
beautiful colors, shining. I don't know but it . . .
I think it's
like . . .
It's a shell! I do not know whether it's abalone, but it has
   beautiful colors. Yes, it has.
Even Turtle . . .
     Oh, Turtle.
Turtle's shell is completely . . .
It has the colors of an abalone shell suddenly.
But now they [seaweed fronds] touch it,
it is all gone. But now it is there again. And then when I touch it,
   it is gone again.
There's a teaching there but I don't get it. I don't really want to
   think.
It is so lovely here.
And Turtle
is very *playful.*
She motions me to look at my
feet,
the nails of my toes are abalone shell. Oh. And when I wiggle my
   feet, it's
gone again.

*Life comes and goes, comes and goes. Everything comes
and goes.
There's beauty
and there's ugliness. You have to love both.*
I know.
I know, Turtle, I know.
I have accepted both.
There's no other way, is there?
Turtle has a black shell again.

I hate to say anything because it is such a marvelous feeling. I
am still underwater.
I have this feeling I want to eat
the seaweed. And, so I'm starting.
Seaweed in all colors. Greenish-red and even white. I take some
of the white and the red.
But the moment I put it in my mouth I have the feeling as if
it is already
not only *outside* of my body but also *inside* of my body. It is sort
of a cleansing
kind of
feeling,
as if, actually it feels
as if I have
dematerialized. And so
it just goes right through me. And yet still I have the feelings
of a
complete
cleansing.
It is so, so soft.
And Turtle seems to have gone.
And now suddenly
I am myself again.
And I pop up like a cork. And there is Turtle. And the water has
left. Everything is . . .

It's not dry, it's moist, but
there is not, not water anymore.
Turtle says to me,
> *You have learned enough for today.*
> *Go back.*
Yes. Oh, thank you, Turtle.

And so, I do not know how I came here. And Turtle says I
  should go back the normal way,
the way I know. And so, even though the drum is still calling,
  Turtle tells me I should go back and so I'm going back now.
There is Raven at the Raven Wall, and he's walking ahead of me.
  He has a strange kind of walk.
> Raven, what is it?
> Do you just want to say hello?
And so, I'm about to leave but
Raven is
standing *right*. . .
Very *sternly* he's staying
in front of me.
> Raven, Turtle told me I should go back. I really should listen
>   to her.
And his eyes are flashing. But, I feel I should listen to Turtle.
And I am out!

So

this is something that never happened to me before. I always
  used to

come out when the

drum was

stopping. Then . . . and, here I am. I don't know, should I stop?
  I'm at a loss. So, let's just see, I'm outside. Maybe I'm, I'm in
  the Middle World. I don't know. Let's see what happens.

It is hot. I'm at the hillside of my home.
Lots of dry leaves.

Raven has not followed me. I think he was *mad* at me that I . . .

Listened to Turtle and not . . .

I, I'm climbing *up* the oak tree. Higher and higher and higher.
The oak tree actually isn't that . . . large, but, for whatever
reason . . . Oh, yes, so now the . . . drum is calling. I think I
climb down.

Some voice calls, and says,

> *Come for a visit.*

Maybe it's my Great Grandmother.
"I will come next time. Yes, I will come next time."

I'm back.

---

 ## Reflections

Ema's Quest. "I like to go to the Abalone Shell Cave to meet Turtle."

Ema's Evaluation (after prompt, "Any comments you want to
make?"). "No, I don't. No, I don't. I do not know what to say. I am
confused [laugh]." [further prompt: "So, how about your purpose?
Did you achieve your purpose?"] "Yes! That's right. . . . Yes. I did.
I spoke to Turtle and I had a nice time really. It's just so different."

Ema's Interpretation. "I was about to go to the sky, you know—
because I saw a little hole and then the drum called me back. And
then a voice says, 'Visit. Come for a visit.' . . . [Great] Grandmother,
in the Upper World? I guess I better do that."

Counselor's Comments. Ema's only purpose is to meet Turtle
in the Abalone Shell Cave. Initially, she is confused by the journey; when prompted, she acknowledges that she accomplished

her purpose. Turtle reminds Ema of various useful matters that she seems to have forgotten. During the journey, Ema recognizes that a new perspective on transformation emerges and integrates with earlier teachings. They are there for her later consideration. For Ema, at the time of discussing her journey, the invitation from Great Grandmother to "come for a visit" is prominent. Ema affirms that she "better do that."

# Into the Void

*I would like to go to the Upper World to visit.*

*I would like to go to the Upper World to visit.*

*I would like to go to the Upper World to visit.*

I am going down the hillside.
Lots of snakes;
the little brown ones. Some are climbing up my legs. I happen to
  like them, because they are sort of
like the little lizards.
I have difficulties walking because there are so many snakes
and, I don't like walking on them. So, what
I have to do is sort of
*push* them aside
gently
and take a step.
They fill the space right away.
And now I trip because I try to be careful and
I'm just rolling down the hillside.
And leaves and snakes and
everything is just flying about.
And, so I am landing
right in front of the entrance to the oak tree. And I am rolling
  into the oak tree.
I am pushed by the . . .
The snakes seem to have formed a ball
and I am *pushed down* the tunnel.
I just let myself go.
It seems to be so powerful

that I am supposed to . . .
I don't know.
I said it was a big ball
but I seem to be part of the ball
because we are just rolling slowly.
So we are just rolling
down and down and down.
Well, huh, I don't really quite know . . .
All right,
I have landed in the room.
And in the middle of the room is a golden pole.
A metal
pole. And I am supposed to *climb* that pole. It is a sculpture,
a snake sculpture.
And I can go up easily because the scales of the snake are like
   straps and I go up rather quickly and I go higher and higher
   and higher.

And now I am out of the cave. And the pole is still going higher
   and higher and higher. I am now in the clouds.
When I look down I can't see the land anymore.
It is cool.
I'm in the clouds and I can't see anything. It is very dense.
I have to push through some kind of a . . .
I suddenly had to stop because there was something
that stopped me. But when I
just lifted my arms and
I could wiggle through.

I am suddenly in a completely different environment, so
I don't really know
where I am, to be honest. I had never been here.
     Oh, Snake, where am I then?
It's an emptiness. That's all I can say. I am in an empty space.
A voice says to me,

*Envision what you like to see, and it will be there.*
    Well, I like to see
    a river.
    And I like to see
    a green meadow.
And I sat.
I like to see Turtle, because I want to ask Turtle what this is all
  about.
No Turtle.
Ah! Snake is there.
    Snake, what is this all about?
I swim to the other side of the river, and . . .
Well, I would like some
cat-of-nine-tails in the river,
I need some
and some seaweed also.
That has always helped me.
What I am doing at the moment is
I just try to . . .
All right, I have green seaweed and I also like some red seaweed
  and some white one. And I hold it in my hand.
I wish Turtle was here. That would make me happy.
The voice says,
    *Do you want anything else?*
and I . . .
    No, I'm really happy. I don't need anything more.
    I'd like Turtle.
But Snake is there again.
    Oh, Snake, I really shouldn't . . .
    I love you, too.
Snake can swim. It is a different kind of snake. I mean, no, it
  looks like a snake
but it is swimming one.
She opens her mouth wide and bites me

slightly
in the *legs.*
In my arms.
I'm not at all scared. And
it feels almost like a massage.
And whilst Snake was at first small, it has become larger. And
   she can take my leg . . .
her mouth is so large that she can . . .
My calfs . . .
The calf muscles are in her mouth. She just goes very quickly up
   and down
and up and down my legs.
And then my arms.
And my hands.
I have a lightness within me.
I can see my blood rushing.
My, my whole system . . .
My whole inside is . . .
Oh! It is,
like electrified.
Whatever
Snake put into my body is racing in my body but it feels really
   good.
And I'm still lying in the water, too,
amongst the seaweed.
There . . .

Oh, oh. The drum is calling and I have to go back.
    Oh, Snake, how do we get back? I don't really quite know how
      we got here.
And so, Snake just takes me in her mouth. And it is
all dark.
    Oh, Snake
    I have to go back; please bring me back.

Oh. And now
she's spit me out and I'm right at the entrance of the oak tree.
I'm out.

 ## Reflections

Ema's Quest. "I would like to go to the Upper World to visit."

Ema's Evaluation (after prompt to work with the journey). "I don't
know what to say. . . . I don't know whether I was in the Upper
World . . . I could have been . . . it was . . . there was nothing there
[sounds puzzled]. I was just there—in the air, and it could have
been far, or it could have been close . . . nothing . . . I got a little
apprehensive . . . I was told 'Envision what you like to know.'"

Ema's Interpretation. "Sort of like a vacuum . . . very strange
place . . . emptiness . . . no horizon."

Counselor's Comments. Accepting the invitation from Great
Grandmother to "come for a visit," made at the end of the previous
journey, Ema enters an entirely new environment, "an emptiness,"
via a golden pole in the Lower World. Upon reviewing the journey,
she describes it as void-like, and to be reckoned with further. As
she says, at this time she is not sure she is in the Upper World.

Since Ema is uncertain about whether she journeyed to the
Upper World, it is a good time to remind her that she has been
successful making Upper World journeys starting from a different place. There is value in cultivating a few *known* pathways and
landmarks so that the journeyer can use them reliably to enter
the Upper World or Lower World and accomplish the purpose of
any given journey.

# A Middle World Healing

*I—would like to go to the Lower World—and, to meet Turtle—to, and ask her for a healing—of my left hip.*

*I like to go to the Lower World to meet Turtle, ask her for a healing—for my left hip.*

*I like to go to the Lower World—and meet Turtle and ask her for a healing for my left hip.*

> I am still in this room. I can't get off.
> I am walking down the
> hillside.
> The oak tree is not there.
> I don't quite understand. Maybe I should start again. I don't
>    want to be in the Middle
> World.
> I am looking.
> I am already somewhere. It is a very
> mountainous area, and . . .
> but I do not know how I arrived here, and doesn't seem to be
>    quite right.
> And don't quite know how to get out of it.
> I have to start again. I'm sorry. It's just not right.
> Okay.
> I start again.
> I like to go to the Lower World
> to meet Turtle
> to ask her for a healing of my
> left hip.
> I like to go to the Lower World

to meet Turtle
to ask her for a healing of my left hip.
I like to go to the Lower World
to meet Turtle
to ask her for a healing of my left hip.
I am again in this landscape. I think I just
see what happens.

It is
like the Tibetan landscape again. I mean, it is in the
mountains but, there is just
no life. I mean
just rock. And where I am at the moment there is not even . . .
Ah, normally I see a river, but there is not even a river. It is a
  completely different landscape where I used to be,
which I know.
I am followed by something but, when I turn around, it is not
  there. When I'm turning around there is nothing there. I
  seem to be alone and yet I have the feeling something is
  following me.

Oh! I do see the landscape from above and I now realize that I
  have wings, actually.
I think I am Vulture.
And my eyes . . .
I am
flying on one spot and my eyes have . . .
I'm *seeing*
something from above, something *very small*
like a white sort of . . .
I go closer and closer. And it is a . . .
It's a rabbit.
It's just not right.
No, it's not a rabbit. It's a sort of a . . .
It's a white . . .

It, okay,
it is actually a rock. It is just *lighter* than the others.

I suddenly have this strange idea, since I don't seem to get any
  where
and I was Vulture but now, I, when I went down suddenly I am
  myself
and the rock has the form
almost, like a turtle. And I suddenly got the idea, because there
  are lots of other rocks around—
to make my own turtle. So I'm, I'm just . . . I'm, I really don't
  know what else to do, 'cause I have never been in this situation.
  So I will just make
my own turtle. So, I am just banging along
with the rocks to smooth
the rock that is already sort of roundish, but just to
make it more turtle-like.
I try to make the ridges
really nice and *even*. Because I would like the rock to look nice. I
  mean, *really turtle-like.*
Vulture is standing
there and he's watching me.
    Oh, Vulture, I really wanted to see Turtle today, but I was not
      received, so I really don't know what to do.
Vulture didn't seem that interested in what I was saying.
He seems to be very interested
in what I'm doing. And, in fact, he's coming with a different
  kind of rock
which has a certain sharp edge, and he just throws it
in front of my feet.
    Thank you, Vulture, that is a nice stone to work with.
There is a little,
just a *teeny little* protrusion and I think I gonna make it the tail.
    I always like turtles' tails.

So, I
give
this rock
a teeny tail. A real cute one. I'm working rather
*fast.* I find out the faster I work, the nicer
the lines
look.
I'm still working on it.
And of course now the shell is pretty much done. But of course I
   don't have a head, because
there is no rock there
for a head.
So, I
just envision the
Turtle,
that it has gone
within its shell.
There is some
shrubbery growing and
there is one with a particular strong
fragrance
and I brush a few of these
and rub it into the shell.
The whole area is
perfumed with this
strong, strong smell. It's not sweet; it is very strong. Yeah, *almost*
   like sage, I would say.
And I also take the sage . . .
I break some more of the sage and the leaves are
sort of dry,
to the dry side, and I can crumble it and I put it over my whole
   body. And I am sitting opposite the "Turtle Rock." And I
   just feel
I should *say*

to this rock
that
I am having pain in my left hip. Is there any way?
No. I would like a *healing*
of my left hip.

> Turtle, I would like to have a healing
> of my left hip.

I feel I should lie down. And I feel I should close my eyes. And,
in fact, I'm putting some, sprinkling some, let's say sage. It is
*not* sage but some of the *herbs,*
on my eyes.
A slight wind is coming up.
I have the feeling I should
*not* open my eyes. So, I'm not supposed to see what's going on. I
just should *feel.*
I do not know whether it is the wind or whether it is Vulture's
feathers
that *make* the wind. Because it is not very strong
and it is sort of uneven, as if somebody . . .
like it is done with a *fan.* Which makes me feel that might be
Vulture's wings.
But, the
wings,
I mean
the wind
is drying my body
out. Completely.
All the flesh has fallen away already from my skeleton. It is now
only my skeleton left.
Oh, ohh.
I have the feeling as if
something is rearranging, or
doing something
at the bones of my left hip.

I do not know
what is done, but
there seems to be a rearranging, or
there is something done
to the *bones* of the left hip.
I have the feeling as if they don't really *belong* to me.
I can only feel; I cannot see anything. But I know that, for what
   ever reason, that
I have become a skeleton,
a dried-out skeleton.
Oh, oh.
The wind, I do not know whether it is the wind now, but it
   becomes so strong
that parts of my bones are just blown away. So, my whole body
   is in disarray.
I find myself
under the earth. I think it is a hollow.
And now, as if
the bones . . .
I really don't
like to try to figure out what happened to me. It's probably not
   that important but
what happened now to me is.

I'm *lying*
in the earth. There is a hollow.
As if
I have become a big root. And, the root, uhhh . . .
I don't really know what happened to me. Because
I seem to have become a plant.
And the plant is,
I think was a *seed*
and then I became a root, I guess. And now I am a plant and I
   am outside. So, I grew out of this hollow

and I am now . . .
right next to the turtle shell, actually.
That's where I came out,
myself again. Strange!

The *smell* of the herb is very, very pronounced. Hmm.
It just goes through my whole body.
I am tapping on the
shell and the shell sounds, even though it is stone, it sounds
*very hollow,* like a drum almost.
I try the same beat
as the drums.
I try the same beat as the drums
on that shell. Ohh, oh.
I am alone again. Just with the sound of the drums.
Whilst I felt very light when I came out of the earth, so light
  almost that every wind
could have blown me away,
now with my drumming,
I seem to fill out. I seem to become heavier. More full of life.
My whole body is *drum.* My whole body is
*sound* of the drum. Ummmm. I have to stay in this without
  talking for a while.
All surrounding sound of the drum fills me up.
It makes me *see* things.
Ohh!
The whole valley that was empty,
it's full of spirits. Plants. Green. Fruits.
The drum is calling. I have to go back and I do not know how to
  get back.
Oh, I do not know how to get back. I am standing on the turtle
  rock.
    Please let me go back. Vulture.
It's like a whirlwind that's picking me up.
And I'm back.

 **Reflections**

**Ema's Quest.** "I like to go to the Lower World to meet Turtle to ask her for a healing of my left hip."

**Counselor's Comments.** Ema repeats her purpose several times to focus her intention, having started the journey a second time. She finds herself in the same place as at first, so she continues from there. Not actually meeting Turtle, she decides to sculpt a turtle image from a rock, with Vulture's participation. She addresses her request to "Turtle Rock." First she asks, "Is there any way?" and then she adjusts her request to clearly reflect that she is asking for a healing of her left hip, as stated in her original intention. Events, familiar but not identical to others she has known in journeys, follow until she returns to her starting place in ordinary reality. Because of technical failure to record the latter parts of this session, Ema's comments remain with her alone.

# Quan Yin in the Upper World

*I like to go to the Upper World to meet Quan Yin.*

*I like to go to the Upper World to meet Quan Yin.*

*I like to go to the Upper World to meet Quan Yin.*

> I am walking down the hill.
> Snakes are coming
> from all over the place out of the earth.
> Now that I have arrived at the opening of the oak tree, I am
>     completely covered by snakes.
> This time I almost feel like [a] snake myself. We are already in
>     the tunnel.
> And instead of walking, I am slithering on the ground. But not
>     as a single
> snake, I mean, there are many, many, many snakes,
>     enveloping me.
>
> I'm entering now
> the cave and
> the golden
> statue
> has really disappeared. So obviously . . .
> I really destroyed it.
> All right, so I have to go.
> I am slithering
> up the walls toward that opening where the golden
> statue was to go up
> but the opening is still there,
> so I'm slithering right through that opening.

I am completely surrounded by . . .
By fog. I can't see anything.
So I don't really quite know,
since that
*rod* isn't there, how do I get up into the
Upper World?
Well,
nothing is happening because I
try to
get to the place,
that empty place.
But I don't know
how to find it this time.
Before, I just climb.
And then I sort of . . .
And then I did, go through . . .
Yeah, but that is taken from me.
I feel I am not really entitled to call her as I really should come
    to her, not she to me. Quan Yin, that is.
I have a great respect for her.

I don't really know where I am at the moment. Because I'm not
standing on one
place actually. The *fog* is just . . .
Well, actually, I don't really know. The fog is just
going by and I,
I just . . .

> Quan Yin, I am sorry. I probably should not have asked
> to come.

I seem to see in the
way, way . . .
I seem to be like in middle point in the far, far distance and I *try*
    to get to her.
I'm coming toward a

sort of a rocky
outcrop.
Emptiness. Emptiness, all over.
I'm climbing up the rock and I . . .
I'm *sitting*
on the rock.
Emptiness.
Nothing there.
The fog has lifted, but
with the exception of the rock, there is nothing else there.
  No color.
No color. No color.
Nothing, no Quan Yin. What is the meaning?
I hear a bell, in back of me, and I turn around.

It draws me into the rock. There is no cave there. It *just*
draws me into,
*straight into* the rock.
I think it is a . . .
There is a fragrance, also.
A lovely fragrance. I cannot explain what kind of fragrance it is.
I am dissolving.
I am dissolving to fragrance . . .
And this
bell . . .
I
am
dissolving
into
the
fragrance, and into
the sound of the bell.
My whole being is dissolved.
I am
rock,

fragrance, and the sound of the bell.
And I hear also water in the background.
Water.
In the background.

I am suddenly scared; I cannot hold it together.
It seems to be so important that I stay the way I am.
Rock.
Fragrance.
Sound of the bell.
This is I.
Water in the background.
I have lost myself
completely. Oh, God.
Some voice said to me
I shouldn't be scared.
        Yes.
They *sending me* on a different journey, they said.
It's somewhere . . .
I don't have an insight anymore.
I have become nothing
but fragrance
and sound.
At first I enjoyed it,
then I got scared.
And now I'm enjoying it.
Emptiness around me.
Sound. There is a high-pitch sound.
It seems to collect . . .
I suddenly *feel*
I am myself again but I don't know, 'cause I have the feeling as if
    the *sound* of the bell is collecting [at] the top of my head.
Sound of the bell is collecting [in] the top of my head.
And
now it seems to

burst open and

and when I look up

I see

thousands of

*tiny Quan Yins. Tiny particles. Ohh. Ohh.*

How gorgeous!

More and more. Coming out of the crown of my head. *Tiny, tiny*
    particles. All Quan Yin. No color. No color!

No form?!

That can't be!

I am reminded that I'm in a different place. Reality has nothing
    to do with this.

> *You are . . .*
> *You are in the realm of mystery.*

Yes!

> *You have to learn*
> *to think in different ways now.*

Oh, yes! Yes!

I'm surrounded

by Quan Yin

in tiny particles. My inner eye is seeing it.

A voice says, I should not think anymore, just enjoy it.

> *Be in this place*
> *and enjoy it.*
> *Don't try to verbalize it.*

I can't talk for the moment. I just can't.

*Ohhhh.*

Emptiness.

Fragrance.

Sound.

Quan Yin. Thousandfold.

What a journey!

I am crying

and I think . . .

No. I am
the waterfall.
I suddenly have become
waterfall.
The rushing water.
Somehow
I am now
running
from this place as water.
To what?
I am falling as water
down
into the
cave
I started in.
Ahhh!
And I'm filling the cave with water.
Higher and higher.
Higher and higher.
Suddenly the
cave is dissolving.
It's like a little lake.
Lake . . .
The drum is calling; I have to go back.
I have to dive down in order to get to the
path.
And I'm running. I'm running back. And I am out.

---

## 🐢 Reflections

Ema's Quest. "I like to go to the Upper World to meet Quan Yin."

Ema's Response (to prompt asking if Ema would like to make a brief statement about her journey, before playback). "No. [laugh]"

Ema's Interpretation (after playback). "She [Quan Yin] just accumulated with the sound. And teeny little . . . it was beautiful . . . very different. And a very beautiful journey. I started to cry and . . . Now I really have to accept that there are mysteries and not really try to . . . explain. [Laughs]" (To prompt regarding whether she was successful in her purpose): "Yes, I think so—thousands-folds. . . . It has taught me I should embrace the mysteries. I am on the journeys and mysteries are shown to me."

Counselor's Comments. Using her most recent method of reaching the Upper World through the Lower World, yet no longer able to use the golden pole as before, Ema attempts Upper World access by climbing the walls to the opening, finding herself lost in fog. Her journey takes on new dimensions as she searches for Quan Yin, awake to the paradoxes that present themselves. Ema expresses, in her own words above, their profound messages for her. Some years later, Ema recalls this as "one of my favorite journeys."

# A Teaching from Quan Yin

*I like to go to the Mystery Chamber to meet Quan Yin.*

*I like to go to the Mystery Chamber to meet Quan Yin.*

*I like to go to the Mystery Chamber to meet Quan Yin.*

I'm walking down the hillside toward the oak tree and I walk
  into the opening. And I walk into the tunnel.
The tunnel is very small.
I have to crawl.
Whilst I'm crawling, I collect some of the roots
and plants.
I, for whatever reason, feel I have a need for a lot of plants and
  roots.

It is dark, with the exception of the fire pit.
I am putting all the plants and roots into it. It gives a wonderful
  aroma and the chamber is filling with smoke.
Quan Yin . . .
She is standing next to the fire pit.
At first she was like a woman. I shouldn't have done it.
I was about to leave, then a voice said,
        *Stay.*
I see Quan Yin in the female form
and in the male form.
I am so startled.
I wanted to ask a question.
I am so startled I do not know what to say.
I do not know what's the matter with me.
The room is clear again, so I am putting more plants and
  roots . . .

Again, it fills the little chamber with smoke, but it is really
   pleasant.
I feel *good*. I really should relax. Now I see Quan Yin again,
in male and female form.
   Why can't I speak?
Whenever the smoke subsides, I put again the roots into the
   smoldering pit.
I like the smoke around me. I feel safe.
When the smoke is there, I can see Quan Yin.
   Oh, Quan Yin, where do we go from here? I like more
      teachings, but I don't know what to be taught about. I need
      your guidance to overcome my
   pain.
   To overcome my fear. There was a time when I had done this.
Meanwhile I am putting roots into the fire pit.
   *You need something,*
   *something substantial to hold your attention in the*
      *ordinary world.*
   *There's nothing wrong with it.*
   *Even here, if I wasn't here you wouldn't ask questions.*
   *You need an image to get your teachings. It is not possible*
      *for you. There is nothing wrong with it.*
   I know. I don't know why I'm thinking that. Because I'm quite
      happy. I feel I'm taught a lot.
   And yet
   I have this longing for more, for more understanding.
   You know I am in front of another door.
   I'd like to go through it.
Quan Yin shows me
a *lot of doors*. I guess these are doors I have gone through
in the course of my
life.
There's more to understanding. And she reminds me that
none of them

to pass, to go through, has been easy.

    Why would I

    lose my patience now? Or

    if not patience, why would I

    give up understanding?

She says that the seed is planted

in me

and it is growing more and more. But it needs

time.

    I know.

Meanwhile, I'm still putting

roots into the

pit.

And Quan Yin is changing from being female to male all the

  while.

I like her

in the male form because

she seems to be

so strong.

And

just whilst I was saying it, the male form has disappeared and

she is there

in the female form, smiling.

> *You are still impressed*
> *with what you see. Male [is]*
> *stronger. That's your mistake. You should be impressed with*
> *what you don't see. The Energies. You should concentrate*
> *on the Energies.*

  Yes, I know. I think

strength means so much to me, because I'm losing my

  strengths. I am getting old.

That's why I'm impressed by strength.

> *That's no good. It's the Energies you have to*
> *make your own.*

How?

How

do I go about it?

The Energies

with me?

And now, Quan Yin says that

for the Energies I have to go back to my

guiding spirits.

They are the primeval forces. I should *not*

abandon them.

I have been made to understand that

if I want to

go further

in the knowledge I'm seeking, I will have to go back

to the primeval forces.

Only they can make me understand.

Thank you, Quan Yin.

You are right. I have been carried away.

Meeting all the boddhisatvas was just something new for me. I saw in them something that isn't there.

I mean, in ordinary

world I see something that isn't really there. But I understand that I can use it as a tool. But not be too absorbed.

But it seems to be so easy now. I understand it now, but

right there, I couldn't before. I just had to be told.

I am so grateful that you did. Thank you so much.

I shall go back to Turtle. Vulture. Yes, the vulture. He is always in my mind.

I was

on the path.

I am glad, however, because it brought me to you.

I will go back. I don't know,

do you want me to go now?

I finally run out of
root material and
the chamber is . . .
All the fragrance is gone and the
smoke.
And so is Quan Yin.
I am all by myself and I just wonder whether I should go
today
to Turtle
or Vulture.
I'm leaving.
Actually
I know a way,
how to go to
outside
where Vulture might be and so I'm just going.
I'm going
through a side door and
to the chamber
of the stone Buddhas. And, now I'm going
out of this
stone temple.
I'm walking down the path toward the river and
I have the feeling I have to cleanse myself, so I'm just
going right into the cold stream. And I have the feeling as if a lot
   of anxiety and
*doubt* I had within me is
sort of washed away. And, it is such a marvelous feeling. And,
now that I turn around
*Vulture* is there.
   Vulture!
   Quan Yin told me that I
   should see you.

I have not forgotten you, as you know, in the ordinary world.
  But I have not come for teachings
to you. I was
sort of
sideswept. I
cannot do two things at once, as you know. I just needed to
know more about
the bodhisattvas and creatures that came to me.
I wanted to know why. And that is not the question I asked
  Quan Yin, did I? That's probably the question I should have
  asked her.
Vulture doesn't say it, but
he transmits it.
He transmits it to me and says that
I should definitely
do a journey on it.
If I want to know why these
bodhisattvas and
*creatures* came to me,
if I want to know
*I should ask.*
And now
the drum is calling.
  Oh, thank you,
  Vulture. I will do it. Yes, I will do it.
  You have to bring me back, please. I do not know how to get
  back.

And Vulture is picking me up and bringing me to the Summer
  Cave.
And I am
going to the vortex.
And I go through the Turtle Cave and
there now, I'm out!

##  Reflections

Ema's Quest. "I like to go to the Mystery Chamber to meet Quan Yin."

Ema's Response. "What a journey! . . . Suddenly, at the very last moment, I know what I should have asked, 'Why the bodhisattvas seem so special to me, over the time.'"

Ema's Evaluation and Interpretation. "I am really very grateful."

Counselor's Comments. This is a similar, but not the same, request as in the previous journey. This one specifies a meeting in the Mystery Chamber, rather than in the Upper World. Ema explores her desert landscape for more teachings, overcoming physical pain and fear. She seems to recognize that she is at a new place in her personal growth. Quan Yin's teachings at this point direct Ema further on her own path.

# Asking for Spiritual Balance

*I—like to meet Vulture—and ask him to give me my spiritual balance back.*

*I like to meet Vulture—and ask him to give me my spiritual balance back.*

*I like to meet Vulture—and ask him to give me my spiritual balance back.*

I have difficulties
because
normally I go through the oak
but today
this little creek
on my right
is
intervening. My thoughts are following the water
of the creek
and I cannot
concentrate. I cannot concentrate
on the oak.
Well, I may as well just try
following the water, because it seems to be stronger than
the other opening I use to go to the Lower World. So, I'm
. . . I'm, I'm still, well,
I just tell it the way it is with no thinking.
I am already a leaf. I am a leaf and—I am following the little
   creek.
I am banged
all over the place because

I'm hitting
little rocks and
I'm hitting
branches in the
water, but I am *not* caught up in them. There seems to be some
  heaviness in my leafiness. I am carried . . .
This creek
is emptying
into the ocean.
Into the ocean.

Now what?
I feel so lost.
I feel so *lost.*
*Oh, God, I feel so lost.*
I have merged with the waves, I think.
The waves
*bring* me to a lonely place.
It's just *all right,* but I have to go down. I can't find anything to
  go down.
Well,
there are some rocks. Maybe I should go and see whether there
  is a . . .
an opening right there! And I am already . . .
I fell into this opening!
Not very deep.
Oh, I shouldn't say that.
I'm still going down, but *so slowly* that I didn't really realize it.
  I'm
like a feather.

    Oh, Vulture, I don't think I will meet you today. That is all right.
    I may just enjoy the feeling
    going down.
I landed

in a . . .

dark place. I don't know what it is. Raven.

Raven is there!

> What are you doing here?

It is as if he looks at me sort of . . .

Well, as if he sort of feels sorry for me.

> Raven, I really need to go to Vulture. You know, to get my
> spiritual balance back. Please bring me to Vulture.

He takes me by the neck.

I must be kind of small. And he *flies* with me. In the dark!

Now he drops me. It is still dark. I can't see anything.

It is the first time

that I don't know . . .

whether the moon or the sun . . .

I am outside and I think

I don't know whether the moon or the sun is coming up. It is
very bright. But I think it is the moon because it does not come
any heat with it. And when I look around . . .

> Oh, Vulture, my God.
> You really gave me a fright.

I must be very small.

I think I am in his nest. And he is terribly tall,

towering over me.

> Oh, Vulture, you know my situation. I would like you to help
> me to get my spiritual balance back.
> I mean, it is okay; I can live without it, but
> I seem to be stuck. And I don't want to complain. I remember
> that poor little
> heap
> I was shown the other day. I don't want to be that one. And yet
> I do need your help.

I only see his feet.

He's so huge. Oh, God!

Vulture, that's not fair. I want to see your eyes.
I do not know whether
he shrank or I
got taller, because
I do now see
his beautiful face. His eyes are so wise.

> Oh, Vulture. I don't know why I get hot and cold. Ecstatic and
> depressed. I don't understand it.
> I'm still confused. I am not confused
> when I'm with you, but I'm confused when I go
> to the ordinary world,
> where I have to live most of the time.

He asks me straight out whether I feel sorry for myself.

> Well, I . . .
> Well, I . . .
> Well, sometimes, yes, I think I do, sometimes.

He asks me why.

> Well, I never really thought of it, but I guess,
> getting old, and
> losing my physical strength, and,
> being in pain.
> I know this is all
> the normal way. But, yes, I feel sorry for myself at times. I hate
> to admit it.

He says to me I should not pay too much attention to myself.
  My ego is so strong still
at times. I should throw my ego away.

> It is so easy to say, Vulture. I do not know how.
> The ordinary world is not an easy world to live in, you know. If
> you threw your ego away, then
> who would take care of me? I mean,
> I know that you are helping me. And, and, the sp . . .
> and here, the Lower World, it's fine, but the ordinary world it's
> not. Not everyone is nice. Not everyone is compassionate.
> And so

you need a certain kind of ego to survive here,
in the ordinary world, I mean.
Vulture looks at me. And he says,

> *Yes, you are right. You need*
> *the balance.*

Yes, I need the balance.
He's saying something to me but I do not know how to say it,
unfortunately.

Oh, Vulture.
I think that he said to me . . .
He said,

> *It is not good to have a*
> *life that is always*
> *running smoothly. One has to have upheavals*
> *in order to keep . . .*

What he means I think, I don't think I express it right.
How can I say this now?
I think,

> *You need hot and cold.*
> *You need wet and dry.*
> *You need both*
> *in order to understand*
> *where the balance lies.*

Yes, yes, that is true.
I thought I had done well for a while.
And so, he says to me,

> *Yes. But now you are at the point*
> *where you have to come up again. You were in the ocean,*
> *now you have to climb the mountain. Slowly. Wisely.*

Yes. Yes. That is true.
He suddenly . . .
I thought he would pick . . .
He . . .
I can't talk.

I can't talk.

> Oh, Vulture, I can't talk.

He says to me, I should not be too hard with myself.

This is a mistake I'm making over and over. I'm asking too much
  of myself.

What he says is that I live in the ordinary world

and I am too harsh with myself.

Mistakes are made to learn. And it's my mistakes or way of
  thinking

about mistakes

that brings me forward. That brings me in front of the door.

And then they open. But they will only open

whenever I feel compassion for myself.

> Oh, Vulture. I always think I do things wrong, I know. And it is
>   so sad.

> How can I possibly . . . ?

I need a handkerchief, please. Thank you.

The drum calls. I have to go back.

> I do not know how to get back, Vulture.

He just pushes me out of the nest.

And Raven picks me up.

And

I'm back.

---

 ## Reflections

Ema's Quest. "I like to meet Vulture and ask him to give me my
spiritual balance back."

Ema's Initial Response. "Nothing is the same, is it, when you travel?
[Laughs] I just couldn't get started."

Ema's Evaluation (after prompt about what Ema understood of the
journey). "Well, I think what Vulture was telling me was that . . .
I'm too strict with myself. I'm asking too much of myself . . . He

said that . . . asked me if I feel sorry for myself and I hated to admit it. I guess sometimes I do. . . . Getting old. [He said] my ego is still too strong . . . bottom of the ocean, now to go to the mountain—that is the normal way to do it. I understood that."

Ema's Interpretation. "He has never been so affectionate . . . and then is when he said I'm just too hard with myself—mistakes we have to make in order to get forward on the way. . . . It fell all into place again. . . . It takes a while to take it all in. . . . Too much crying today. Nothing is the same when you travel [journey]."

Counselor's Comments. This journey is reminiscent of some of Ema's early journeys, such as *Journey on Balance* and *Ego and Harmony*. Ema revisits those earlier teachings in the present one with new details, to integrate them into the now that is hers. When the contents of different journeys reveal the same images or messages, it is useful for the journeyer to contemplate their particular relevance.

JOURNEY 64

# Tara at the Mystery Chamber

*I would like to meet Tara—in the Mystery Chamber.*

*I would like to meet Tara—in the Mystery Chamber.*

*I would like to meet Tara—in the Mystery Chamber.*

I am sliding down the hillside because it is wet.
I sort of lost my footing.
I'm sliding right into the opening of the oak tree. I'm sliding
*down* the tunnel, my feet first, and
I just
grab some of the
roots
that are hanging from the
small tunnel.
And
I am already in the Mystery Chamber,
feet first.
Oh, God. The Chamber is still green.
I put the herbs into the pit.
And a voice says to me,

     *Speak.*

  Oh, Tara, I
  I had this wonderful
  journey this morning. But
  when I was sitting in the flames,
  I don't know for how long,
  there was nothing there. I mean everything disappeared.
  What happened to me there?
Maybe I shouldn't have come again.

I'm sorry. I really shouldn't have come. I'm sorry.

Oh, Turtle, I think I made a terrible mistake.

I'm sitting at the lower seat. There's a high seat and there's a
lower seat. And suddenly Turtle has appeared. And Tara is
sitting right on top of Turtle.

Oh, Tara

and Turtle.

You always surprise me. And then I'm always without words.

I still wonder, what happened to me

this morning

in the journey when

I was *sitting* in the fire. I was engulfed in it and then every
thing disappeared.

The voice said,

> *But that's where you always wanted to be. You wanted to
> find out what emptiness was.*

Ahh. Oh. Well, you mean . . .

Well, well, yes,

I mean there was nothing there.

> *Yes. Exactly!*

Is that all?

Tara

has become her wrathful form and she's just *laughing*.

And

it's echoing in this

chamber.

My ears are almost splitting.

Stop! Stop!

Tara asked me what I thought would happen.

I really didn't think, I guess. I really didn't think.

For me, where I was,

I mean emptiness,

I was not thinking then. I mean, my mind was

not really working.
I think I didn't get the teaching.

There is an answer, but
I think it comes out of
Turtle's belly.

> *Emptiness is so easy*
> *that it is difficult.*
> *In order to grasp it*
> *one tries all kinds of*
> *metaphors*
> *and teachings.*
> *But what*
> *you went through this morning is just it. That's all there is.*
> *You are disappointed.*

No.
I mean,
maybe I
wasn't ready for it, I don't know,
because it was so easy. Yes, I guess so. I mean I have thought
  about it for a long time.
Is this then
one of the mysteries?
Yama always talked to me about mysteries. Is that one of
  them?
It was a very good feeling.
Can I get this feeling again
when I come here
to the Mystery Chamber
and ask for you,
Tara?

She is now in her beautiful form, and she smiles and says,

> *Maybe.*

Yes, of course. That is all right. That is all right. I don't mind.

The
chamber
is not a chamber anymore, I think, because the walls are gone.
And yet the fire pit is still
there and I did run out of . . .
I did not grab as many roots and so I ran out of it.
Out of the roots.
So it is
crisp.
I mean, there is no smoke any more
in the chamber and it is *crisp* and *clear.*
And
Tara
and Turtle
have become statues. They are not alive anymore.
I see myself sitting,
opposite
Tara and
Turtle.
And I myself, also
have become
rigid
like a statue also.
I don't quite know what to make of it.
I feel I should go back.
Yes, something is within me that makes me go back
to the tunnel and I'm getting more
*roots.*
And, coming back, I throw these roots, into the fire.
And
suddenly
we all three
are
engulfed

in flames.
We are all merging together,
and
like a spiral.
A *spiral*
comes out of us.
or *we* have become the spiral, I think.
Power.
It's power.
It's an immense power, an immense power, an immense force
that is driving this spiral
upwards.
Upwards.
My God, what a power!
And now the power is just sort of
dissolving
into nothing.
However, my mind is still functioning
at the moment
because I see it all.
The *drum* is calling. I have to go back.
Oh, I have to go back. How?
Oh, how?
    Tara!
I'm out. I don't know how.
I don't know how.

---

 ## Reflections

Ema's Quest. "I would like to meet Tara in the Mystery Chamber."

Ema's Summary. "I am very grateful that I'm allowed to go there. . . . I hope I get it right. . . . still one can misunderstand sometimes, you know. I wanted to know about this strange thing, this interesting . . . Maybe that's just it. [laugh]"

Ema's Interpretation (after reviewing the recording). "Already a lot has changed within me . . . in my everyday life . . . what bothered me then . . . now I'm not afraid. I'm not afraid of death . . . if I have to die, I die. I have overcome a lot of human obstacles that I used to have . . . anxieties and so, and so. . . . it has all come back. I have become pretty much myself, again—and more . . . just fine.

"The teachings I got have strengthened me immensely. My whole mindset has been changed. . . . Now I get really *new* teachings—completely new sources, which is quite remarkable in a way. . . . It is such a sacred thing to me. I am so grateful for it.

"The main thing was . . . when I thought I saw myself as this poor little package and Vulture took the [blanket] away and there was nothing. I thought, 'My God!' It was as if something in my brain was just a little bit off. A veil was just taken away. . . . I will never forget it, because it was just so powerful . . . so it comes together, as it has over the years . . . like a puzzle. . . . It is getting more and more finished; well, it will never be one hundred percent finished . . . it is at least halfway finished. All my journeys before, they have not been random, they have always come toward my evolving. That is nice to know, in a way. . . . I appreciate it very much.

"At first, I really didn't, but later on, I have taken quite some things from the nonordinary world into the ordinary world. I mean, many of the teachings, because I wanted to know how I could be stronger.

"In effect, ever since I was told, 'Time has no bearing on this,' I have gotten much farther than I thought I would, because I don't have this time frame . . . this thing in my *mind* that I'm not capable of understanding things. . . . Since that is all gone, I just think I'm more relaxed about taking things in, which is *great!* Because I was told by Yama, because I'm so slow to learn with the teachings, he said, 'Time has nothing to do with it.' He asked me what was time and I said, I couldn't answer. He said, 'Time has nothing to do with it. And, of course, it is true. What is time? Time has nothing to do with it. It really doesn't. To understand the higher things or whatever . . . it just comes to you or it doesn't, and . . . it's really true, time has nothing to do with it. It really doesn't. That's it! It's no more explaining to do."

Counselor's Comments. Ema requests help in understanding a specific journey experience of earlier in the day. In this current journey, she travels to another world, dialogues with familiar spirits, merges with them and transforms, and obtains knowledge. Alongside a variety of spiritually enlightening circumstances, Ema wrestles with her question and finds her personally emerging potential, in unity with her helping spirits. In her interpretation above, she notes that much has changed in her ordinary life, that she is not afraid about obstacles and things that formerly bothered her.

# EPILOGUE:
## REFLECTIONS ON
## OPENING THE CIRCLE

Ema passed through several stages or phases of evolving skill and confidence in interpreting the meaning of her journeys or the answers to her questions. Although her stated intention often was to make a journey of exploration without any other purpose, still she wanted to find meaning in such a journey. Training to select her journey's purpose required considering exactly what it was that she wanted, often a difficult task for her. Exploration is a quite legitimate purpose for a journey. You have the opportunity to learn the territories of the Upper and Lower Worlds and their assets, which you can employ as needed in the future. As with all journeys, keep in mind your purpose.

With journeys of exploration, it is more difficult to maintain the discipline to journey purposefully, especially if there is not a pivotal need to help someone else, as there is with healing or divination. Therefore, it is easy to lose focus in the journey and in understanding of the meaning of the journey. Even in the case of journeywork for others, where there is an overriding need, there are potential pitfalls in interpreting meaning. The alert shamanic journeyer is aware of the possibility of misinterpreting meaning.

Ema's modesty, humility, and gratitude for the aid of her spirit helpers have stood her in good stead, as she sincerely struggled to understand the meanings of her journeys and the answers they provided to her questions. Generally, the path to understanding is not a smooth, linear one. Ema, however, persisted and gradually increased her confidence in both her spirit helpers and in her ability to discern the meanings of her journeys. In addition, the journeys built up, each bringing additional knowledge or content that, over time, also conveyed a sturdier sense of the reality of these worlds in which she found herself. Finally, she realizes she is at the beginning of a new adventure, excited to have the opportunity and the tools to meet it.

# APPENDIX

## ABOUT HARNER SHAMANIC COUNSELING[1]

### BY MICHAEL HARNER

Harner Shamanic Counseling (HSC) is a *spiritual* method, a system of *shamanic* counseling that follows the ancient principles of shamanism, not of psychology or of other Western systems. As a method of spiritual counseling, HSC has at its goal *life-enlightenment,* not the treatment of psychopathology. It is a problem-solving system for discovering one's own spiritual power and the wisdom to deal successfully with daily life.

HSC is a copyrighted system based upon classic shamanism with the addition of certain important innovations created by Michael Harner through years of his own practice of shamanic counseling. Concepts, practices, and goals used in Harner Shamanic Counseling include: non-ordinary reality; the shamanic journey and shamanic divination (both undertaken by the client); the realization of one's own personal spiritual power; and the discovery of one's ability to obtain extraordinary, very practical, spiritual wisdom and answers to important personal questions.

In essence, the client becomes a practitioner of divinatory shamanism, with the help and guidance (in ordinary reality) of the shamanic counselor. One of the features of HSC is that the *real* shamanic counselors are in *nonordinary reality.* These are sacred teachers the clients spontaneously encounter in their shamanic journeys who provide the nonordinary reality answers to the clients' questions. The ordinary

1 Reprinted by permission of the Foundation for Shamanic Studies.

497

reality HSC counselors, in contrast, do not provide substantive answers or interpretations for the client, but are essentially experienced shamanic facilitators who provide encouragement and methodological shamanic advice based upon their own more extensive experience in shamanic journeying and shamanism.

HSC uses the electronic sonic-driving technique originated by Michael Harner to alter the state of consciousness of the client in order to go "outside of time" to utilize the ancient shamanic problem-solving methods. The client is trained in the unique Harner-invented simultaneous narration and recording method of shamanic journeying in order to amplify the quality of experience and to have an on-going recording of it. Through his/her experiences in the shamanic journey, the client has the opportunity to overcome inhibitory fears and to gain self-confidence while acquiring heart-felt wisdom. With this, the client commonly experiences a sense of personal empowerment and a new-found joy in existence.

Since HSC is a spiritual rather than a psychological system, it is not necessary for an HSC counselor to be a professional in clinical psychology, psychotherapy, or a related field. Indeed, sometimes it is confusing for an HSC counselor to be operating under the burden of another conceptual system that may unconsciously intrude into the shamanic one. What does seem to be essential is for the counselor to be well-trained and experienced in practical shamanism and to be an individual of sensitivity, intelligence, character, and compassion.

To preserve the integrity and standards of the Harner Shamanic Counseling system, and of its teaching, unauthorized use of the Harner name is prohibited by law. Permission to employ the Harner name in this context is limited to those who have successfully completed the week-long Harner Shamanic Counseling training. The Foundation also reserves the right to withdraw such use of the Harner name at its sole discretion at any time. Other individuals may, however, use the generic term, "shamanic counseling," to describe their work.

The teaching of Harner Shamanic Counseling in any form whatsoever, whether under this name or any other, in part or in whole, *to two or more persons at one time,* including by oral, as well as written, audio, video, or film means, is prohibited without advance written approval by Michael Harner or Sandra Harner and is subject to conditions set forth by him/her. This applies to Certified Counselors as well as to all others.

As of 2008, the Foundation for Shamanic Studies ceased offering certification in Harner Shamanic Counseling. This cessation does not affect those who already are Certified Shamanic Counselors (C.S.C.). Note: Certified Shamanic Counselor and CSC are registered trademarks of the Foundation for Shamanic Studies.

For more information on training in Harner Shamanic Counseling, please see the website for the Foundation for Shamanic Studies: www .shamanism.org

Photo by Stephanie Mohan

# ABOUT THE AUTHOR

Sandra Harner is cofounder and vice president of the Foundation for Shamanic Studies (FSS) and is on its international faculty. Actively involved in the FSS, she worked with her husband, Michael Harner, in the development of Harner Shamanic Counseling (HSC) and directs the HSC training program for the Foundation. Since 1964, she has engaged in field research among native peoples of North and South America and the Sami people (Lapp) of the Scandinavian Arctic. In addition to her work in shamanism, she is a licensed psychologist, with special interests in health psychology and existential-humanistic psychotherapy. She lives in Mill Valley, California, with her husband.

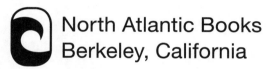